MANAGING THE SYSTEMS DEVELOPMENT FUNCTION

MANAGING THE SYSTEMS DEVELOPMENT FUNCTION

Robert O. Peterson

VAN NOSTRAND REINHOLD DATA PROCESSING SERIES

VNR VAN NOSTRAND REINHOLD COMPANY

New York

Library of Congress Catalog Card Number 86-18912
ISBN 0-442-27345-2

Printed in the United States of America

Van Nostrand Reinhold Company Inc.
115 Fifth Avenue
New York, New York 10003

Van Nostrand Reinhold Company Limited
Molly Millars Lane
Wokingham, Berkshire RG11 2PY, England

Van Nostrand Reinhold
480 La Trobe Street
Melbourne, Victoria 3000, Australia

Macmillan of Canada
Division of Canada Publishing Corporation
164 Commander Boulevard
Agincourt, Ontario M1S 3C7, Canada

16 15 14 13 12 11 10 9 8 7 6 5 4 3 2 1

Library of Congress Cataloging-in-Publication Data

Peterson, Robert O., 1947–
Managing the systems development function.

(VNR data processing series)
Includes index.
1. Computer software—Development—Management.
I. Title. II. Series: Van Nostrand Reinhold data processing series.
QA76.76.D47P48 1987 658.4′038 86-18912
ISBN 0-442-27345-2

To
Lea, Bobby, Heather, and Matt

THE VAN NOSTRAND REINHOLD DATA PROCESSING SERIES

Edited by Ned Chapin, Ph.D.

IMS Programming Techniques: A Guide to Using DL/1
Dan Kapp and Joseph L. Leben

Reducing COBOL Complexity Through Structured Programming
Carma L. McClure

Composite/Structured Design
Glenford J. Myers

Reliable Software Through Composite Design
Glenford J. Myers

Flowcharts
Ned Chapin

A Programmer's Guide to COBOL
William J. Harrison

A Guide to Structured COBOL with Efficiency Techniques and Special Algorithms
Pacifico A. Lim

Managing Software Development and Maintenance
Carma L. McClure

Computer-Assisted Data Base Design
George U. Hubbard

Computer Performance Evaluation: Tools and Techniques for Effective Analysis
Michael F. Morris and Paul F. Roth

Evaluating Data Base Management Systems
Judy King

Network Systems
Roshan Lal Sharma, Paulo T. deSousa and Ashok D. Inglé

Logical Data Base Design
Robert M. Curtice and Paul E. Jones, Jr.

Decision Tables in Software Engineering
Richard B. Hurley

CICS/VS Command Level with ANS COBOL Examples, Second Edition
Pacifico A. Lim

SERIES INTRODUCTION

This is a big book in many ways. It is big in its coverage of managing software development. It is big in seeing managing software development as more than project management and in putting project management in its proper place. At the same time, this book is big in its coverage of software project management, going well beyond the usual cookbooks.

This book is big in its practical emphasis on the realities of managing software development, such as political pressure and keeping the staff. It is big in the range of the topics the author presents in the three parts of the book: managing the process, managing the people, and managing the technology. It is big in the insights into managing software development. And it is big in both its depth and its breadth of coverage.

These and other features of this big book provide a wealth of useful and stimulating ideas. As we read, we see in new and important ways the situations which we face in our managerial work. Sometimes these insights are disturbing, sometimes reassuring. In either case, we are the better for being able to see these situations differently.

The author offers us a broad view of the practical arts of management, as in Chapter 7, which deals with the establishment of a department personality. So often authors ignore the impact of the culture of an organization on the performance of the work. This author recognizes it, and for that this book is bigger in value.

Ned Chapin Ph.D.
Series Editor

PREFACE

The writing of this book was motivated by the perceived need for information on managing the systems development function. For the new or aspiring manager of systems development, there is little literature. There is a wealth of material on how to manage the development of a system, how to design a database and the principal criteria to use in developing interactive systems. However, there is little to help the manager who is running a department rather than developing technical solutions to business problems.

Several years ago, I managed the systems development department of a large manufacturing firm. I had the benefit of working for a forward-looking MIS director; the firm was doing very well, and there was a talented and dedicated staff of analysts and programmers working for me. We were in the technical forefront in many areas, and we had most of the facilities needed to progress in the areas where we were deficient.

I recognized early in my tenure that the function I was managing had changed substantially. I was no longer able to deal closely with the intricacies and technical complexities of any one project. We were running too many projects simultaneously, and I did not have the time for close involvement. I found that I was no longer able to manage people the same way as I had in the past. I was now forced to deal with them as a group rather than as individuals.

I also found that the definition of technology had changed. Previously, technology had been what we, the development group, brought to the user department. When we implemented components of a new technology, it altered the way the user department did business. The change always flowed from us to them. I was now running a department the same way the users ran theirs. My technology consisted of the procedures and process controls which allowed my department to operate efficiently and effectively. Some of the procedures were automated and some were not. Nevertheless, they represented technology.

My technical background had not prepared me for these new managerial responsibilities and perspectives on development. Being reasonably intelligent, I sought to learn from the experiences of others. I first read as many current management books as I could find. Unfortunately, the emphasis in these books was executive management or on the procedural aspects within established limits. While valuable, these works did not address my most pressing need—managing a group of programmers and analysts.

The material on the data processing discipline was even less helpful—at least for my specific need. I found no end to treatments on programming techniques, analytical processes, database planning and a variety of other subjects on isolated aspects of the process. Some were very good, but none addressed my problem. Managing the systems development function of a company is definitely not the same as managing the process of developing systems.

As luck would have it, I survived, learning by trial and error with the help of my staff and management. The department did very well, but I was struck by the fact that so many of my predecessors had found these same conditions when they became managers. Surely there should be some material available to smooth the way.

Later, as a consultant, I found that my situation was not unique. I also found that the need was not specific to new managers. The development managers I dealt with had brought different talents to their position. Some were excellent personnel managers, some were experts in managing the process of developing systems, and others were able to install procedures effectively and maximize the use of technology in their departments. Some were more successful than others. For those who eventually failed, it was not their strengths which caused problems but rather those aspects of running a department to which they brought either no interests or no skills.

Three situations stand out as particularly noteworthy and partially explain the organization of this book—managing the process, managing the people, and managing the technology. In none of these situations did the company fail due to the development department's inability to perform well. Also, the managers of those departments were doing the best they could. They were talented, dedicated people.

The first situation took place in a medium-sized to large textile firm. The company had concentrated on acquiring the latest state-of-the-art hardware and software available. It was felt that, with this equipment, they could accomplish two things. First, they could attract high-quality technicians who wanted to work with the best equipment possible. Second, by having the most advanced software, they could install sophisticated systems faster and at lower cost than they could with the equipment more typical of other companies of their size.

For a while, this strategy worked very well. Two or three major interactive database systems were implemented which put the company ahead of its competitors in its ability to respond quickly to customer demand and to control inventories. However, no time or effort was spent in developing an atmosphere that would motivate people to remain with the firm. The pay was relatively low and the benefits were minimal but, worse yet, no sense of esprit de corps was developed. There was no sense of identity with corporate goals and no feeling of advancement in the craft. Staff members considered themselves mere resources for maintaining and developing systems. Turnover was tremendous; anyone who stayed for 9 months was a long-time employee.

As if this was not bad enough, no effort was made to implement procedures or methods for the development of systems. All of the emphasis was placed on the specific system need to be satisfied, and therefore each new request was serviced independently of all previous requests. Since turnover was so high, few systems bore any resemblance to previously implemented systems. This meant, of course, that the time needed for maintenance or enhancement grew to the point where there was no time available for true development. All staff members were dedicated to keeping existing systems running. This situation remains today, and the initially sophisticated systems which were implemented several years ago have atrophied to the point where they are no longer competitive. The firm still maintains state-of-the-art hardware and software and, to the joy of other local firms, has become a very effective training ground for development personnel.

The second example concerns a state agency (not the author's home state) where the principal concentration has been on people and procedures. People are treated well, personnel conditions provide nearly total job security, and employees can partake of a number of options such as flexible hours, which makes it a very comfortable place to work. To ensure consistency and to limit the possibility of systems failure, procedures, methods and other aspects of technology are defined to the letter. Every system looks the same as every other, all code is consistent and users invariably receive precisely the system they requested.

However, while all the pieces are in place, management has failed to recognize a basic premise of systems development: that the function itself is in transition. The very nature of the discipline has implied that transitional state since its inception and for the foreseeable future. Development departments must be ready to change constantly and take advantage of emerging technologies. In the case of this state agency, the systems being developed have followed the same identical process, using the same tools, for the past 10 years. While there have been no major failures, there have been no major successes either.

Users make relatively few requests for improvements or new products because they know that by the time their requests are completed, the usefulness of the system will be long past. Therefore, this agency is mired in inefficiencies which are easily eliminated with computer systems. Its failure consists not only of not recognizing the need for transition but also of not understanding the department's principal reason for existence—to provide rapid system solutions. Procedural integrity exists, but not toward that goal. Consistency and continuity are admirable attributes for a systems development department, but not at the sacrifice of flexibility and natural evolution.

The final example deals with a department in a somewhat unique situation. It was part of a statistical research firm whose computer outputs were direct products. Whereas many development departments begin as overhead, cost-reduction groups, this one was seen as a direct contributor to profits.

Partially because the company dealt with statisticians (a difficult, competitive group to recruit and retain), there was an atmosphere quite conducive to retaining people. Company benefits were excellent and opportunities for advancement were good. Visibility was high, and the systems development group presented a dramatic contrast to the conventional "backroom" mentality.

Since the output of development was direct product, procedures were stringent but not counterproductive. Effective quality control gates were established, and the procedures were periodically reviewed and enhanced to ensure maximum efficiency. In fact, the development department itself never actually implemented a system. All products were turned over to an independent group whose sole function was review and verification of quality and adherence to specifications.

Despite this excellent atmosphere, the management of systems development made some serious errors which had catastrophic results. The basic error was that the process of developing systems was virtually ignored. When projects were received, they were immediately assigned to the person with the most experience in the affected area. That person was then basically on his own. No methodologies existed, and project management was, by and large, up to each individual. In fact, the next time the project was seen after assignment was when it was turned over to the quality group.

Due to this isolation of project efforts, separate forms of project management techniques and development methods began to emerge. The effectiveness of each approach was governed entirely by the individuals involved. Each implemented system required the attention of the developer for maintenance, since there was little or no commonality between systems. Developers became frustrated due to the increasing maintenance load and, despite the benefits and career potential, turnover increased.

With the limited management of projects, implementation was either late or incomplete. The development department learned that its success was judged on its ability to complete projects on schedule. Difficulty in implementation was considered an indictment of the quality group, not of development. It was not unusual to see programs and subsystems turned over to quality with no operational code whatsoever.

What made this situation so catastrophic was the fact that the product of development was the product of the company. Over a 5-year period, the company went from the acknowledged industry leader to a third choice for its customers. It was recently acquired by a larger firm, and the development department is being slowly disbanded.

The intent of this book is not to prevent situations of the type described. In many cases, there are circumstances which will prevent even the most dedicated manager from successfully managing the department. The intent is to provide enough insight into management of the development function so that the manager can understand the implications of his or her actions.

More than anything else, the intent of this book is to bolster the contention that managing a functional department within a company is not the same as developing a system. The manager is removed by administrative requirements from the day-to-day management of projects and the physical development of an implementable product. Therefore, while the skills honed in those activities are valuable, they are not the skills which will provide success in managing a department.

One note on mechanics should be made before proceeding. When I first prepared the draft for this book, I totally avoided the use of gender implications with pronouns. Everywhere a gender was implied, I used "he and she" or "his and hers." In reading over the drafts, that style sometimes proved unwieldy. Since there is, as yet, no simple gender-neutral pronoun, I chose to use "he" and "his" where explicit reference to both sexes proved distracting. There is no implication here beyond style. The skills and attitudes necessary for a good development manager are intelligence, sensitivity, well-organized thinking and imagination. These characteristics are certainly not possessed by either sex in more abundance than the other.

ROBERT O. PETERSON

INTRODUCTION

Systems development has undergone extraordinarily rapid changes and a dramatic increase in importance to the corporation. This evolution has been spurred by two interrelated factors: the increasingly competitive nature of business and the accelerating advancement of technology. The rapidity of this growth and the continual obsolescence of yesterday's accepted approaches have left systems development with an impressive set of challenges in meeting its responsibilities.

Just a few short years ago, computer systems development was relegated to a "back room" role of constructing and implementing products purely in response to utility activities. Labor distribution, payroll, accounts payable, and the other basic activities of a company were the principal thrusts of development, and then only as it applied to purely clerical human replacement activities. While extremely important in its own right, this work lacked the visibility and strategic importance we see today.

Over the past two and a half decades, the competitive atmosphere of business and advances in technology have allowed and required the development of systems to rise in importance to the corporation. The importance of information to the company's very way of life requires that systems be developed not only in line with business plans but often as primary drivers of those plans. Today systems development is a major concern of most executives. How well systems are produced, how well they support corporate growth and how flexible the development group is are now discussed at the senior executive level.

Where development once consisted of a group of technocrats under the control of whatever business unit made the greatest use of them, it is now as critical a business function as marketing, planning or operations. That transition is important, and its implications are dramatic. Whereas before the manager could concentrate on the technical aspect of developing systems, there are now broader issues to be faced. The skill and creativity with which that manager directs the development function now has a direct and pervasive effect on the health of the corporation.

A business function represents an integral part of the corporate purpose, direction and method of meeting competitive challenges. Its activities relate implicitly or explicitly to all other aspects of the corporate operation. Its internal workings may be hidden from view, but the effectiveness with which they are managed is reflected in its relations with all other functions. In this situation, the manager must be concerned with all aspects of the function; there cannot be a concentration on any one aspect at the expense of others. There must be a clear understanding of the function's purpose, the resources necessary to fulfill that purpose, the mechanisms necessary to achieve control and consistency and how dynamic the function itself must be to evolve in step with the business.

In development's case, this goes far beyond constructing any one system. The successful manager of development creates an environment in which all projects are managed well, not just the high-visibility, technically satisfying or high cost/benefit ratio projects. This requires that a constant project flow be maintained so that all serviced departments can evolve through the use of technology. It also requires a department consisting of business specialists but of workers with a mix of skills and expertise who can shift with the business. These people must be retained for a long time and must display the personality traits that allow shifts of direction.

Also required is administrative talent on the part of the manager. Functional integrity requires control. At the managerial level, that control is maintained by the appropriate application of procedures and internal technologies that allow the manager to control at a distance.

Much of the development manager's administrative and leadership requirements are applicable to any corporate function. However, any successful manager must understand what makes the department unique. In the case of systems development, there are a number of characteristics which make managing that function substantially different from managing other departments. The service nature of the department, the relatively high educational level of the personnel (with correspondingly high expectations), the constant transition between today's approach and tomorrow's and the crucial nature of its products all contribute to the manager's need to concentrate all skills and attention on that function. There is little historical precedent to guide the direction of systems development.

For these reasons, the department must be managed for the long term. Viewing its management simply as a short-term step in a career path will not satisfy the responsibilities of the department. Few managers in any company can boast as high an impact on the corporate future as the development manager. As such, this position can represent the culmination of a career whose goal is to influence the destiny of the corporation. Even when performance allows promotion of senior management, the development manager must recognize the department's impact on the corporate future.

Therefore, the department must be directed as if that manager will fulfill long-term career goals within the department.

Much of the development manager's approach is governed by senior management's philosophy and culture. Nowhere is this fact more evident than in the implications of political pressure and stress. Certainly political pressure is exerted, in varying degrees, on all departments of a company. However, the service nature of development and the technological orientation of most of its personnel make these pressures especially difficult to handle. The manager is charged with providing information service to all functions, regardless of the political strength of each. As pressure is exerted from one area, the manager must respond to it, since pressure is one of the ways the corporation stamps its priorities on the organization. However, despite this reaction, the manager must remain proactive in dealing with the entire corporation. Today's political strength may be tomorrow's business liability as the enterprise and the business evolve.

The development manager is faced with a basic dichotomy. On the one hand, it is necessary to manage a project process, which is, by its nature, unstable. Needs are assessed and enormous resources applied to one goal—the completion of a specific project. When that is done, an entirely new project is initiated, possibly in a new direction, which requires the same dedication and attention as the preceding one. This produces enormous ups and downs both for the staff and for performance. One project can be successful and another a failure despite the use of the same approach, people and priorities.

On the other hand, the manager must achieve stability and consistency both in maintaining what exists and in ensuring some commonality of direction. Without this stability, constant project shifts will inevitably create chaos. Out of that chaos will come such confusion that the company will no longer be able to react quickly to competition. In today's environment, this could spell disaster.

All of these factors make it extremely important for the manager to understand what is required in order to manage the development function aggressively. It is not good enough to be a fine technician or a superb politician. The manager must be a business generalist, a technical specialist, and a stable leader to fully meet corporate responsibilities. The manager must also thoroughly understand these responsibilities, how they can best be met and how they will change in a dynamic, transitional discipline. Such a charge defies a simple "cookbook" approach. It requires adaptation to specific situations and environments. That adaptation starts with an understanding of the basic issues.

This book is organized to provide that basis of understanding for the manager. Its three major divisions reflect the three principal factors in managing the development function: managing the process, managing the people, and managing the technology.

Part I, "Managing the Process," deals with those aspects of systems development which focus on the management of projects. It includes the receipt of work requests, the classification of those requests, and the measurement of the department's effectiveness against its charter.

Chapter 1, "Responsibilities and Scope of Systems Development," discusses the process of establishing a charter for the department, translating stated responsibilities into specific goals and communicating those responsibilities and goals to the staff. While seemingly basic, the establishment of a framework for the department's goals has a pervasive effect on its tasks and plans. All too often, little attention is paid to defining the purpose and charter of the development department. This chapter tries to put that issue in perspective.

Chapter 2, "Classes of Work," defines the basic classification of requests for development's resource dedication. The basic unit of work is the project, but projects are further broken down for application of performance expectation and service guarantees. Each class has its own special approach and implications for the department's success, and each requires specialized skills to ensure proper service.

Chapter 3, "Project Management," marks a departure from the conventional project management textbooks; it focuses on the development manager's new role. Most text books deal with the management, planning and control of a specific, start-to-end project. While effective management of these large projects is certainly important, the manager of development more often deals with a queue of projects, not single ones. Success is measured as much by the proper management of many projects as of any single one.

Chapter 4, "Organization," discusses options for forming, developing and maintaining a department for maximum effectiveness. Several variations of organization are discussed, together with their pluses and minuses. In order to establish an effective organization, the manager must tailor it to match both company characteristics and technology. That organization should not be created accidentally or simply because it has always existed. It must represent the best possible arrangement for the company. That tailoring requires understanding and planning.

Chapter 5, "Performance Measurement," discusses the need to measure the effectiveness of development efforts. This goes beyond determining how well systems perform to consider how effective the process itself is. If development is to maintain an effective posture within the company, it must be able to both improve and display that improvement to upper management. The measurements described in this chapter bear the same emphasis as the balance of this book—measuring in terms of the function's performance, not abstract technical metrics.

Part II, "Managing the People," addresses the issues involving the personnel in a development department. It is through people that the manager ultimately achieves his goals. Managing development people requires unusual efforts both to provide a satisfying environment and to merge these diverse personalities into an effective department personality. Historically, the demand for skilled technicians has exceeded the supply. Despite the trend toward end user development, this situation is likely to remain for the foreseeable future. Managers must address themselves to their staff's needs while operating the department in the most cost-effective manner possible.

Chapter 6, "Personalities," discusses the characteristics of the typical development department. It is important for the manager to understand what skill sets and general traits are displayed in order to maximize the department's output. Available skill sets must be matched with perceived future trends. Edicts regarding change are of little good if one cannot ensure that the people are available to make that change successful.

Chapter 7, "Establishing a Department Personality," discusses ways to meld the diverse personalities discussed in Chapter 6 into a cohesive, supportive single personality. Naturally, people are individuals. They display unique personality styles, and the manager cannot hope to eliminate that individualism. Nor should it be eliminated. However, successful departments always display a common thrust and set of values and philosophies. Success is invariably tied to how effective this group thrust is. It fosters support and channels drive to a single goal. When this occurs, the value of the whole exceeds the sum of the parts.

Chapter 8, "Hiring and Career Pathing," addresses both the acquisition of new talent and the maintenance of a group of long-term employees. Development people are typically career oriented. They measure success as much by the future they perceive as by the short-term challenges and gratification they experience. The successful manager provides opportunities for advancement while bringing in the most appropriate (not necessarily the most technically skilled) people to keep the organization populated and fresh.

Chapter 9, "Politics, Pressure and Stress," deals with the reality of working in a development department. It is important for the manager to understand how these factors affect the development process. As a technical group, developers react to pressure well, but generally only when they perceive a logical direction and benefit from that pressure. Oriented to cost/justification and associated product quality issues, they must be shielded at times from the realities of politics and at other times immersed in them. This chapter discusses ways to shield employees and ways to bring them into satisfying contact with politics and pressure while avoiding debilitating stress.

Chapter 10, "Perks and Benefits," discusses the imaginative ways in which the manager can make the development department one of the acknowledged best places to work. This goes beyond the conventional company benefits and, in many cases, includes ways for the manager to transcend the limitations imposed by corporate policy.

Part III, "Managing the Technology," discusses the various aspects of technology which affect the development manager both today and in the future. It does not deal with state-of-the-art hardware but rather with those components of technology which are controllable by development itself. It includes factors which one may not immediately perceive in terms of technology—procedures and methods. However, these are the technologies of development. They further and enhance the function's ability to fulfill its responsibility, just as sophisticated systems allow user departments to fulfill theirs.

Chapter 11, "End User Languages," deals with the coming transition of development. End user languages are a direct response to two factors in the reality of developing systems: an independent department cannot hope to keep pace with the systems backlog, and the end user is far more capable of preparing systems solutions to business problems. The opportunities created by this technology involve high risks if not properly managed. Invalid information can be presented for executive strategies if not properly auditted and controlled. One of development's chief challenges for the future is to provide this control—albeit at arms length.

Chapter 12, "Procedures, Methods and Standards," reviews the principal mechanisms the manager uses in directing the department. The manager cannot hope to manage every aspect of every project directly. Procedures, methods and standards allow the direction and consistency of projects to be maintained by the staff. It is important to strike a balance between bureaucracy and freedom when developing and maintaining these mechanisms.

Chapter 13, "Managing in the Database Environment," addresses the impacts felt by the development manager in a growing database environment. The database is a major component of the future development staff. Through years of theory on comprehensive, fully integrated databases, there has been little practical success in achieving the original goals of the database concept. This chapter steps back from the concept and focuses on the pragmatic issues involved in establishing the database.

Chapter 14, "The Information Center," concerns the concept of providing professional assistance to the user/developer. When combined with end user languages and a pragmatic database approach, the information center presents a picture of development's future role in the corporation. Today its application varies widely. In this chapter, options and potentials are discussed, as well as the transition from a conventional department to an information center.

Chapter 15, "Planning for Transition," focuses on imaginative ways to position the development department for the future. Development is a unique function in the business community. Technology and competitive pressures drive it to constant change. While its future is today somewhat vague, certain characteristics of development in the future can be postulated. The development manager must place his department in a position to realize the benefits of the future. This requires imagination and creative application. Chapter 15 discusses some of the ways this can be done.

Systems development is a difficult and challenging business function to manage. It is subject to extraordinary changes, and there is little opportunity for the manager to rest on yesterday's laurels. Methods of operation must change in step with the technology flooding the discipline daily. The need for sophisticated computer systems is quickly becoming an overriding factor in corporate success or failure. The increased visibility and importance of development brings with it increased pressure and requires a comprehensive, well-balanced approach to management.

The purpose of this book is not to provide pat answers to the challenges facing the development manager. The intent is rather to paint a broad picture of what management of this critical function means. The development manager of today cannot simply be a technocrat or a superior project manager. It is necessary to understand the implications of decisions across all of the department's responsibilities. Only through this understanding can the corporate need for information systems be filled and the future of the corporation safeguarded.

Acknowledgments The author gratefully expresses his appreciation to the following for their contributions to this work.

Thomas M. Danninger
Vice President, Data Management Center
Aspen Systems, Rockville, Maryland

Thomas W. Johnson
Vice President, Information Systems Division
State Street Bank and Trust Company
Boston, Massachusetts

Chester R. Smith
Manager of Training
Northern Telecom Inc.
Research Triangle Park, North Carolina

CONTENTS

Part I
Managing the Process

1
RESPONSIBILITIES AND SCOPE OF SYSTEMS DEVELOPMENT

The responsibilities and scope of systems development are shaped by the political imperatives of the company and the strengths and conceptual subjectivity of MIS management. Seldom does the MIS executive have the opportunity, or luxury, to determine objectively what the development department should accomplish, what services can and should be provided, and how to go about providing them.

Buffeted by company politics, MIS is viewed sometimes as a bottom-line business group and at other times as a collection of technocrats. Unable to understand and cope with the complexities and evolution of the discipline, corporate management veers from close surveillance of MIS through steering committees to a nearly total ignorance of its activities. MIS management responds by installing reactive organizational structures such as end-user computing support groups. In this environment, it is impossible to establish and develop a sensible definition of the responsibilities and scope of MIS.

This is an unfortunate situation. Without a definite strategy and clearly defined responsibilities, a systems development group loses effectiveness and viability. To proceed effectively, its responsibilities must be clear and the scope of its activities universally understood.

In this chapter, we will discuss the responsibilities of MIS. These include defining development, tracing its evolution, and discussing the importance of a charter for the function. Once these issues have been clarified, we will discuss how and why systems development work is allocated.

DEFINITION OF SYSTEMS DEVELOPMENT

Since this book is intended for professional MIS personnel and those with an active interest in systems development, a detailed definition will not be given. However a few comments are in order.

First, surprisingly few organizations have formally defined the role of systems development. Given the dramatic evolution of this function and its importance to the company, its purpose must be clearly understood. Otherwise, opportunities to use developmental skills will be missed. Second, without a formal and universally understood definition of systems development, managers find it difficult to fulfill their responsibilities to the organization. And conversely, the organization does not know what to expect from the development department. Third, unlike other corporate disciplines, development is new enough so that its definition is far from clear. In an age when the future of many companies lies in the effective use of technology and information, an explicit definition must be provided.

Defining the development function is not something for which the development manager is likely to be applauded. However, it is important enough to receive the manager's careful and deliberate attention. Appendix A analyzes the components of the typical definition of development. This is also the definition assumed in this book. It bears some study.

DISPERSEMENT OF THE DEVELOPMENT FUNCTION

The development function has been dispersed in myriad ways across the business community. More and more, we see the infusion of business analysts in many departments. In some cases, these analysts form subdepartments and are seemingly in conflict with the MIS development charter. This has been the cause of much consternation and conflict, not to mention confusion of roles. These attitudes can be attributed more to the newness of dispersement than to its suitability or unsuitability. Most often, the conflict is caused by the development department's perception of its reduction in scope rather than by abuse by users. In reality, the analysis of business needs is the province of functional experts. Accounting departments, for example, are far more capable of evaluating their computer system needs than development personnel. They are immersed in the subtle nuances of their activity and gain an implicit understanding of its workings as much by osmosis as by explicit analysis. MIS workers cannot hope to attain their level of understanding.

The ability to evaluate system needs, however, does not imply the ability to design solutions to meet these needs. Design and selection of alternatives requires the training and expertise of the professional analyst. Regardless of the functional understanding of the user, it is not a substitute for expertise in the process of development.

Professional systems analysts in user departments do not threaten the development group; they aid and extend the group's delivery capability. However, there must be compliance with a set of rules governing the development and support of systems. There must be free and frequent communication, project control must be equalized, and consistent methods must be followed for the relationship to be truly cooperative. Without this compliance, it is impossible to develop long-term strategies; the result is hopelessly fragmented, redundant systems.

RESPONSIBILITIES TO THE COMPANY

Most companies today find the business world very different from what it was 20 years ago. Consumers are far more demanding, government regulations are quick to stifle drastic price strategies, and product obsolescence occurs almost immediately after introduction. In this environment, two elements are essential for survival: the ability to analyze vast amounts of information rapidly and the ability to provide increasingly sophisticated technological services.

Therefore, corporate success is intimately related to the growth and continuity of systems development. This is a far cry from the situation a few years ago, when MIS was considered a necessary evil—and, for many persons, not totally necessary. That is a heavy responsibility for a discipline that has matured quickly and sporadically.

This heavy responsibility of MIS is linked to satisfactory fulfillment of its role. This means not being all things to all people. Although the scope of development is broad, it is not deep. The definition of MIS involves specific responsibilities which are fairly easy to predict from its charter. The five most critical responsibilities will now be discussed.

Supporting Current Systems

Most of the attention of MIS is devoted to new systems development. Nearly all the material published on methods, procedures and mechanisms is aimed at developing new systems more effectively. However, the first and foremost responsibility of development is to maintain the continued flow of existing information systems. Regardless of how obsolete a system becomes, it must be kept running until an acceptable alternative is developed. Typically, this includes a substantial investment in enhancements and extensions which far outstrip the original investment and, equally often, outstrip the cost of a replacement system. Although this situation seems illogical, it actually occurs all the time. We replace automobile parts, for example, long after the economical life of the car is over. This is true simply because there is no dramatic signal that it is time for a change. Better ways can always be found to invest funds if one can make due with what is already available. It is the prime responsibility of development departments to provide management with the options to make this investment choice.

Maintaining Business Currency

Since technology leads to innovation, systems development departments must keep abreast of industry advances and assess and implement those advances in the company. Often this effort can appear to run counter to the priorities of upper management, which is frustrating to the development manager. However, the effort must be made and imaginative ways found to implement these features and enhancements with the lowest possible cost and human impact. Over time this effort will become increasingly fruitful as management begins to recognize the advantages of technological currency.

To be technologically up-to-date, one must understand what is occurring in the local market. What is being done by area MIS organizations with which the company competes? How does this affect the business environment, including competition for competent people? This information can be found anywhere from local newspapers to meetings of professional organizations. Gathering it does not imply a need for corporate espionage. It merely creates a healthy state of professional competition from which everyone benefits.

Understanding Information Technology

The advent and legitimatizing of fourth-generation computer languages, decision support facilities, and personal computers gives the user an incredibly rich variety of options in solving systems problems. With these tools, the opportunity to bypass the corporate role of MIS and establish purely endemic systems at one's own pace enhances the user's capability but can jeopardize corporate health.

Regardless of the "user friendliness" of the facilities, there is a need for expertise in information technology which goes well beyond computer literacy. The economics of scale, single vendor support, data integrity, and a number of related issues can be handled competently only by professional MIS workers with a strong background in development. In addition, MIS provides an independent and, hopefully, objective perspective on corporate priorities.

Development personnel must remain the experts. With the variety of systems solutions and the low-cost availability of independent computer power, the development of information technology has become a major aspect of the developer's responsibility. In many organizations, this role is defined as user services, the information center or consulting services. Often it is independent of the development organization. Regardless of the company's organization chart, however, it is a development function and requires the perspective, experience, and technical expertise of a development analyst.

Understanding Technological Opportunities

As often as business problems spur the investigation and implementation of technological solutions, technological opportunities go in search of a problem to solve. In the early stages of the discipline, MIS professionals were constantly accused of creating problems with their myopic concentration on technology and were lectured on the need to be business minded.

In fact, truly innovative firms—those that lead their field—constantly evaluate emerging technologies to see if they can be used to competitive advantage. As competition stiffens and product variations narrow, the use of technology to gain the upper hand is becoming the only way of increasing the company's market share. With the high level of systematization of production which exists in most firms, the systems development perspective is essential to fully understand the implications, cost, and effort involved in implementing these opportunities.

This is not an isolated role for development. It must work in concert with the traditional responsibilities of planning and engineering to apply and implement new technologies. However, the increased reliance of companies on information and rapid status analysis make this a vital systems development function.

Providing New and Expanded Services

This is the responsibility typically associated with development: the implementation of new systems and the enhancement of old ones. A few years ago, it would have ranked first in importance on this list, but given the user-oriented facilities discussed earlier, this is no longer true. This ranking will continue to slip. It is a simple matter of the pace that can be maintained and how well the development discipline adapts to its evolving role.

As businesses become more and more dependent on computer solutions, it becomes more difficult to implement new systems or enhance old ones. The interrelationships of existing systems and data becomes increasingly complex and sensitive to error. The impact of computer technology also widens to the point where a seemingly minor enhancement affects the entire organization. As much time is spent in announcing the change as in making it.

The most popular solution to this problem has been the "integrated database" with its array of detailed information, which supposedly provides total security, unambiguity, and insensitivity to change. However, database technology and its implementation have fallen woefully short of this expectation. What we see is a database for accounting, one for payroll, one for manufacturing, and so on ad infinitum, until the difference between databases and independent files is blurred.

The only effective way to implement an integrated database across the organization is through a substantial independent effort or a steady, long-term strategy. However, the first is too expensive and the second too lengthy for most firms. Therefore, the integrated corporate database is not likely to help us in the near future.

The developer is left, then, with the same tools as before for developing and enhancing systems. Databases, sophisticated methodologies, and enhanced computer literacy are all available to help, but the basic approach of careful attention to detail, formalized, dynamic planning, and hard work still remain the most effective tools.

To sum up, the support of current systems, maintenance of business currency, understanding of information technology, understanding technological opportunities, and providing new and expanded services are the five primary responsibilities of systems development. However, evolution being what it is, that ranking will remain dynamic. Table 1–1 lists additional responsibilities of most development functions today. Many of them are situational and the list can be extended or reduced. The important thing is that every organization that hopes to succeed should create such a list and be aware of the relative importance of each item on it.

Table 1–1. Prime Responsibilities of Systems Development

1. *Purpose:* Contribute to Corporate Health

   Assures the growth and continued stability of the corporation

   Support current systems
   Maintain business currency
   Understand information technology
   Understand technological opportunities
   Provide new and expanded services

2. *Purpose:* Assess the Viability of Information Usage

   Relates and maintains computer use for company goals, policies, and strategies

   Assure appropriate use of computing resources
   Certify externally developed system solutions
   Provide a strategic framework for technology
   Extend computer literacy throughout the corporation
   Provide systems expertise to business functions

3. *Purpose:* Internal Productivity

   Maintains a leading-edge posture for systems Development

   Measure, maintain, and improve service-level commitments
   Provide preventive maintenance for systems
   Assure maximum flexibility for systems to match changing business needs
   Improve system life-cycle costs
   Replace technically obsolete systems

EVOLUTION OF MIS

Evolution is a natural progression from one stage of development to another. It is an inevitable process which we can alter, for good or bad, but never stop. The one certainty is that it will continue. The role and validity of development in the business environment tomorrow depends on the priorities we set today and on how well we plan that evolution.

The phases of MIS evolution have often been described. Its expanding and contracting responsibilities will be considered here. Those responsibilities are related to technological evolution. Most of these technologies, including database capabilities, enhanced communications capabilities, and microprocessors, are external to MIS. Each has had a dramatic influence on development responsibilities and thrusts, and each was originally driven by influences not directly related to systems development.

That fact in itself breeds dangers. A viable organization must develop its own level of importance within the corporation in order to assure a reasonable place for itself in the enterprise's decision-making process. The alternative is for the more critical responsibilities to be parceled out in response to each competing area's power structure. This leaves development with the dregs—those things no one else wants.

For this reason, an objective understanding of how and why development has progressed is paramount to formulating clear strategies for the future. With this preamble, we will discuss the three stages of development.

Stage 1: Manpower Substitution

The first stage of development, which ended with the implementation of operating systems around 1965, set the stage for the project justification process. It was almost totally concerned with the substitution of computer systems for repetitive and human-sensitive processes. Almost all of these were clerical activities such as payroll, accounting, billing, and check posting.

Historical filing took one of three forms: card files, tape libraries, or computer reports. In terms of their impact on the company, the maximum value of such systems was provided by removal or reallocation of personnel. It was during this phase that cost/benefit principles were used in deciding whether to initiate such projects.

Cost/benefit analysis showed that a computer system provides quantifiable savings over time. A delta factor between the cost of development and the savings produced by the system solution determined the benefit. Based upon staff size, projects were ranked by the magnitude of their benefit. Conversely, staff size was determined by the number of projects available over a certain return on investment (ROI) threshold—say, 25%.

The prime ingredient was the number of people displaced, either directly by obsolescence or indirectly by avoiding staff increases. With the many opportunities to trim staff, the stage was set to make this the prime, and almost total, determinant of project initiation.

MIS was also the sole dispenser of computing solutions. There was little general computer literacy among outside personnel, and developers did little to change this situation. Rather, they reveled in it, assuming the role of technical gurus with their own language and mores. The opportunity to educate others about the emerging technology was, by and large, ignored.

The overriding emphasis of cost/benefit analysis has not waned, despite recognition of the strategic nature of information technology. Project justification continues to be less important than avoiding costs, improving methods, and increasing cash flow. In reality, far more is to be gained by improved information availability and increased competitive advantage than was ever achieved by displacing workers. However, in most cases, forced cost/benefit thinking still remains.

An unwillingness to develop a common language and to define the position of MIS in relation to the business community was another problem resulting from the manpower substitution phase of MIS evolution. The barriers and mistrust which were created at that time have never been completely destroyed. The reluctance of users to accept MIS evaluations has been a significant price to pay. Even more damaging, however, has been the exclusion of MIS and development management from the management fraternity.

This exclusion has forced MIS executives to learn the trade in spite of upper management. It has caused them to react to corporate strategies rather than becoming involved in their formulation. While this situation is now ending, it has had a major impact on the evolution of development through its next stage, as well as its relative immaturity in today's management structure.

Stage 2: Information Custodians

With the advent of operating systems and the additional controls they provided, the roles of developers changed drastically. The controls and disciplines spread to the development process itself, making the efforts of MIS workers far more predictable.

Work began, and progressed at a dramatic rate, on the formalized methods and the scientific approach to systems development. Predictability was a key ingredient in the evolution of development. It allowed the user/customer to see and sometimes understand where the work was. It also provided visibility and offset the skepticism created earlier by MIS.

Most of the methods stressed (in some cases, beyond reason) the heavy involvement of the user in the development process. While methods are discussed later, suffice it to say that this situation was exactly the reverse of the earlier MIS practice. The user was generally less than enthusiastic about the high level of involvement required and either paid lip service or refused to participate. While this rebuff generally created an atmosphere of ill will, the final result was positive: A vehicle was created for active and cooperative communication between the user and the developer. A common ground had been established. The result was a far more dependable system which met the user's needs.

An additional benefit of this work in development technology was the disciplining of the process itself. A judgment could now be made on what constituted a good product or a bad one. Steps were designed to ensure that good systems were the result of development projects, and systems maintenance and enhancement were simplified.

This stage was also marked by the spread of database technology. It heralded the concept of the information specialist and the use of corporate data as an accessible resource—the same as capital. It was at this time that the idea of integrating all corporate information-producing activities into a single hierarchy was spawned.

As we mentioned earlier, and will discuss in detail in Chapter 13, integration has never been achieved. The emphasis on the database as the be-all and end-all solution had the unfortunate effect of causing us to ignore other opportunities. It did, however, provide another major benefit. Because the database provided stable data relationships, it allowed the development of decision support and ad hoc inquiry facilities.

This stage created an atmosphere in which users could develop some of their own solutions—albeit in a limited fashion. It broadened knowledge of systems and placed the MIS person in a position to become a steward of data rather than merely a dispenser of systems.

The final major outgrowth of this stage was provided by academia. The computer science curriculum began to be integrated with business as well as engineering. These graduates became aware of the potential of information technology in this competitive world. While they were not in a position to direct the strategy of their companies, they brought a new perspective to executive management. Today they are chief executive officers in many corporations. As a result, the stature of MIS and systems development roles has greatly increased.

Stage 3: Integration

The third stage of MIS began in early 1982 with the introduction of the IBM personal computer (PC). It was not the first PC, or the best, or the cheapest. But it was IBM's. Thus, it legitimatized the PC as a viable business machine. More important, given IBM's ability to market the PC in huge numbers, it spawned the development of an enormous variety of software products.

This was the ultimate form of the decision support product. Now not only could user-managers look at data in any way desired, they could develop and implement any systems needed. All this could be done with a minimum investment and a high probability of meeting one's needs directly and immediately.

Granted, the solution was likely to be limited to the department/function involved, to ignore existing data, and to involve a high risk of error. But it had been developed in time to solve immediate problems. This was significantly better than the typically longer development procedure.

The reaction of MIS personnel was quick and short-sighted. Equipment purchases were disallowed in favor of performing development on centralized mainframe computers. Requests for help were met by quotations of standards which limited the acquisition and deployment of the PC. Promised MIS solutions were slow in coming—if at all.

Aggressive users purchased PCs anyway, either as office equipment or for their own use. Then they either bought software or developed it themselves and set to work. The development department was neither consulted nor coordinated with. This created a potentially disastrous situation.

Recently, things have begun to change. A prime example is the advent of the business analyst, often in the user area, to consolidate and coordinate user and MIS development efforts to achieve a common solution. Another is the creation of the information center, software clearing house, and the like—healthy harbingers of truly cooperative development. Much still needs to be done, but the stage is set.

Since we are still in stage 3, the impact of the PC revolution is hard to determine. However, three major developments have occurred which, if analyzed, point to major evolutionary steps in development.

1. The first, as previously mentioned, is the advent of the business analyst, or, stated another way, the existence of development practitioners in the user community. This indicates a willingness to participate in developing information technology and a recognition of its value in creating business strategy. MIS must carefully foster this new role to ensure that it does not evolve into a replacement for the development analyst. That level of expertise and objectivity is still needed despite the ease with which the new tools can be used.

2. The second major development concerns dispersement. The creation and acceptance of fourth-generation computer languages has extended the potential for systems development to nearly everyone in the organizaton. This can be risky, since not all parts of systems should be developed by the casual computer user. However, it does increase significantly the resource pool available to implement systems far more responsively than in the past.

Dispersement should not be confused with distribution. Dispersement involves the movement of the development process into areas not controlled by MIS departments. Distribution is the movement of components of the MIS function, such as hardware itself or localized variations in software, to remote facilities. In general, control is still exerted by MIS professionals although those remote sites may have substantial variations in upward reporting and authority. Distribution can include anything from hardware to decision processes.

Dispersement brings risks—in many ways, far more pervasive risks than distribution. However, it is inevitable. One of the challenges to the future development department is to direct and support dispersement and distribution as effectively as possible.

3. Dispersed development could not be considered reasonable without the third dramatic contribution of stage 3: the spread of computer literacy. Exposure to computer fundamentals, through either education or osmosis, has created a user community capable of assuming the responsibilities inherent in systems development.

More important than speeding dispersed development, widespread computer literacy creates an environment in which the developer must propose fundamentally sound systems. Users will no longer be fooled into accepting unworkable solutions. This environment of knowledgeable users is healthy for the company as a whole. It challenges the computer professional to provide stronger, more germane designs and strategies.

LESSONS FOR THE FUTURE

Evolution is progressive. Understanding that progression, and what lessons have been learned, is crucial to planning future steps intelligently and solving problems. For a variety of reasons, not the least of which is the speed of technology, MIS development has been progressing rather spasmodically. This situation contributes to the development group's continued operation in a reactive rather than a proactive mode. Unfortunately, with the development options available to the user today, a reactive mode is a guarantee of failure—for the development staff and the organization as a whole.

In Part III, planning for the future is discussed, based on the pragmatic realization that systems development is in constant transition. It should be

Table 1-2. Key Issues in the Evolution of Development

Stage 1. Manpower substitution
- Institution of a cost/benefit orientation
- Concentration on replacement/reallocation of personnel
- Isolation of the technocrat from the business community

Stage 2. Information custodians
- Formalization and discipline
- Movement to involve users in development
- Growth of the information orientation: database introduction
- Decision support/ad hoc inquiry growth
- Computer science as a business curriculum

Stage 3. Integration
- General use of the business analyst
- Dispersement of development
- Extensive computer literacy
- Development as a transitional function

emphasized that maintaining a posture which allows technological advances to be exploited is often more advantageous than pure business strategy.

Table 1-2 summarizes the key issues that have arisen in the evolution of development. Knowing these issues, and the ones focusing on the specific organization, we can determine how the responsibilities and scope of development have been defined. If this definition does not match the role perceived by management, steps must be taken to achieve alignment.

THE DEVELOPMENT CHARTER

In a smoothly operating, cooperative organization, there is an implicit understanding of the responsibilities and scope of every department; in many cases, of every individual. This is one of the prime strengths of the small company. It allows concentration of skill sets, maximal flexibility, nonredundant activities, and a minimum of contention. It is one of the first characteristics of success lost as the company grows.

In order to avoid the problems associated with growth, organizations take steps to formalize responsibility and scope. Unfortunately, this is typically done at the individual level via job descriptions. Seldom, except in the very large company, is parallel formalization made at the department level. This situation creates confusion and an atmosphere of conflict.

Since most departmental functions are well established, the conflicts do not become overwhelming. However, MIS does not have a long, stable history. In order to overcome this problem, it is necessary to create a charter in order to define explicitly the responsibilities, scope, and characteristics of this department.

Format and Style

Like any written document, the development charter should be prepared with its audience in mind. This audience is twofold: the members of the MIS department and the end users who require its services. In addition, care must be taken to assure the department's ability to evolve along with the organization.

All too often, MIS personnel prepare documents in playscript fashion. This is a holdover from stage 1 of clerical function replacement, when each step had to be followed precisely and without variation. The purpose of the charter is to define responsibilities while making it possible to adapt that definition to new and unanticipated situations. Without flexibility, the charter is doomed to rapid obsolescence.

The complete charter should occupy no more than two pages. Studies have shown that people tend to lose interest after that point and ignore anything longer. Embedding a mass of detail in the body of the document will accomplish nothing more than causing it to be unread. If the responsibilities and scope of MIS are such that a lengthier definition is required, it is best to provide separate section attachments or references. In this way, persons with specific interests will have the opportunity to focus on the material of relevance to them.

The charter should be written in a crisp, concise fashion. Brevity is more important than grammatical purity. This helps to keep the charter short and allows for a reasonable amount of situational interpretation. If clarification is essential, separate attachments should be used.

Content

The charter should cover a minimum of six topics in order to properly define development's relationship with other MIS organs, as well as with the balance of the company: definition, organization, responsibilities, scope, sources of work, and references. With extensively split development groups, several charters may exist. However, taken together, they should give a complete and accurate picture of the development function.

Organization has a significant impact on the way the charter is structured and worded. Management separation by business function may make it necessary to write independent charters for the finance and marketing development groups. If this is the case, as much of the charter as possible should be common in order to ensure a consistent approach.

Figure 1-1 depicts the relationship of grouped charters across sample organizational lines. Figure 1-2 is a sample organization charter which can be reviewed, along with a sample discussion.

Definition. The definition provided in the charter is the previously discussed generic definition. Added to it are components tailored to the organization, as seen in Figure 1-2. An assumption is made regarding the defi-

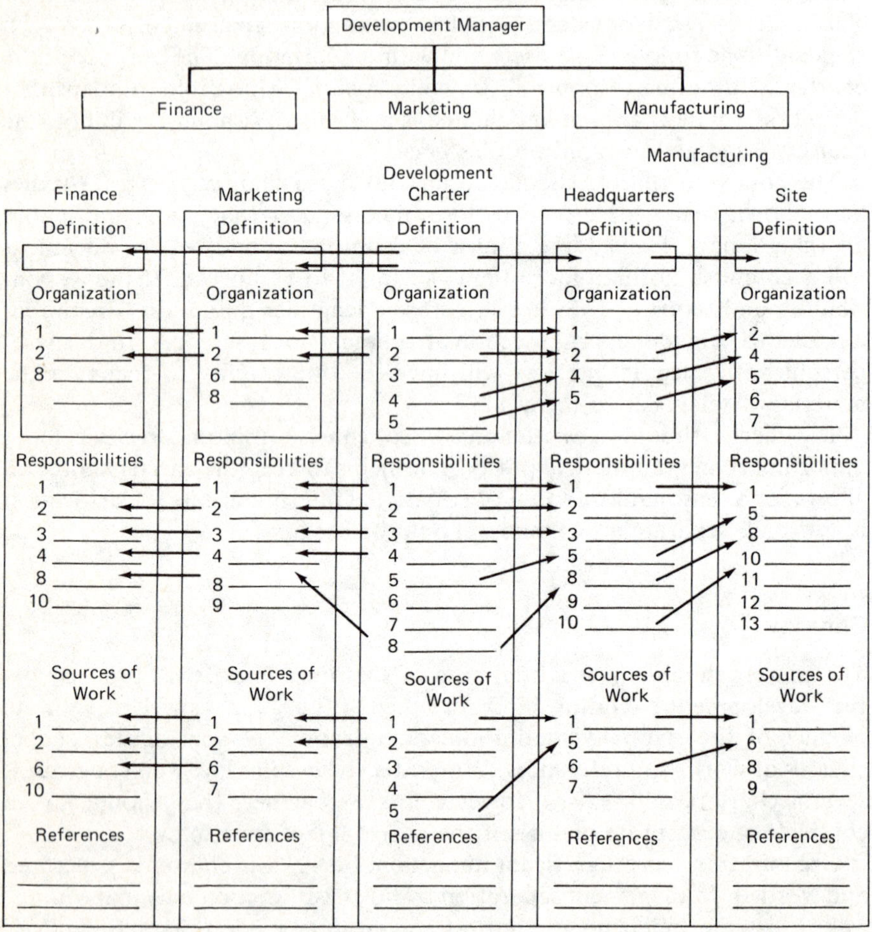

Figure 1-1. Dispersed Organization Charters.

CHARTER OF OPERATION—SYSTEMS DEVELOPMENT (DEPARTMENT 21XX)

DEFINITION

MIS systems development is responsible for the construction, implementation and support of all certified application systems.

ORGANIZATION

The department reports administratively to the vice-president for MIS. Within the department are four separate wings, which report to the vice-presidents of those business lines:

Financial Systems Development —Vice President of Finance
Marketing Systems Development—Vice President of Sales/Marketing
Plant Systems —Vice President of Manufacturing
Corporate Systems —Vice President of Planning and Administration

RESPONSIBILITIES

1. Evaluation of all work requests, categorization of these requests, establishment of priorities for estimation and presentation of those requests/recommendations to the appropriate steering committee.
2. Maintenance of an applications portfolio in regard to system value, competitive state, technological currency, and performance. Report on portfolio status to the quarterly Management Steering Committee.
3. Assure maximum efficiency in the development process through evaluation of new technologies, adaptation of new techniques and internal working committees.
4. Construction and implementation of new and enhanced computer systems. This may take place through the dedication of development resources, coordination of external efforts or adaptation of package software.
5. Support of production software and correction of failures and problems occurring in normal operation. Problem solution coordination from identification of failure through final solution, including communication of status to the service center.
6. Maintenance of service-level commitments, by project category, as defined in MIS service-level commitments. Reporting on service-level performance to the Management Steering Committee.
7. Evaluation of emerging technologies and reporting on potential adaptations of those technologies which may provide competitive advantage, expanded customer services and/or increased operational efficiency. Coordination with corporate strategic planning to integrate those opportunities into the planning cycle.
8. Provide information consulting services to the user community at the standard corporate charge-back rate. Requests for services will be fulfilled following corporate procedures.

SCOPE

Development is responsible for the construction and implementation of all new systems and enhancement of existing systems, with the following exceptions:

1. Localized personal computer (PC) and decision support applications,
2. Engineering design applications,
3. Internal auditing systems.

Support is provided for all applications which have passed certification procedures.

(*continued*)

Figure 1-2. Sample development charter.

Consulting support for application exceptions and noncertified systems is provided as time permits and at the standard consulting charge-back rate.

SOURCES OF WORK
Work requests are made to Development by one of four methods:

1. Completion of the work request form for new development or enhancement of existing systems. There are two types of work requests forms:
   a. Standard Form AB-123
   b. Interactive Project Request (see the opening system menu)

   All requests will be briefly evaluated for feasibility. Further analysis, and entry into the request queue, require department manager approval.

2. Evaluation request from the Management Steering Committee.
3. Request for support of system failures made by calling User Support Problem Reporting.
4. Analytical support-level commitments from members of work committees established within standards guidelines.

REFERENCES
Corporate Policies: 1.2, 1.5, 1.9, 4.6
Corporate Standards: 1.0–1.19, 3.0–3.12
Corporate Procedures: 12.0–12.35

Figure 1–2. (*continued*)

nitions of many terms (e.g., "certified"). It is hoped that these terms appear in a standards and procedures manual.

Organization. It is imperative to describe the reporting structure of the group. Without this, readers may be able to figure out what the group does, but will be unable to determine who they are or where to go for more information. If corporate organization charts are maintained, they should be referenced but never attached to the charter. The description should, once again, be short.

Obviously, Figure 1–2 represents a matrix arrangement for the company. A number of systems may appear to service each organizational unit. This is inevitable in a highly systematized environment. However, the majority of the systems will qualify readily for the proper reporting lines.

Responsibilities. In a limited document such as a charter, the total responsibilities of the group cannot be described in detail. To some extent, the descriptions should be generic, so that detail issues can be referred to the relevant ones. However, the descriptions should not be too general. They should be germane to the organization and should cover the most commonly experienced situations.

If separate documents exist to clarify these responsibilities, they should be referenced. Most commonly, they appear in standards manuals and may include commitments to performance, required forms, steering committee charters, and other relevant information. The responsibilities listed in Figure 1–2 are fairly representative.

Scope. The advent of the PC, increasing computer literacy, and the increasing dispersement of the development function over the last few years have increased the need for a strict definition of the scope of development. This is especially important at a time when the phases of the development cycle may be addressed by a variety of departments, with little or no control exerted by the professional development staff.

After a blanket statement is made, this section of the charter most often takes the form of disclaimers and exceptions.

Sources of Work. For a development group to maintain its viability, there must be an explicit mechanism to request work and an expectation of getting a response. Informal discussion will not satisfy this requirement in terms of either resource allocation or user confidence. In nearly every organization, work requests follow a specific pattern. This section of the charter simply formalizes that process.

References. One of the limitations of documentation is its susceptibility to obsolescence. To limit this tendency as much as possible, items covered in higher-level documents, such as standards or policies, should be referenced rather than repeated.

The final section of the charter should be an index of all standards and higher-level documents which are referenced in the charter or required to understand it.

The creation of a development charter will inevitably breed the need for charters in other areas of MIS. Once the development charter has been written, the MIS executive can describe all internal requirements and relationships to avoid conflicts within the department.

The charter is crucial for the development department to fulfill its organizational role. It defines the department's function for the balance of the organization and allows an intelligent transition to new or expanded responsibilities without degrading its current service commitments.

CONCLUSION

The responsibilities and scope of MIS development vary widely across industry types and company cultures. For example, management's attitude and the level of strategic involvement in high-technology industries are very different from those found in manufacturing companies.

The level of formality in different firms has an impact as well. There are many firms whose procedures and policy manuals are developed solely for the benefit of the auditors and the board of directors. An entrepreneurial, shoot-from-the-hip approach is favored. In such an environment, stringent coordination of a development charter with the policy manual is obviously an exercise in futility. By contrast, firms with a heavy involvement in government contracts require stringent procedural adherence to secure and maintain those contracts. In such cases, the formality of the procedures and policies can have as important an influence on company health as the product itself.

There are universal givens, however. One of them is that the development of strategic systems is essential to the life of the company. In order to ensure the production of those systems, there must be a well-understood division of responsibilities within MIS. Otherwise, those systems will either be delayed or of less than optimal quality.

The culture of the company helps determine how effectively the development function is integrated into the organization. Regardless of the adequacy of integration, however, development must ensure that its own level of formality adequately reflects its *real* levels of responsibility and that it can meet that responsibility. With that foundation established, building the framework of the department and enhancing its function becomes significantly easier.

2

CLASSES OF WORK

In order to manage the development process, it is essential to understand how work flows into, through, and out of the development department. The set of activities which ensures a smooth, productive flow can then be identified. However, as the discussion of charter development in Chapter 1 reveals, and as experience in any environment teaches, work flow varies widely depending on what type of work is being performed.

Each task requires a different approach, measurement criterion, and estimating mechanism. Often individuals perform at significantly different levels of proficiency depending on the type of development work in which they are involved. The only effective way to manage this diversity is by appropriately classifying work as it is received and adhering to procedures that are sensitive to each class.

Classification is important for many reasons. During the life of a corporation, priorities for resource allocation vary based on a variety of external conditions. Economic slowdowns are marked by staff reductions (later, we will discuss how to ensure that this does not affect permanent staff) and concentration on support and preventive maintenance. When a recovery is sensed, a dramatic shift occurs to gain a competitive edge by introducing new services. With acquisitions and product-line expansion, new emphasis is placed on specific application enhancements.

The criteria for determining performance also vary substantially among different types of work. Measures and reports on the performance of large, complex, new systems are dramatically different from those used for enhancements. In the first case, the schedule-performance ratio predominates; in the second case, the emphasis is on the number of units produced.

The degree of visibility also varies substantially. Major projects achieve maximum visibility only at specific times: major milestones, user tests, and implementations. Enhancements provide more steady but less dramatic visibility. Support produces high visibility generally in negative terms—a failure to meet service levels. Consulting support, probably the most important form today, generally receives only spotty reviews.

Table 2–1. Purpose of Classification

Allows independent application of priorities by eliminating competition for resources
Allows independent application of service levels by separating goals by work characteristics
Increases visibility of high-level business needs by highlighting requests across multiple priority levels
Segregates requisite resource allocations by classifying requirements by risk and complexity
Ensures flexibility to match business needs by allowing demand servicing to match economic conditions
Provides a smooth flow of request servicing by preventing blockage of queues with high resource efforts
Simplifies assignment of external resources by insulating of low-risk efforts
Allows the development of meaningful estimating methods by matching historical trends to types of efforts

The key purposes of classification are shown in Table 2–1. This list can easily be adapted to the specific environment.

As discussed in Chapter 1, the development function is often dispersed among a number of organizations. However, the characteristics of classification remain constant. It is important to deal with these characteristics consistently in terms of measurement, priorities, methods and implementation if the process itself is to remain consistent.

In this chapter, we will discuss the management of four broad classes of work: support, enhancements, maintenance and new systems development. We will also consider the subdivision of classes into categories and the management of project queues by class and category.

SUPPORT

Support encompasses those activities that ensure consistent functioning of the production environment, including correction of system failures, interpretation of unusual situations, and assisting in unusual cycles. With the growth of end-user systems, support now includes system consulting, which provides expert information to users.

The skills necessary for both situations are the same. The concept of "information resource management (IRM)" implies that the management of information usage is just as important as the running of programs and application systems. The management of these two types of support is significantly different, however, and each will be discussed separately.

Production Support

The prime responsibility of systems development is to keep production running, as noted in the definition of responsibilities in Chapter 1. Often production support is classified with computer operations because it is related to the steady-state environment. This arrangement is viewed as solving the typical problem of "letting the fox guard the henhouse" by separating the support, or production, role from that of development.

The development manager must remain sensitive to the key role of support within the organization. However, the competing activities of development and support must be separated to ensure that the development department's responsibilities are fulfilled. The way this separation is maintained depends on the size of the organization.

In the larger department, development and support are generally separated at the development manager level. Support personnel are assigned to specific applications in order to ensure a thorough and intimate knowledge of these functional areas. Their separation from new systems development is total; in some cases, an adversary role is purposely created. This provides a system of checks and balances between the typical change-oriented developer and the steady-state–oriented support person.

In the smaller department, development and support are often separated along business lines, such as finance and manufacturing. Separation also tends to occur at a higher level and to become somewhat blurred. In this environment, the support person can serve as a developer as well. This decision is nearly always based on resource availability. Dispersal of support leads to many problems, typically causing one role or the other to be sacrificed. Their fate is determined more often by the desires and interests of the staff than by the needs of the organization.

In Chapter 4, this and other issues of organization are discussed. In this chapter, however, the key issue is that support and development are substantially different and must be handled as separate entities. Regardless of how artificial this separation may seem, it must be maintained. Without it, both capabilities are compromised and their differing priorities blurred.

Consulting Support

The development department's response to user requests and problems is now being handled increasingly by consultation. The user's ability to direct and correct his own problems and find his own solutions shortens the production cycle and eases the pressures on MIS. To ensure that the user's efforts will be guided along safe and profitable lines, the professional developer's response must be as rapid and effective as that seen in the failure of production systems.

With computer languages for users, databases, and PCs, any use of the computer system for business purposes can be considered production. Therefore, the same techniques and priorities are used for providing consulting support. Priorities and urgency are established, request queues are managed, and support cycles are maintained. There are some exceptions, however, which make the management of this activity somewhat unique.

The differentiation between consulting and new development can become somewhat blurred and their demarcation difficult. Basically, once the direction of a project is established and a needs analysis is completed, the project moves from consulting to development. This boundary is not always clear but in operation is fairly easy to manage. The consultant's responsibility for providing new solutions consists of bringing the project to the definition stage. This may involve a considerable commitment on the part of development, or it may reside almost entirely with the user. The consultant attempts to clarify the decision factors involved.

During problem resolution, the consultant attempts to use the facilities of the system to solve the problem without making substantial changes. This may bring two results: a correction process and a request for system enhancement. The fact that system/program changes are not immediately necessary to restore operation is of major benefit.

In helping users solve problems or develop new systems, the allocation of time is not as straightforward as it is for the support person, who works from identification to postmortem and is then done. The consulting role may involve a long-term commitment throughout a strategic project. However, in terms of time allocation, the same rules apply. All allocations must be based on the release of requests from the project queues, where they are held for review. This release is based on priority and urgency. Therefore, a significant amount of the consultant's time should remain available for true problem resolution.

Visibility of Support

No development process is as visible as support. Yet, unlike the other processes, its visibility involves the avoidance of negatives. In this respect, it most closely parallels computer operations. It is most effective when no one notices that problems have occurred because they were corrected so quickly. The consultant's contribution is to give the user the confidence to undertake independent problem resolution. Development's contribution is intentionally deemphasized to enhance the user's sense of self-reliance.

This low-key posture has kept many upwardly mobile persons out of the support role. This function does not provide the extraordinary visibility necessary for rapid advancement which other roles in MIS provide. This topic will be discussed in more detail in Part II as a function of managing development personnel. At this point, suffice it to say that, in spite of the negative perception of the support role, the key role of any development

Table 2–2. Key Characteristics of Support

HIGH VISIBILITY OF FAILURES
Failure to produce an adequate level of support results in severe business problems

LOW VISIBILITY OF SUCCESS
Success in support involves invisibility; problems are averted before they become acute

HIGH-PRESSURE ENVIRONMENT
Once a support problem occurs, there is little leeway for mistakes

REACTIVE TO CURRENT SITUATIONS
Little planning can be done

MINIMUM INPUT FOR ANALYSIS
Situations must be resolved quickly with whatever information is available when the problem occurs

HIGH-PRIORITY RESOURCE DEMAND
The user expects the expert to take charge, and invariably that expert is needed

MULTISTAGE CORRECTION PROCESS
The system is brought back on line and then the real problem is corrected

SUSCEPTIBILITY TO DESIGN LIMITATIONS
Every limitation in system design results in a support problem, either by creating the problem or by inhibiting correction

GENERAL LACK OF UPWARDLY MOBILE PERSONNEL
Support does not typically attract aggressive people; they tend to focus on new systems

MINIMAL OPPORTUNITY FOR PRIORITIZATION
Severe problems must be corrected immediately, not when it is reasonable to deal with them

"MEATBALL SURGERY"
Support solutions cannot wait for elegant or even technically sophisticated procedures

member is to support the existing systems. This is accomplished not only by effective support of production systems but also by the user's development efforts.

The key characteristics of support are summarized in Table 2–2.

MAINTENANCE

Maintenance is the process of modifying the system in response to changes resulting from either planned cyclical situations or external events. Most typically, these modifications are mandated by regulatory changes or expansion/contraction of the business. In most cases, there is substantially more lead time for maintenance than for support, leading to more comprehensive and less risky implementation.

Maintenance is classified separately because it is vital to the *continued* health of the operational systems. In a well-managed maintenance process, system obsolescence through atrophy is minimized. By contrast, with poor maintenance, the system slowly becomes mired in exceptions and add-on features. These inevitably force extensive revisions or enhancements long before the competitive replacement stage occurs.

One goal of maintenance is to avoid replacing systems before their time. This can be accomplished only by ensuring that the expanded features of the system fit the original design criteria of the product. The impetus which drives any such change creates impacts which have characteristics that are common based on the business situation.

The expansion of the business, with larger production or new services, has the highest impact on the system. At times, this change provides the shortest lead time as well. The announcement of a new company purchase is often shrouded in secrecy until the final details are completed. When this finally occurs, the emphasis is on rapid integration to achieve the quickest profits and forestall the loss of customers due to uncertainty.

Maintenance requests, like those for support, have priorities. Urgency is a less important factor because all projects are equally urgent—they *must* be done. This causes a marked variation in the amount of maintenance work throughout the year. It tends to be cyclic and unbalanced.

An option which provides substantial benefits in all but the most extraordinary situations is known as "scheduled maintenance." With this approach, each department is given a specific period in which all maintenance requests are serviced. Only that department is addressed during its period, and only during that period is it addressed. The period in question may be scheduled as often as resources and needs dictate—yearly, quarterly, or even semimonthly. The key elements are the predictability and concentration of the cyclic schedule.

Scheduled maintenance has a number of dramatic benefits. First, all available resources can be assigned to the requests. This ensures that all necessary personnel are available and that larger maintenance requests are not deferred due to resource starvation. It permits the user manager to state his or her needs honestly rather than attempting to split requests arbitrarily in order to ensure continued flow through the queues.

Second, scheduled maintenance makes it feasible to consolidate similar requests into version levels of application software. This is the principle employed by most software companies to minimize the number of changes introduced in the field. It simplifies distribution, lowers the expense of testing, and reduces the potential for failure.

Finally, scheduled maintenance increases the confidence of users that their systems will be maintained and developed in pace with their needs. In general, users will wait for their turn if they are confident that their requests

Table 2–3. Key Characteristics of Maintenance

GENERALLY LONG TO MODERATE LEAD TIMES
Most maintenance requests are known long before the need for a solution arises

LOW VISIBILITY
Visibility is seldom high; the quality of maintenance is recognized but not highlighted

SUSCEPTIBILITY TO DESIGN LIMITATIONS
Designs that do not recognize the characteristics and needs of maintenance produce significantly longer cycle requirements than those that do

SHORT LEAD TIMES LEAD TO HIGH VISIBILITY
Major, extraordinary events such as company acquisitions tend to create a situation in which development *delays* the success of the event

FLEXIBILITY FOR PROJECT COMBINATION
Due to longer lead times, there are many opportunities for consolidation, if they are properly managed

DIFFICULTY IN BALANCING REQUIREMENTS
Maintenance requirements are all top priority, and it is seldom possible to balance them

will eventually be serviced. They can then coordinate their activities with software implementation dates and establish appropriate priorities. This system also allays any fears that they are being ignored or politically shuttled aside.

The key to successful maintenance lies in the design of new systems. It is essential to externally define as many of the potential variables as possible so that they can be altered without modifying the core of the system. In addition, as many of the variables as possible should be controlled by the users. This effectively separates development from maintenance loop (with the exception of consulting support). Accomplishing these goals in developing new systems takes planning and imagination. However, these efforts are well rewarded. By extending the life of the system, their benefits greatly exceed their costs.

Although the definition of maintenance varies across organizations, its characteristics are fairly common. Those discussed here, and a number of others, are summarized in Table 2–3.

SYSTEM ENHANCEMENTS

System enhancements are alterations in or extensions of existing systems to increase their functionality. Functionality generally is increased by making the product more effective, bringing it to a broader audience, or encompassing a more general process. Enhancements differ from new development primarily in two ways: their size and the basis on which they are developed.

In general, enhancements represent small to moderate resource allocations. This can range from an hour-long change to a multi-man-year effort In a few cases, enhancements take longer and involve more resources than new development due to the second criterion—the base upon which they are built.

Enhancements involve changes in an existing system. The changes may be insulated from the core of the system by type (reporting, inquiries, etc.) or by design (selected subfiles, database structures, etc.). Alternatively, they may involve the core itself, with extensive testing and peripheral modifications. However, there *is* a basis upon which to make changes and judge test results, and, most importantly, a broad and extensive set of preconceived judgments on how things work.

The advantages of having an existing system upon which to build are enormous. This fact, unfortunately, gives rise to the general opinion that any enhancement is relatively simple. It causes users to favor many enhancement requests over system replacement simply to avoid long, costly development efforts. Thus, the advantages of having a system can be quickly eroded by poorly coordinated attempts to modify design concepts in order to encompass new approaches. Nothing destroys a sound design more completely than an attempt to install the uninstallable.

The Enhancement Environment: Advantages and Disadvantages

No component of development creates more steady visibility than enhancement. Of course, this visibility can be negative as well as positive, and the success of any development department is linked to its success in performing this class of work.

At first, it might seem that new systems development is the crucial step. However, this is simply not the case. New systems provide visibility only at selected points in the process, and since user involvement is high, the implementation of a new system is nearly an afterthought. The recipient has already developed a list of needed changes (he or she has had time to develop this list while testing and compromising during the development cycle) and is committed to stressing them in order to ensure continued attention. Therefore, the new system is fated to provide less than complete user satisfaction.

Enhancements are a different matter entirely. They are generally developed from working systems, and each solves a specific problem. Enhancements tend to be precise and to the point, as well as taking far less time than new systems development for completion. Therefore, the probability of satisfaction is higher due to the freshness of the idea. In addition, rapid gratification always provides a higher positive visibility.

An active backlog can bring positive visibility, but can also make it difficult to maintain a constant, meaningful flow of request servicing. An undisciplined flow of requests can make it difficult to shift resources and alter priorities. As one functional area pumps in requests, so does another, and the requested changes can often conflict. In addition, the same request is often serviced twice due to misspecification.

Surprisingly, the larger the department, the more difficult it is to manage a heavy enhancement load. More requests can be serviced, but since the skills of department members vary widely, so does product quality. In this situation, a system can be unalterably changed before anyone realizes that the system's design has been significantly compromised.

However, the greatest danger lies in periods during which requests cannot be serviced as quickly as usual. This usually happens because of major project conflicts and the drainage of needed resources. However, in cases of resource commitment, corporate managements and users have a very short memory. The only thing they remember at the end of a month that has seen a reduction from 40 requests serviced to 4 is that 4 requests still remain in the queue. It becomes imperative to continue servicing the enhancement queue, and this must often be done against seemingly insurmountable odds.

Maintaining Positive Visibility

It is this dramatic swing between positive and negative impacts which makes management of the enhancement process so critical. Without proper management, frustrated users do not make requests or, worse still, tend to concentrate on the inability to service any single request. With this heavy stress on single requests, the ability to balance and consolidate development time becomes extremely difficult.

The most important aspect of managing enhancements is to maintain a constant and predictable flow of projects. This is accomplished by balancing high-resource efforts with minimal ones. Priority control must be established, but basic servicing must also be provided in order to continue the flow. It is crucial to ensure that this process does not raise accusations of favoritism or failure to meet bottom-line business needs.

There is often a tendency to service one area in favor of another. Friends reside in a specific department, one system is more enjoyable to work on than another, or politics allow one user to exert more pressure than another. The development manager must ensure that this trend does not get out of hand by carefully monitoring the nonpriority requests that are serviced. Projects pulled in priority order balance favoritism, since the business dictates the order of service. Nonpriority requests (those serviced to maintain project flow) must be balanced by personal intervention.

Project queue management is discussed at the end of this chapter. The important thing to remember here is that the management of enhancements is designed to maintain project flow while ensuring service balance. It ensures a perception of service on a broad scale rather than concentration on one business area. In addition, it accustoms users to submit large numbers of requests.

It is extremely important to develop an extensive backlog of requests. Typically, development managers complain about the multiyear backlog of requests for services. That backlog is their most important tool, however, and is far worse to have no requests at all. Backlogs show a healthy user community and a strong need for information resources. They allow the development manager a number of options for resource allocation as well.

Allocation can take many forms. First, if all requests are kept in an active queue, they can be consolidated. This not only ensures technical efficiency (merely maintaining and reimplementing a program involves a substantial overhead even if nothing is done) but, more importantly, it allows consolidation of requests which can carry the group over the justification threshold. With this consolidation, one gains the benefits of the request at a substantially lower cost. It also gives users the impetus to continue submitting service requests. Without an ensured project flow, their imaginative ability will be stifled.

This process implies, of course, that projects are kept in the queue even if they are not justified technically. When enhancement requests are received, they should all be reviewed with the same amount of care regardless of the probability that they will be too costly. If they fail to be justified, they are held in the queue until their characteristics change. In this fashion, they simply await proper timing and resources. Unfortunately, projects are all too often eliminated too soon simply to keep the queues clean.

There is no need for clean project queues. There may be reporting mechanisms requiring that only a selected class of work or only active projects be reviewed. This is simply a reporting mechanism, however, not a management priority.

Categorizing Enhancements

More than any other class of work, enhancements must be carefully evaluated as they are received. The objective is to ensure that they really are enhancements and not new systems in disguise. Often this is the most difficult evaluation to make because, if an effort is classified as new, it may languish behind many long-term, high-priority efforts and be doomed from the start. Users understand this very quickly and tailor their requests to the utilization of existing products, thereby eliminating the need to justify new development.

Once a project is classified as an enhancement, it is reviewed with a primary emphasis on the cost, since the benefit should have been provided by the user. The effort dedicated to the project's estimation should be in proportion to its benefit. Often requests are made with no benefit indicated—at least, no quantitative benefit. An estimate should be made anyway, but not with the detail associated with quantified requests.

For requests of unquantified benefit, a cost should be predefined at which the project will be considered regardless. This should be done because it is sometimes more costly to search for benefits or bend implementations to seek benefits than to service the request. It is also consistent with the concept that the development department exists to service user needs. At times, development should fulfill requests simply to meet this responsibility regardless of the benefit involved. Of course, this practice can be justified only for requests under a predetermined cost threshold.

Requests are best categorized by impact (either on the business or on the systems which will be changed) rather than by the cost of service. The reason is that the cost of servicing a request is seldom directly related to the benefit associated with its implementation. Categories should be kept simple—high, moderate, and low impact are good examples. The queues will then be serviced based on preestablished priorities, first-in/first-out, or time to produce. Most often, a combination of these three categories provides optimum results. The categories should be evident to the requestor very early in the process. This allows the requestor to reassess the approach and perhaps bring new factors to bear on the issue.

Often these factors are either political or represent a respecification of the request so that an additional benefit is provided. In either case, the alteration must be respected by the development department. Development is responsible for servicing users, not for righting the wrongs of misapplied company power. That task is the responsibility of upper management. One of the major fallacies in MIS departments is that they are responsible for ensuring that the highest-benefit projects are being serviced. That is simply not the case and only leads to conflict.

The key characteristics of the enhancement class of work are summarized in Table 2–4.

NEW SYSTEM DEVELOPMENT

New system development consists of the analysis and development of applications not previously automated, replacement of existing applications,

Table 2–4. Key Characteristics of Enhancement

HIGH VOLUME OF REQUESTS
The development department's work consists largely of adding enhancements to existing products

WIDE SPECTRUM OF RESOURCE REQUIREMENTS
Requests can vary from a few hours to multi-man-year efforts; benefits preclude balanced allocation of needed resources

HIGH VISIBILITY
Most of the reasons for development's failure result from an inability to service enhancements; most of its success is based on the ability to service a large number of enhancement requests

WIDE RANGE OF COMPLEXITY
There is little relationship between benefit and complexity

BUILT ON EXISTING SYSTEMS
The advantages of having an existing base to build upon—stable processes, known operations, etc.—represent a major advantage over unproven products

UNDISCIPLINED FLOW OF REQUESTS
The flow of requests is driven by a variety of forces, many external to the company, and is difficult to forecast

PRIME IMPORTANCE IN MOVEMENT OF VOLUME
The expectation is that, given a relative staff size, a certain number of requests will be serviced; if the staff is increased, the number of service requests will increase

PRIORITY SENSITIVE
Priorities established at request time may alter for a variety of reasons—but never in the requestor's eyes

POLITICALLY SENSITIVE
User managers use the enhancement class of work to exert influence and power through the level of sevice they receive

or major extensions of existing systems. It differs from enhancement primarily in the way the current system (if one exists) is addressed and the relative size of the effort. In the typical company, a relatively small backlog of new development requests occurs. If a large number exists, this is due either to an understaffed or low-achievement group or to a misrepresented class of work.

Of all the types of development work, new development projects are the easiest to manage. Their size provides the flexibility necessary to alter the process in response to changing conditions. Their reduced visibility (on a constant basis) allows ample opportunity to prepare for the times when visibility is acute. Most publicity is reserved for new development efforts. This generally results in the prime personnel talent of the department being reserved for this class of work. In addition, the preponderance of books and trade magazines concentrate on new systems development.

Most of the methodologies and management mechanisms developed over the past several years are geared to new development projects. New development is the only meaningful way in which these methods can be adapted to a specific organization. For the development department, this is its major advantage; it provides a way to try new variations on what has been done in the past so that the department can evolve. While in many cases this has occurred at the expense of the other classes of work, new development is the best option because it includes all phases of the project cycle. If a new mechanism is effective in a new project, it can probably be adapted to the other classes of work and provide consistency throughout project services.

Chapter 3 discusses the management of development projects in detail. Here our concern is with those characteristics of a new development effort which make it unique in the classification of work. In establishing procedures and policies for development, it is crucial to understand how each class of work differs from the others in order to anticipate and control exceptions.

Maintaining Work Flow

The staffing of most development departments makes it impossible to address many new projects simultaneously. In this book, we consider projects that require two man-years or more major projects. Beyond the number of persons involved, the expertise which a major development project requires must be considered. This includes a project leader, a good allocator of personnel, systems analysts, programmers, and a person with an intimate knowledge of how the systems are interrelated. Few organizations can run more than two or three of these projects simultaneously.

However, every development department should have at least one major new development project underway at any given time. This ensures the perception of change and advance on the part of upper management, allows management skills to remain honed by constant exposure, and ensures a continued state-of-the-art posture toward development technologies. Once a lag develops in the new development queue, it is often very difficult to reestablish the momentum necessary for project flow. There is a tendency to become overly conservative and less flexible.

User Involvement

New development projects invariably produce the highest percentage of user involvement over time. This involvement tends to involve a higher level of management as well. There are more decisions to make, more trade-offs to address, and a more extended period of time which allows greater involvement without slowing the process.

This involvement, however, is a two-edged sword. It provides the optimum forum for users to make their needs known and to gain ownership of the product. However, it may also create an atmosphere of conflict in which incidental issues gain preeminence out of proportion to their true value. It is an unfortunate fact of human relations that the more contact that occurs, the higher the probability of conflict. Political needs must be satisfied, vagaries of personality dealt with, and conflicting priorities rationalized.

Calendar Time

The most important characteristic of a major project is calendar time. It overshadows resource expenditure, cost/benefit analysis, and impact on the business. The longer a project lasts, the higher the probability that the environment will change enough to endanger it. Since new development projects typically account for the bulk of the large efforts, they tend to be affected by calendar time more than any other class of work.

It is impossible to maintain high positive visibility for a long time. Given enough time, major components of project success such as key personnel, business competition, resource availability, and political impetus are fated to experience major alterations. It is nearly impossible to account for such potential impacts adequately at project inception time without driving up the costs beyond reason. Therefore, such costs are seldom included. They do occur, however, and with dependable frequency.

Visibility

On an ongoing basis, the visibility associated with new development is significantly lower than that of any other class of work. At specific well-separated periods, new systems development ranks at the top of the class. These periods include the key decision and milestone events throughout the development life cycle. During the interim periods, however, visibility is quite low—unless schedules slip.

When schedule dates begin to be missed, the visibility of the project increases dramatically. This visibility is generally bad and invariably results in continuing negative visibility throughout the balance of the project. Positive visibility occurs at only two points: project start-up and implementation. At these times the drums are rolling, energy is high, and the primary effort is centered on the project itself. Project start-up is almost always a positive experience. Not so implementation.

The positive aspect of implementation occurs when all anticipated components of the system are being implemented. This includes both explicit and implicit definitions. This can occur only if no major trade-offs have taken place during construction and if the perception of what the system will do equals the reality. Very seldom do these two situations occur. There is nearly always a user who is not getting what he was promised or thought he was promised.

In new development, it is essential to deliver what was promised. Since the freezing of specifications is a totally unworkable solution, the key to success is to promise only a portion of what is possible. The core of the system represents a total commitment and cannot be compromised. In contrast, the peripheral components, reporting, inquiries, and subsystems are produced in a predetermined priority sequence. For this reason, the inevitable changes which occur during the development cycle do not alter the delivery dates. The users may not gain everything they desire, but at least they have understood from the beginning that there was some chance that certain components would lag.

A variety of options exists for completing the project. Incomplete components can be added as enhancements, a second-stage project can be initiated, or external workers such as consulting or contract personnel can be called in. With end-user development mechanisms in place, users also have the ability to develop those components themselves and to provide the necessary balance to limit development resources.

The characteristics of new systems development, and others, are summarized in Table 2–5.

MANAGING PROJECT QUEUES

A healthy development function depends on the effective management and balance of the queues in which projects are placed. This is true, in fact, of any business function. A manufacturing function attempts to balance production so that every class of product has a representative inventory. Fast food chains must balance the preparation of different types of hamburgers to ensure that they will reasonably match the flow of orders received. In the world of systems development, one must make sure that the appropriate support level is maintained, maintenance is adequate to support the changing business, the flow of enhancements is continuous, and new systems are being regularly implemented. As with any other business function, this is easier said than done.

The first step has been discussed: classifying project requests as they are received into appropriate classes of work. Each of these classes should be associated with service-level commitments which are meaningful and rep-

Table 2-5. Key Characteristics of New Systems Development

- GENERALLY HIGH RESOURCE DEMAND
  - Most new development requests require extensive resources and a wide variety of skills
- VISIBILITY OCCURS AT KEY MILESTONES
  - Visibility tends to exist in wave fashion—wide crests and troughs
- MINIMAL NUMBER OF CONCURRENT PROJECTS
  - Few development departments can handle many new development projects, if for no other reason than the lack of a large number of senior analysts
- PRIORITY DRIVEN
  - The predominant factor in choosing the next project to address is its relative priority
- PREESTABLISHED OF SERVICE SEQUENCE
  - Request sequencing is established by management, either formally by committee or informally by political means
- SELF-BALANCING
  - The availability of resources and upper management's attention, not development managers, tend to balance the new project queues
- MANY ADJUSTMENT OPTIONS
  - The length and scope of most new development projects provide maximum opportunities for adjustment during construction
- HIGH USER INVOLVEMENT
  - Users at the management level tend to consider the time they spend on new systems more important than that allocated to any other effort
- LONG CALENDAR TIME
  - Projects tend to run longer than other classes of work due to the number of outside forces involved
- SUSCEPTIBLE METHODOLOGY
  - Formal methods are most often used for new projects than for any other kind of work

resent achievable goals on an ongoing basis. These service-level commitments define the level of attention given each class of work. Every class is assigned at least one queue in order to ensure that there will be an opportunity to meet the commitments.

The definition of service levels varies among the classes and queues of work. Some of these definitions have a bearing on the success of others and often change with the calendar or with business conditions. The end of the year, for example, generally requires a reemphasis on the maintenance and consulting support classes to ensure smooth annual closings. The acquisition of a new business line has an impact across the board, upgrading some classes of work and downgrading others. The only way to determine how well the development department provides service, and the only way to direct the servicing of competing projects effectively, is to associate service levels by class of work and queues.

Service-level commitments are generally broken down further into categories within each class. This is done to allow the flexibility of addressing different sets of priorities, since in order to manage a queue class properly, one must deal with each as an independent entity. How these service-level commitments can vary is outlined in Table 2–6.

Category 3

This is the lowest level of work within the queue. It involves the least return, shortest time, or lowest resource demand for the class. Typically, the least attention is paid to requests in this category both by the requestor and by the development department. Since only minimal testing is required, requests in this category often bypass the testing process entirely. While purists may shudder at the thought of changes being implemented without testing, one must consider the costs involved. Testing is expensive and should be related to the amount of trouble that can be anticipated if the changed product fails.

In the support class, category 3 includes reports whose line spacing occasionally fails, an inquiry which cannot parse a parameter string if a certain character is used, or a casual information request from a user (e.g., "How do reports break down by lines of print across my department?"). They generally have such low priority that they are not prioritized, and when a new system reaches the analysis stage, they are often purged to await the replacement system. As in most of the classes, this category is often assigned to new, inexperienced personnel so that they can gain familiarity with the process without doing much damage.

For maintenance, requests are generally assigned to category 3 based on the simplicity of change and the lead time to implementation. They include end-of-year date changes, which take two hours and must be completed within the next six months, or expansion of the master control file to accommodate a new service bank by year-end. Like all maintenance requests, they must be serviced, and serious consequences attend their failure, but there is so much lead time that failure is nearly impossible (assuming they have been properly predicted and appropriately evaluated).

For enhancements, the optimal criterion for category 3 is the impact of the request. However, several variations exist, ranging from the number of man-hours needed to complete the work to the level of management making

Table 2-6. Sample Service-Level Commitments

SUPPORT

PRODUCTION SUPPORT
- Category 1—Severe service interruption
  - Response in 15 minutes
  - Identification in 2 hours
  - Correction in 6 hours
- Category 2—Moderate service interruption
  - Correction in 24 hours
- Category 3—Productivity reduction
  - Prioritization in 6 hours
  - Maximum of five projects in backlog

CONSULTING SUPPORT
- Category 1—Project membership requirement
  - 16 hours per week dedication per project
- Category 2—Technical information requirement
  - 5-day response
- Category 3—Technical review requirement
  - 5-day response

MAINTENANCE
- Category 1—Business requirement
  - 1-week lead time requirement (30-man-hour week)
- Category 2—Cycle requirement
  - 4-week lead time requirement for monthly maintenance
  - 8-week lead time for others
- Category 3—Cosmetic change
  - Maximum of six requests per month

ENHANCEMENTS
- Category 1—High impact
  - 10 requests per month
- Category 2—Moderate impact
  - 5 requests per month
- Category 3—Threshold benefit
  - 5 requests per month

NEW SYSTEMS DEVELOPMENT
- Category 1—Major project
  - Maximum 2 requests in flight
- Category 2—Minor project
  - Maximum 4 requests in flight
- Category 3—Threshold project
  - As time permits—priority sequence 50% of the time

the request. Some criteria are more objective than others but in the final analysis, the primary factor is the requester's level of concern.

New systems requests in category 3 are represented by low-priority system extensions, those with borderline cost/benefit advantages, or "nice-to-do" requests. In the typical development environment, such requests are never worked on because higher-priority problems exist. However, there are some major advantages to working category 3 requests into the normal flow of work.

First, these requests are excellent for training new project leaders or analysts. The risk is generally low, the request is not difficult, and there is far more leeway for compromise, from the user's perspective, than exists in higher-category work. Users understand that if they do not compromise and keep the request simple, they will not get anything.

Second, a category 3 request can be most effectively used to try out a new technology or method. It provides the perfect environment for process analysis, and users are generally receptive to this procedure. The existence of several category 3 requests provides the opportunity to choose one to be serviced based on its characteristics rather than business needs.

Category 3 requests are managed with flow as the prime consideration, once the absolute requirements are met (the maintenance change must go in by year-end, etc.). They give the development manager the opportunity to assign work based upon departmental, personnel, or visibility requirements. Category 3 should be viewed as a "job jar" to be dipped into whenever the opportunity arises.

For this reason, priorities should be established with the understanding that they represent group priorities. Requests are not handled serially; instead, the priorities represent general ranges of measure. For instance, a project received, classified, and placed in a category 3 queue must be serviced within 3 months (an arbitrary figure). Within that limitation, development personnel have the option of working on nearly any request they desire. They will choose projects for reasons ranging from whim to familiarity to challenge. This flexibility allows the staff to schedule their own work while fulfilling their commitment to the project. As long as the queue is serviced, the sequence is incidental (within limits).

It is the responsibility of the development manager to control and balance the service sequence. The servicing of requests should not concentrate on a single user or department, requests should not languish in the queue simply because they are considered unexciting, and staff members should display sensitivity to the general improvement of the systems. By properly managing the category 3 queue, a development manager can create a commitment to service while satisfying the department's need to grow technically.

Category 2

Since three service categories are defined, the position of category 2 implies that it receives requests which fall somewhere between small and large, critical and noncritical. That fact makes it the most difficult queue to manage and the one with the most danger. The priority structure which dominates category 2 has a marked effect, but relegation to a lower level still provides the development manager with some degree of flexibility.

When requests are placed in category 2, the usual reason is that their size or cost/benefit ratios do not justify high attention. This does not imply that they cannot provide major benefits for the company. Rather, it indicates that their value represents a mixture of strategic and cost avoidance/reduction justification. Since cost tends to be the overriding management consideration, their strategic value is often ignored. Also, category 2 tends to have more requests than any other category. This brings us to the most important factor—visibility.

Just as enhancements provide the maximum visibility within classes, category 2 requests tend to attract the most publicity. The reason is simple: due to the nearly automatic assignment of resources to category 1 efforts, projects in this class depend on the good faith and dedication of the development department to ensure that they are addressed. Since users are not comfortable with that arrangement, they are most vocal about category 2 requests.

If users want to ensure an appropriate flow of requests, they tend to believe that a noisy approach is more likely to push the work through. Therefore, aggressive users bring long lists of requests to steering committee meetings, with a litany of why their departments are doomed to fail if these problems are not solved. This process creates enormous pressure to ensure a constant and equitable flow of projects in this category. As with category 3 requests, the development manager is confronted with the need to recognize the business priorities associated with each effort, as well as to maintain a constant and perceptible flow of projects. It is this decision process which ultimately spells the difference between success and failure in development. There are two key elements in ensuring success.

The first element is to ensure that priorities are dealt with in groups, as discussed earlier. As with category 3, the priority system must not be considered absolute. The need to consolidate, preempt, and rearrange priorities in light of personnel availability, competing resource demands, and business cycles requires constant attention and maneuvering. This often includes political give-and-take, with promises to address a user's high-priority item next month (along with a few low-priority ones) in order to allow a lower-priority item to slide through for the sake of efficiency.

Realistically, there are no priority 1, 2, and 3 projects. There are simply groups of the highest, intermediate, and lowest priority. Cost/benefit or whatever mechanism is used for ranking is simply not precise enough to provide a significant amount of detailed comparison. What really matters is that, in any performance period, it is unwise to allow too many higher-priority items to remain unserviced.

The second key element in success is to allow the staff to pull a number of projects from the queue as they wish. The priority mechanism in category 2 makes it impossible to do this to the same degree as with category 3. However, if only a portion of the department's total resources is dedicated to filling prioritized requests, the remainder can be used to fill requests in a more random, internally motivated fashion. Careful management of the randomness of that selection will ensure the maintenance of an optimum flow of work.

There is little difference in the way in which category 2 and category 3 requests are managed. Priorities established when the request was placed in the queue must be honored, but some flexibility must be allowed. Requests at this category level generally do not spell the difference between corporate life and death. Flow must be maintained and business strategies must be followed.

Category 1

These requests are the most critical to the company. Because of the executive attention involved, this category is the easiest to manage as well. Most of the servicing decisions rest not with the development manager but with steering committees and procedural directives. Therefore, the development manager is left only with the decision of staffing and method. This is certainly not a trivial activity, but it does remove much of the decision process from the manager.

Within the support class, category 1 represents severe system failures which demand immediate and dedicated attention. Realistically, little queueing is involved. A problem or request is highlighted and is worked on at once. If more than one problem occurs, more staff is assigned until the resources are exhausted. Once again, the prime responsibility for development is to keep the ship afloat. If this means that everything halts until the problem is solved, so be it.

In both maintenance and enhancements, category 1 involves projects which must be completed by a specific date. That date is established either on the basis of outside influences, such as cycle times or acquisitions, or by the request's rising to the top of the queue and the original estimate being mapped to the calendar. In either case, a completion date is set.

This can create significant problems, especially when resources do not match demand. When that happens with category 1 requests, other efforts such as new development must suffer, temporary resources must be applied, or extra hours must be put in. Generally, scope trade-offs are not possible since category 1 requests have relatively clear bounds when placed in the queue.

Temporary resources are usually the best way to deal with bloated category 1 queues. Unfortunately, their expense is high. The best solution, of course, is to avoid the problem entirely by keeping ahead of the demand dates. As in the other categories for maintenance and enhancement, it should be possible to work on other requests in the queue in a less structured fashion. Thus, smaller, high-priority requests would never cause bottlenecks because they would have already been addressed.

New development queues are established by planning and prioritized by management. This can be done formally through steering committees or informally through political imperatives. In any case, pulling projects from the category 1 development class is part of a long-range, predesigned plan. There is very little management involved.

Managing the project queues, coupled with the proper classification of project requests upon receipt, guarantees a consistent flow of work through the development department. The categories tend to manage themselves once appropriate procedures and standards are established and an adequate degree of commitment is achieved. Users tend to design requests to fit into certain classes and categories based on the service-level commitments associated with them.

3
PROJECT MANAGEMENT

Most of the development department's resources and time are used to work on projects. Whether those efforts are directed to new systems, support, enhancements or maintenance, all are project oriented, with discrete start and finish points for each. Project management is also the focus of the department's improvement and evolution.

MIS development is one of the few departments of its size where this orientation is so complete. For this reason, the group is somewhat out of synchronization with the balance of the company, making it difficult for other groups to relate to it.

The majority of textbooks on development have focused on project management. This activity has spawned an industry of methodologies, techniques, languages and education specifically designed to improve and control the factors involved in developing computer systems. With few exceptions, this process has encompassed what has become known as the "project life cycle."

The project life cycle is the period of time during which a request moves from justification through implementation and review. While the activity during this period does not account for all of the development department's responsibilities, it does represent an enormous portion of their visible delivery of product. As such, it deserves careful consideration.

In this chapter, the development life cycle is discussed in terms of process management, rather than focusing on any particular methodology. A seven-stage life cycle is presented. The objective is not to redefine the life cycle (enough definitions certainly exist) but rather to study the impacts and key elements of *any* life cycle definition in relation to process management.

One element that is stressed, however, is that there are two independent cycles in any development department: emergency support and normal development. The classes of work they are associated with are distinct enough to justify independent approaches. Therefore, two cycles are defined.

PROJECTS VERSUS ONE PROJECT

The orientation of MIS development to projects sets it apart from the other departments of the typical company in a number of subtle and nonsubtle ways. It places the group in a position of making discrete performance judgments, as well as creating a commitment to single entities. As an example, the inception of an effort to automate the order entry process represents the beginning of a substantial allocation of resources to a single goal. That goal (the implementation of the system) immediately is the only reason for the project team's existence. In a project-oriented department, this immediate, short-term concentration is fostered.

The development manager is under constant pressure to balance competing priorities and available resources. The department's visibility rises and falls with a never-ending series of problems and resolutions which are often difficult to put into perspective and even more difficult to anticipate. This creates not only significant difficulties in internal management but also discontinuity in dealing with users. In most cases, users view projects as exceptions to normal operations, to be dealt with and forgotten. With the development manager, this constant balancing is a way of life.

To manage a development project successfully, some continuity must be created in the multiproject environment. This continuity provides a relatively stable base from which to adjust and improve the process. Without that stability, the manager is left with nothing but an endlessly repeating cycle. Establishing that stability begins with the recognition that the development manager is dealing with two independent concepts—managing *one* project and managing *projects.*

To a large extent, the development manager is distanced from the management of any single project. His or her responsibility typically involves either the interpretation of a specific project's status or the coordination of many seemingly independent efforts. The skills of project management brought to the position protect the manager from poor leadership of any single project but do not guarantee that multiple projects will be properly coordinated.

The successful manager uses the life cycle like any other tool, understanding and dealing with its characteristics and nuances. With critical, highly visible projects his or her involvement will be significantly greater, but it is not detailed enough to manage the project directly.

However, it is important to understand the distinction between management of many projects and management of one. It is equally important to understand when it is necessary to become deeply involved in any single project.

Managing One Project

Regardless of how professional and senior a development staff becomes, the development manager must always closely monitor a single project. Political imperatives, technological newness, impact on the organization and many other reasons will cause the manager to manage the cycle in detail. This may strain that manager's talents, since specific project management skills are quick to atrophy. It may cause conflict with project managers who are more comfortable with independent action. It may even slow the schedule since the department manager cannot give the project his or her individual attention. In spite of these problems, however, the department manager's active involvement may eventually be required.

This is not a bad idea. Peter Drucker, in his landmark book *Management—Tasks, Responsibilities and Practices,* stated emphatically that all managers should routinely perform some departmental work related to their responsibilities. Only by so doing can they continue to understand how the process trulv operates. In the case of the development manager, this means management of a project.

The problem occurs in choosing which type of project to manage. It should be a typical rather than a critical one. This ensures that the project will not conflict with the manager's primary responsibilities, nor will the business suffer because the manager could not dedicate enough time to it. Its schedule should be long enough to avoid major deadline slippage due to conflicts in other areas. Finally, it should be relatively self-contained so that the manager does not have to deal with inappropriate levels of the organization.

Often the factors mentioned earlier—politics, technological newness, etc.—will force the manager to become actively involved when conditions are less than optimum. At times, this imperative is even created by upper management because of pressures placed upon them. Examples abound: The financial department needs to close five days earlier this year, or the company is risking its future on the successful absorption of a new acquisition. The development manager must then decide how deep his or her involvement should be.

Obviously, the level of involvement is dictated by the situation. However, the manager must be sensitive not only to the priorities of the department but to the need to avoid compromising the integrity of the development life cycle itself. The manager's lack of direct involvement in that cycle will make forced involvement unwieldy. The cycle was formalized to ensure the manager of its continued effectiveness and of the ability to manage it from a distance. In the unfamiliar role of project manager, these formalities will seem constraining, since the individual responsible for production (the project manager) and the person to be satisfied (the department manager) are the same person.

This is a difficult situation and requires the manager's stringent discipline. Ideally, the actual project managers are allowed to do their jobs, and the upgrading of the project simply means more frequent status meetings and the use of somewhat more frequent executive privilege. When that is not possible and in-depth management involvement is required, there are some guidelines which can simplify the process and lower the risk.

Managing The Life Cycle. The detailed management of a project is an amalgam of technical, design, personnel and scheduling issues. The successful project manager balances these factors, together with the components of the system, to bring the project to a successful conclusion. The constant, detailed involvement required to make this happen is not something the development manager can provide and still fulfill his or her normal duties. Therefore, the approach which best fits this need is to manage the life cycle of the project rather than the project itself.

Managing the project life cycle involves reviewing the check points, approving follow-up planning, and maintaining control of design, programming, and all the other formal components of the project. Of course, this is what the manager does in all projects—at least the larger ones. When managing a specific project, he or she is also involved in planning each phase, as well as being the recipient of reviews. The design is prepared with the manager's involvement, test plans are developed cooperatively, and meetings with users are attended by the manager.

The key ingredient at this level is to manage the elements objectively, according to the rules. All projects require many small trade-offs and approvals which are not documented—the subtle adjustments which make a project flow smoothly. In no way should the development manager attempt to descend to this level of detail. It will only hamstring the effort and result in longer hours, extended schedules, and bruised egos.

Limiting External Interactivity. During the project, the development manager must carefully choose with whom and for what purpose to interact. It is inappropriate for the manager to perform analyses that are usually done by less senior personnel. Projects end, after all, and the manager must continue to operate with his or her peers. If the manager gets the reputation of being an analyst, he or she will be treated as such by senior management.

The most effective way to avoid this problem is to operate within the development group as much as possible. Analysts should perform the evaluation and analysis with the users. The manager should direct that effort from within the development department itself or deal with the proper level of management in the user areas and allow the user manager to collect the needed information.

Designating a Project Manager. Regardless of the desire of upper management for the development manager to handle the project personally, the manager must assign a project manager with all the normal responsibilities of that position. It may be necessary to give this person a different title in order to screen the true role, but a full-time project manager who can react to the needs of the project at unanticipated and critical points must exist.

Assigning a project manager fills a number of needs and avoids some significant problems. It ensures that consistent leadership is provided if upper management suddenly decides that there is a different project which requires the development manager's attention. It bridges the gulf between the results-oriented manager and the process- and people-oriented project leader. It ensures the presence of a technical expert in the process. Finally, it avoids improper delegation of responsibilities when the development manager is not totally familiar with staff strengths and weaknesses.

The development manager must recognize that he or she no longer has the skills required for a lower-level position. The assigned project manager can provide those skills and allow the project to flow smoothly while the manager fulfills the pro forma requirement of direct involvement.

Identifying Key Decision Points. Detailed project involvement implies an active participation in key decisions. This can include anything from the structure of user-controlled variables to whether the initial stage is implemented in a prototype fashion. While a delay in making minor decisions may slow the project down, missing key decision points, or not knowing that they were key, can bring it to a halt. The more the decisions represent gating points, the more important it is to react to them immediately.

Most key decision points can be identified early in the planning process. They include the final review of the design documents, the prioritization of requests, acceptance meetings, and many other steps which are easily recognized as major events. When management assumes the active involvement of the development manager, they have these decision points in mind. This involvement cannot be deferred. Therefore, the manager must handle these points as they occur, not when his or her schedule permits.

Understanding the Difference Between the Roles of Project Manager and Department Manager. Project managers do not interact with peers in the same way as they do with subordinates. The manager must understand this difference in order to ensure a proper balance between the project and other projects in flight. The fact that the manager is active in any one effort does not imply that the priorities or mode of operation has changed. The manager's interactions with temporary peers must reflect that situation, and this is not easy.

In addition, this peer relationship is not the kind that the development manager finds with peers in his or her normal environment. In that environment, resources exist, the level of detail is much less, and political pressures are far more significant. Project personnel do not function with the same perspective. It is crucial that the development manager make this transition in order to operate effectively in an active project role.

Table 3–1 summarizes these and other guidelines for actively managing a single project. It is not an easy role to fill and can be quite frustrating, both for the manager and for the rest of the staff. The fact that it is necessary does not ease this strain. It is also important to understand why the manager is being asked to operate in this mode. Table 3–2 lists some of the more typical reasons.

As we can see, most of these reasons are negative. It is very important for the manager to understand completely why management wants his or her active involvement. If it continues, a serious problem is indicated and steps must be taken to correct it.

Finally, managing a project of high visibility can be fun. Probably more than anything else, this represents the greatest danger in the exercise. After a few years of administratively managing a department, a detailed, hands-on effort can be most satisfying. This is fine for managing selective projects with low visibility, as discussed earlier. It is less effective if it becomes the norm for the more critical projects.

Managing Projects

The new development manager has typically come up through the ranks of analyst and project manager. The role of project manager provides a combination of administrative, personnel, and technical management skills that flows fairly well into the development manager's role. The greatest shock almost invariably comes when a number of projects must be managed, coordinated, and evaluated from a distance, precluding painstaking attention to detail.

The problem goes beyond the obvious one of relying on the skills, professionalism and dedication of subordinates. It involves the need to balance and understand the interrelationship between the single project and the development life cycle. The shortcuts which the new manager perceived as

Table 3-1. Guidelines for Managing a Single Project

1. MANAGE THE LIFE CYCLE

   Since the development manager has become the expert on the development cycle, the more he or she can stay within these bounds, the higher the probability of success.

2. LIMIT EXTERNAL INTERACTION

   The limitations created by atrophied project leader skills are a fact of life and understood by management in general. There is no need to prove this to the organization in general.

3. DESIGNATE A PROJECT MANAGER

   Projects require constant attention. A development manager cannot provide the necessary level of attention. Therefore, make sure that someone is in a position to do so.

4. IDENTIFY KEY DECISION POINTS

   Project flow is largely dependent upon key decisions made at key decision points, not at the manager's convenience. They can generally be predicted and schedules set up accordingly.

5. UNDERSTAND THE DIFFERENCE BETWEEN THE ROLES OF DEPARTMENT MANAGER AND PROJECT MANAGER

   The two roles require constant changing of "hats." When this happens, the approach must be changed as well.

6. DO NOT ABUSE THE MANAGEMENT PEROGATIVE

   There is a temptation to avoid steps because the manager is often the recipient of the output. However, those steps have secondary results as well. It is important to go through all the motions as intended.

7. ESTABLISH THE MANAGEMENT REPORTING MECHANISM EARLY

   Upper management wants a combination of senior-level and detailed reporting. It is unlikely that they truly understand this fact. Establish the ground rules early and abide by the accepted mechanisms and schedules.

8. CONTINUE PROJECT STATUS MEETINGS AS USUAL

   The fact that the manager controls the project does not change the normal progress reports.

9. DO NOT TRY TO BE AN ANALYST OR A PROGRAMMER

   Even though project leaders normally fill these as well as administrative roles, it is unwise for a full-time manager to do so. Manage the project; don't try to be a technician.

10. MAINTAIN PRIORITIES AMONG PROJECTS

    The manager's responsibility for a project does not increase its priority to their organization. Attempts to upgrade its status automatically will subvert the queue management procedures, whose implementation required much effort.

Table 3–2. Reasons Managers are Asked to Lead Projects

1. THE EFFORT IS VIEWED AS A MAJOR BUSINESS EVENT
   Extensive cost or a competitive posture is at stake. While the project may be important, the department's impact is equally important, and the manager's attention will be diverted.
2. THERE IS A LACK OF CONFIDENCE IN PROJECT MANAGERS
   Either the manager will reestablish the project leaders' reputations or very little departmental progress will take place. In addition the quality of procedures and methodologies should be questioned.
3. THE MANAGER IS BEING KEPT OUT OF THE WAY
   This is a fairly common occurrence and is obviously extremely negative. It allows management to make organizational changes without interference.
4. THE DEPARTMENT'S PERFORMANCE IS CONSIDERED UNACCEPTABLE
   The manager is being forced to confront his or her problems. It is hoped that, by seeing the situation firsthand, the manger will correct the situation.
5. DIRECT CUSTOMER CONTACT IS EXPECTED
   This is a perfectly reasonable situation, assuming that it does not become the rule rather than the exception. Customers may feel that they are being given exceptional attention, and additional business may be generated.
6. A NEW TECHNOLOGY IS INVOLVED
   Management invariably views development as a technocracy—which is not totally unreasonable. Therefore, the manager is the ultimate technocrat. This attitude implies a less than optimum view of the manager's skills.
7. CORPORATE SECURITY IS AN ISSUE
   Often the knowledge of events is to be limited. Unfortunately, this approach also limits the manager's ability to plan and react.
8. A TOUCHY POLITICAL SITUATION EXISTS
   This is a risky situation. The manager can quickly find that political problem being shifted to himself when he tries to apply technical and political skills.

major strengths now appear as negative traits in former peers—who are now subordinates.

There are a number of methods which should be utilized to ensure proper management of projects. Each one assumes a stable, well-defined, well-managed development life cycle. Without this process control, effective management of a large number of projects is difficult—if not impossible. Table 3–3 lists these methods and discusses the relative importance of each. The most important methods and their critical elements are then discussed.

Project Status Meetings. These meetings are conducted with the level of management immediately below that of development manager and consist of a status review of all projects within each person's area of responsibility.

Table 3–3. Methods for Managing Multiple Projects

1. PROJECT STATUS MEETINGS

   The prime formalized method for assessing project status. The results of the meeting can be directly translated into management-oriented status presentations.

2. PROJECT MEETINGS

   Review of the details of individual projects. Has the advantage of including project staff members so that they achieve a certain amount of visibility.

3. STAFF MEETINGS

   The principal orientation is towards process improvement and review, as well as coordination with strategies.

4. PERFORMANCE STATISTICS

   Periodic measurement of performance trends of the department in general and of individual projects as exceptions to the trends. The manager should analyze the statistics thoroughly before review at staff meetings.

5. TIME ACCOUNTING

   The distribution of personnel time during a project can give a revealing picture of its progress. These figures have very little meaning in themselves but are a useful component of management.

6. USER MEETINGS

   The outside's perspective of any project can be substantially different from the internal perspective. User meetings reduce the dependence on analysts or lower-level managers for the manager's understanding of the group's performance.

7. MANAGEMENT BY "WANDERING AROUND"

   As described in *In Search of Excellence* by Thomas J. Peters and Robert H. Waterman, Jr. this can be an invaluable way of judging the department's real view of itself and of intermediate managers. Be careful that it does not degenerate into management by spying.

In small organizations, this may involve senior analysts who fulfill project leader roles. In large organizations, it may represent managers who, in turn, hold project meetings with their own staffs.

There should be a formal agenda which covers all key topics for any specific project. Projects will be reviewed in differing fashion depending on their life cycle status. The depth of their review will also differ depending on their category and visibility. These levels should be predefined when the project begins to allow the reporting manager adequate opportunity to prepare for the meeting.

This predefinition also ensures that key components are addressed. For example, a schedule of meetings and a capsule report on their results can help the manager determine how well the user is being involved in the decision process. A statistical review of test results reveals how comprehensive the test plan was and how well it is being followed.

An understanding of how project progress will be judged transforms the review process from a subjective to an objective exercise. Each staff member is given the same consideration and provides a factual picture rather than a personal perception. If the review process is established intelligently and parallels the life cycle, proper reporting can provide assurance that if the project is managed well, the resultant product will probably be on time and effective.

The timing of project status meetings is important. They should be regularly scheduled and timed so that the results can be communicated to upper management in a timely fashion. In other words, if the development manager must attend a staff meeting every other Thursday where status is important, the project status meeting should occur on Wednesday morning. This allows adequate time to prepare and to follow up on key questions.

The agenda of the meeting should be standard and designed to move swiftly. Prepublished material should be provided to attendees so that it can be reviewed prior to the meeting and only exceptional conditions highlighted. Very few organizations have enough time to do this, but it is much more efficient and profitable than performing the complete review verbally and in person.

The frequency of the meetings is largely dependent upon staff size, number of active projects, and reporting requirements to upper management. Certainly, as described above, at least one of the meetings should take place immediately before the next meeting with upper management so that a proper upward information flow can take place. The frequency of meetings also depends on how many other meetings take place on a normal, scheduled basis. After all, the purpose of the development department is not to meet but to support and develop application systems. I have seen project status meetings take place as frequently as weekly and as infrequently as every six weeks. As a starting point, too many meetings are often better than too few.

Project Meetings. These meetings represent the lowest level of review, with attention focusing on a single project. The format and style are identical to those of the project status meetings, except that there is significantly more detail. Project members should be present and detail schedules reviewed. Obviously, such meetings occur only for major or long-term projects and should be scheduled around major milestones—designing, testing, implementation, and so on.

The meeting should not be presided over by the development manager, the manager should be present. He or she can gain a perception of the project's progress which goes well beyond the normal depiction of status. In addition, the meeting allows staff members to gain visibility before the manager. Since this visibility can be abused, the manager should not attend all meetings, but only critical ones. Otherwise, reporting on project progress can become a matter of mere posturing rather than a true working session.

Staff Meetings. The purpose of this meeting is to review the performance of the subgroups and the department as a whole. It is the culmination of the group's efforts to improve productivity and performance. Projects enter into the picture only as a measurement, not as the central focus. The staff meeting provides an excellent forum for highlighting performances above or below normal and for a group exercise in determining why such performance took place. This is not an exercise in personalities but rather in metrics.

The development manager should preside over the meeting, prepare the bulk of the material, and make the presentations. The department and its capabilities are his or her responsibility—not that of the submanagers. Since they have presented the projects' status, the development manager should present the department's status. All too often development managers choose to become an audience once they reach their new role and force staff personnel to do preparation and presentation. This is a serious mistake. Just as staff members must perform for the manager, the manager should perform for the staff.

THE DEVELOPMENT LIFE CYCLE

The development life cycle includes all the stages of a development project from inception to completion. In order for this cycle to be maximally effective, its steps must be well defined and there must be a clear understanding of the goals and scope of each stage by everyone involved.

In addition to managing the classes of work and proper allocation to and management of the work queues, the development life cycle is crucial in managing systems development. It is amazing how few development departments spend time trying to define this life cycle, much less manage it. In general, projects are entrusted to the professionalism of the project manager, allowing the process to be defined as the project proceeds. This makes the organization vulnerable to the vagaries of individual competence and attitude, as well as to external events. It is unreasonable for development to operate in this fashion since the company depends so heavily on the delivery of timely and effective computer systems.

This textbook is not intended to define the life cycle in precise, explicit terms. That discussion requires a separate book, and many such references exist. A number of them are mentioned at the end of this book. Here we will provide a broad description of the stages of the life cycle in reference to each other. From this discussion, reference to books dealing with life cycles, and *the environment in which they are implemented,* the reader can gain the basic information needed to establish a well-defined life cycle.

It is important to understand that any life cycle, methodology or mechanism must be adapted to the specific organization. There is no universal agreement on how a life cycle should proceed. In all likelihood, there never will be. The life cycle must reflect the culture, mores and priorities of the individual organization.

There are two independent cycles which should be formalized within the development group: the support cycle and the development cycle. Each services a relatively independent set of priorities and should be managed separately. Support (production support) concentrates on correcting problems and getting the system back on line. There is no high priority on elegance or justification. Development combines all the standards, procedures and policies of the organization and concentrates on producing a lasting product.

Attempts to combine the two cycles into a single definition invariably result in unacceptable compromises in one cycle or the other. The development cycle should be the focus of attention. It is also the cycle to which all projects should gravitate. This means that projects requiring support should be directed to development as soon as possible.

The Support Cycle

Theoretically, the support staff waits for a problem to develop. As most professionals know, however, slack time seldom exists. Most often, a backlog of problems exists, to be addressed on the basis of evolving priorities and the business cycle. The support cycle consists of four main stages: problem reporting, analysis, correction, and postmortem.

The Problem Reporting Stage. Reporting can be initiated by nearly anyone who uses development services. It must be formal and must prompt an immediate result, either specific activity or entry into a problem queue. The key ingredient during the reporting stage is immediate prioritization of the problem and recording in a fashion that allows the user to trace the progress toward a solution. It also reassures the user that adequate attention is being paid to the problem.

Once the report of a problem is received, it is immediately routed to the individual most qualified to solve it. The problem's impact on the organization must also be determined to establish its priority. The typical development department handles many problems, ranging from questions on how to understand outputs to debilitating system failures. Therefore, prioritization and proper routing are essential.

The problem's type or class also indicates its relative severity. This perceived severity, in turn, will determine response commitments, reporting requirements, computer time authorizations, and often the level of personnel assigned to the problem. The response prompted by the severity level may vary from shift to shift based upon a number of variables, such as system level (reporting or updating), time of the month (mid-month or closing cycle), and external priorities (e.g., filling orders for new and important customers). Therefore, the pulse of the business must be carefully monitored and understood when setting severity levels for reported problems.

The Analysis Stage. Analysis will often vary based upon staff allocations and interpretations at reporting time. If the problem is deemed to be one of possible misinterpretation, a consultant from the support group may handle it. If it is found to be a crippling system failure, senior support analysts may respond immediately at the expense of in-flight efforts.

In either case, the group providing the resource must respond to the problem based on its position in the reporting queue. It cannot be prioritized based on its challenging nature, personal intervention via direct calls from users, or personal expertise. Only by adhering to the allocation procedures of problem reporting can the system be made to work. Otherwise, imaginative users will easily find ways around the procedure and gain an unfair share of the available resources.

The result of the analysis is a decision on how the problem may be corrected. Depending on the problem's severity, this may involve a number of steps to satisfy the most demanding need first and the less urgent needs in sequence until the problem is completely solved. Regardless of the problem's severity, the transition from analysis to correction should be well defined.

This process allows review by another party before correction is attempted. Often a correction is based on frustration or ignorance ("Let's try this and see what happens"). In either case, the risks are high. With the heavy company dependence on information today, the process should proceed from identification to correction with a complete understanding of what the result will be. Substituting one problem for another via uninspired correction is worse than the original error.

The level and degree of review are usually determined by the severity of the problem. Simple columnar errors in reports do not justify a substantial amount of walk-through and verification before the correction cycle begins.

Some review is necessary to ensure correctness, but much less than with a high-level severity issue. In the latter case, a review would be conducted with at least the development manager present, and would probably include the MIS executive. The more serious the problem, the higher and more exhaustive the analysis and planning should be.

The Correction Stage. Correction of system failures by production support follows one of two paths: normal program development or "meatball surgery." The decision on which path to follow is based on a number of factors ranging from the time of the problem's occurrence to its position in the development cycle.

Normal development of system enhancement implies the time to follow standard life cycle stages. Although a number of these stages—such as justification—are brief, an attempt should be made to follow the normal process as much as possible. This can be done only when time is not the key element. These situations abound—for example, when the correction need not occur before the end of the next month or when the problem is so minor that interim steps have solved it adequately.

Meatball surgery is a quick temporary solution which is followed immediately by a more permanent correction. This situation often involves several types of change, constructed in layers to provide enough time for the final correction to be produced. Therefore, one of the purposes of the postanalysis review is to determine how long the permanent solution will take to develop. The number of changes and their relative complexity are determined by this time cycle.

The first rule in making temporary fixes is that they must be just that—temporary. They must never be allowed to remain in place any longer than is absolutely necessary. Leaving them eventually causes the system to become bogged down and hastens obsolescence.

The second rule in making temporary fixes is to avoid "fooling" the system in order to push the correction through quickly. Pushing negative credits through a system to avoid problems with debit processing modules is a disastrous solution. Always process the exceptional situation in problem correction as an exception. Fooling system auditing and control measures invariably leads to increasingly severe problems later.

For normal problem correction, the usual procedures are followed. For temporary corrections, extraordinary paths are followed and many of the audits are bypassed in favor of speed. Temporary changes are loaded into a "purgatory" library and executed from there—not from the production libraries. When the final correction is implemented, these libraries are destroyed.

The Postmortem Stage. Any time a problem arises, a failure occurred in the normal development life cycle. Many of these problems are too costly to find during that cycle, and the eventual failure is the price paid for the time–quality trade-off. This does not mean that problems are accepted, however. The repetition of problems signals the need to adjust the standard cycle. The postmortem review allows the need for these changes to be highlighted.

This review essentially ends the problem. The results of the review should be reported to and evaluated by MIS management as a measure of the effectiveness of the development/support function. Obviously, key problems which caused significant interruption of service or considerable embarrassment will be more pointedly reviewed than routine problems. As a result of postmortem reviews, sweeping changes may also occur. For instance, a determination that 30% of the staff's time is spent correcting problems which should have been found in change control may result in the creation of a formal change management staff.

The Development Cycle

The development cycle represents the vast majority of the organization's efforts. Most of those activities, in fact, must be made to fit within this framework. Part of the support cycle is defined in order to make this happen by not permitting long-term solutions (other than recommendations) to flow out of the support cycle. Rather, they flow from support into the development process. This ensures that the proper level of review and formality is brought to bear on the effort.

A seven-step development cycle is described here. The stages are kept reasonably simple for the purpose of discussion and, as was mentioned earlier, to allow the reader to develop a set of formalities tailored to the specific organization. For the small company that is expanding, this brief analysis may be sufficient and the stages described should suffice. However, they will eventually be strained.

The cycle begins with the release of a project request from the queue. While some similarities may exist in the steps taken to determine the request's priority and class placement, the efforts, scope, and commitment to schedule set these stages apart from the initial queue placement. Projects at this point become *real*—not only for the development group but for the users as well. The project's definition and goals may change in many ways once it becomes a reality.

There was a time when specifications and other definition statements were frozen in order to keep the original definition of the project intact. The theory behind this effort is valid, but in practice it is seldom viable. The user is the recipient of the effort, and it is far more important to produce a satisfactory product than to force the user to accept only what he or she originally requested. A system request is not a binding legal contract; it is a request to improve the business by assisting an individual component.

Therefore, some flexibility is needed. The stages of the development cycle are defined as integral, discrete entities, but in practice, components may be redefined while the balance of the effort continues. The project manager has the responsibility of rationalizing these variations while adhering to the spirit of the life cycle.

The Analysis Stage. In the analysis stage of a project, the need for the change is evaluated (or reevaluated) to determine affected components, resource requirements (human and hardware/software), priorities of components and the primary path to be followed (languages, database, systems, etc.). While components of the system may require recycling through this stage, the primary work is discrete and nonrepetitive: It is the basis for all future stages. It requires a formal review and acceptance before proceeding further.

There is a high level of user–developer interaction at this stage, with a number of interviews being conducted to ensure that key team members have enough expertise to describe the necessary system adequately. Generally, a formalized methodology is used, such as YOURDON structured techniques, Jackson techniques or various other standard methodologies.

The success of analysis, more than that of any other stage, depends on the level and quality of user involvement. The effects of that involvement will be felt throughout the project. At this stage, a sense of user ownership can be developed, creating a willingness to accept the inevitable trade-offs which will occur. The user can gain a true perspective of what the system can do, so that unfortunate and unfavorable gaps do not exist between expectation and result. Finally, a system can be prepared which adequately matches the business need.

In order to pass from analysis to planning (the next stage), the system must be formally accepted by both the user and the development department. The scope, cost, benefit and ancillary efforts required to bring the system to production must be described. The acceptance agreement should be published by the user rather than by the development department. This ensures that the perspective of the user requesting service from MIS is maintained. The analysis merely defines what is being requested in terms which allow its design and construction.

Table 3–4 outlines the key components of the analysis stage.

Table 3–4. Key Characteristics of the Analysis Stage

PERCENTAGE OF PROJECT LIFE	15%
TIME CONTRIBUTION BY AREA	
Development	50%
Management	5%
Analysis	75%
Programming	15%
Quality control	5%
Users	50%
Management	20%
Line personnel	80%

MAJOR RISKS

- Failure to allow adequate time for analysis will result in a probability that the system will fail to meet the user's demands.
- Active user involvement can be difficult to maintain. Management especially favors a passive role.
- There is a tendency to put off decisions during analysis. The result is a blurring of project scope.

GOALS

- Ensure that the environment or the technology has not changed so much since the original request that the project is no longer justified.
- Define the bounds of the system so that its intent and goals will not be lost in the process of design and construction.
- Communicate the parameters of the system clearly to all persons who will have to interact in the process or with the implemented system.

REQUIREMENTS

- A specification document, in the required form, which leads to the next stage.
- Documented approval to proceed to the next stage.
- Budget estimate of the personnel, hardware, and software resources needed to complete the project.

Planning. The analysis stage defines what is to be done. The planning stage outlines what steps, in what sequence, and by whom the project will be brought to fruition. It is a cooperative effort involving the user and the developer. Like analysis, planning does not commit the company to further dedication to the effort. In fact, with little reworking, the analysis and the plan should be usable whether the project proceeds beyond this stage or not. This is an extremely important aspect of every phase—to produce results which can be reprocessed at a later date.

Most of the planning is done by the development analyst, with the user manager acting as a reviewer. This is done primarily because development is generally the critical path. The user's involvement consists of coordinating his or her schedules with the development department's and ensuring that the desired implementation dates are met and the guarantees are fulfilled. While the bulk of the planning is performed by development, it is important to involve the user in detail.

With the user's involvement, reasonable trade-offs can be made. The option of having the user develop part of the system on a PC using a fourth-generation language may be considered as a viable alternative to having analysts and programmers devote a substantial amount of time to development and reporting. Specialized peripheral modules may be delayed in favor of enhancing core system capabilities. In any case, with intimate involvement, the user/requestor is more likely to be receptive to changes than if such changes are suggested during a management-level presentation.

If a scheduling product is used to maintain the schedule and track progress, the data should be loaded in at this time. Many products are available today to aid and extend the ability to track projects. Their use and effectiveness is discussed in detail in Chapter 11 under "End User Languages." The implication is that the user should track the project—and that is the intent.

The planning stage generally produces a single output—a formalized schedule, complete with personnel allocations, contingency plans and budgets. The stage is generally short enough so that additional subphases are not necessary.

Table 3–5 outlines the key elements of the planning stage.

The Design Stage. Design is the stage during which the specific modules are defined and described so that they can be built by the analysts, programmers or users. Unlike the previous two stages, this stage generally overlaps the following stages throughout the life cycle. In other words, the whole product is not designed before the process of construction and implementation begins. Construction starts as soon as possible, and major phases of the system will probably be in operation before the final components are designed.

Therefore, the project represents a commitment by the time this stage begins. Cancellation of the project, or even short-term delay, involves an unrecoverable loss of resources. Therefore, it is extremely important that the project be approved before it enters the design stage. There is the perspective from the user community that once a project reaches design, they have little need of involvement. Such is not the case.

Although design issues are often technically oriented, the ability to relate

Table 3–5. Key Characteristics of the Planning Stage

PERCENTAGE OF PROJECT LIFE	5%
TIME CONTRIBUTION BY AREA	
Development	75%
Management	5%
Analysis	50%
Programming	40%
Quality control	5%
Users	25%
Management	85%
Line personnel	15%

MAJOR RISKS

- There is often a tendency to overplan and allow little or no leeway. Reality dictates that plans must be extremely flexible.
- If the analysis stage was less than comprehensive, planning will produce a product which is virtually useless.
- If plans are not produced that show separate levels of detail, little attention will be paid to them.

GOALS

- To produce a blueprint of the project schedule that management, users, and development can use to schedule their resources and strategies.
- To schedule budget allocations and recruiting needs.

REQUIREMENTS

- Loading of the schedule components into the project tracking mechanism used.
- Approval of the plan by management. Management must also approve the impact on all other projects as well.
- Approval of the plan by other components of MIS. This should occur before approval by management.

the design to the user's operation is extremely important. Some efficiency must often be sacrificed to ensure that the design meets the user's needs. Although these trade-offs cannot be discussed in a black and white perspective, it is a fact that convoluted designs which do not really fulfill operational needs will eventually cause significant problems. As users turn increasingly to their PC, these discrepancies become even more significant.

Users develop their reporting mechanisms and subsystems based upon their view of how the system should be designed. As time goes on, more and more of the system's framework consists of these external components. Enhancement and maintenance of the peripheral components can become as complex and time-consuming as the core facilities which were the original basis of the design. When there are many conflicts between the user's and the developer's views, the evolution of the system will inevitably cause the enhancements to become more complicated than the system itself and will lead to far earlier obsolescence than if the two perspectives had been consistent.

Ideally, the product should be designed from the user's perspective. The user's involvement should be cooperative, with an emphasis on matching development's views of the product. This not only increases the likelihood of consistent development, both internally and externally, but also allows the design phase to end at the intended point. Thus, there will be no need for the design stage to be followed by a behind-the-scenes internal design phase.

Regardless of the number of iterations of design throughout the life cycle, each subphase must be completed separately. This means that a design document must be produced and approved by both the user and the development department. That document may take many forms, ranging from pseudo-code to specifications, but it must be written in a language which is understandable by both development and the user. Neither party may be totally intimate with all of the terms, but they must be able to understand the concepts. Without that clarity, the purpose of the design may be unclear and the final product can be significantly different from the original intent.

Table 3–6 outlines the key characteristics of the design stage.

The Construction Stage. The construction stage of the life cycle consists of the activities involved in building programs, databases, documentation and communication interfaces to operate the proposed system. The activities are carried out by both user and development personnel when 4GL capabilities exist in the company. Construction normally begins when the design stage has completed (at least for those components being constructed).

Construction is by far the most resource dependent and lengthy stage of the life cycle. It is during this stage that most problems surface in the interaction between the user and development, primarily due to the time frames involved. The key to success, obviously, is to compress the time frames as much as possible.

With a large project, the overall time frames cannot be substantially reduced, assuming that the estimates were not inflated and that planning and design were performed well. In fact, few multiple implementations can be done. True implementation implies a limited need for support, operational independence and a defined level of stability. That cannot be achieved during construction.

However, a state of pseudo-implementation can be created. Here the

Table 3–6. Key Characteristics of the Design Stage

PERCENTAGE OF PROJECT LIFE	15%
TIME CONTRIBUTION BY AREA	
Development	75%
Management	15%
Analysis	40%
Programming	40%
Quality control	5%
Users	25%
Management	75%
Line personnel	25%

MAJOR RISKS

- Much construction is often done under the guise of design due to limitations in designers' conceptual skills.
- Trying to design the *entire* system can result in overly restrictive designs relative to construction trade-offs.
- Failure to involve the user will result in designs which do not closely match the user's view of the system.

GOALS

- A flexible, well-defined picture of what the system will be, how it will relate to other systems, and how the components of the system will communicate.
- What work will be done by whom.
- How the components will be presented for test and review.

REQUIREMENTS

- A formalized design document(s) which can be used for construction.
- A list of potential areas where trade-offs may need to be made in order to meet schedules. This allows an opportunity for a parrallel stage of reanalysis.

product exists in a purgatory library where the user can put the product through its paces. Components of the system may not exist, or they may perform only rudimentary forms of their projected functions. They are linked together in some fashion, though, and the user can begin to gain an appreciation of what the system will look like. Developers can still create new versions at this level of production, as they normally would during construction.

Even though pseudo-implementation is a preliminary step, many problems and idiosyncracies can be uncovered during the construction period. This does not negate the need for formal testing by the user, but it certainly reduces the problems to be expected during that test process. A formalized, final test is generally somewhat artificial; specific time frame requirements reduce its imaginativeness. Testing during construction is far more free and flexible. The combination of these two approaches will yield a far more acceptable result than a purely system test approach.

The most important benefit of pseudo-implementation is not in the test process. It lies in the ability to involve the user throughout the construction stage. It provides a way for the user to keep in constant touch with the product and see it operate in a real-world environment. Once again, it engenders a sense of ownership which more than compensates for whatever overhead is involved in maintaining the system.

The advent of 4GL products and the user's ability to contribute directly to construction have created many changes in the construction of computer systems. Development departments have long struggled to integrate this capability into the development life cycle. This has usually been done by compromising standard procedures for development or has precluded their creation.

4GL products, however, cannot allow the bypassing of good, systematic construction and testing of system components. In fact, errors made in development using 4GL products are likely to produce significant problems simply because they tend to be more forgiving than their procedural counterparts. This means that a bug can lurk in the software for years, affecting the system in extremely subtle ways.

This does not imply that 4GL should be avoided. To the contrary, 4GL is the only way the development department can hope to keep up with the demand for new systems in the next decade. However, it does mean that all system components must pass through the check-and-balance mechanisms always applied to procedural languages.

The procedures of walk-throughs, code reviews, and independent testing should be continued and demanded regardless of the tools used to develop systems. Their use should be enforced regardless of who performs the process. Once again, as noted in Chapter 1, development is a function independent of the organizational group that performs the process.

Obviously, once the system is operational, MIS cannot expect to enforce development standards on 4GL that is used by the user as a stand-alone effort. However, enforcement during the development life cycle provides a reasonably stable base on which to build. System components which are developed later on should pass through a certification process in order to guarantee their propriety. The subject of certification is discussed in Chapters 11 and 14.

Table 3–7 outlines the key characteristics of the construction stage.

The Implementation Stage. Implementation is that portion of the development cycle which begins when final acceptance testing commences as

Table 3-7. Key Characteristics of the Construction Stage

PERCENTAGE OF PROJECT LIFE	50%
TIME CONTRIBUTION BY AREA	
Development	80%
Management	5%
Analysis	15%
Programming	75%
Quality control	5%
Users	20%
Management	25%
Line personnel	75%

MAJOR RISKS

- The actual construction of the system will become remote from the user, diluting the user's sense of ownership.
- Failures in the previous stages will culminate in construction, and the effects of these errors will be hidden.
- Due to the low visibility of this stage, schedules will slip and be unnoticed until they are irrecoverable.

GOALS

- To produce planned systems components which match the specified results of the analysis stage.
- To provide enough flexibility in the components to allow changes during construction in response to problems found during user testing.
- To build a system which matches, as closely as possible, the user's view of the system. Elegance is found primarily in simplicity.

REQUIREMENTS

- Operational system modules which are relatively error free.
- All necessary documentation to allow implementation.
- All required material, in final form, to satisfy implementation gating steps.

the product becomes operational. It generally consists of a series of gating activities intended to ensure that the product will perform as intended.

Flawless implementation will probably never be achieved. Even if the technical errors are eliminated with concise automated test systems, the fact that the expectations never precisely match the results produces systems which are not totally in accord with their intent.

Implementation occurs almost totally in response to meeting the gating requirements. If these requirements are intelligently established and adhered to, implementation will be successful enough to represent an adequate steady-state environment. Since gating consists of checks of development, the requirements should be developed independently, with the exception of production support needs.

The establishment of gates does not fall within the province of this book. Suffice it to say that whatever gates are established must never be a matter of subjective judgment. No third party should be allowed to reject an implementation because it is not technically elegant or because alternative solutions may be superior. The judgments must be objective and appear in standards that are available during development.

Table 3–8 outlines the key characteristics of the implementation stage.

The Adaptation Stage. The adaptation stage is that period in which the implemented system is manipulated and adjusted until it fits the environment for which it was intended. The larger the project the more important this stage, since a large project has far more opportunities to be out of

Table 3–8. Key Characteristics of the Implementation Stage

PERCENTAGE OF PROJECT LIFE 5%

TIME CONTRIBUTION BY AREA

Development	50%
Management	20%
Analysis	40%
Programming	10%
Quality control	30%
Users	50%
Management	40%
Line personnel	60%

MAJOR RISKS

- In the rush to complete implementation, adequate testing and reviews will not be done.
- The discovery of limitations will result in accusations and recriminations.
- Too many compromises will be made in bridging the gap between expectation and the resulting system.

GOALS

- To produce the system in an orderly fashion.
- To provide adequate hands-on experience with the system so that follow-up training is unnecessary.
- To identify limitations and design ways to correct them.

REQUIREMENTS

- Satisfaction of all gating requirements.
- Plans for required adaptations; approximately 50% of the time allocated for adaptation should be planned.

synchronization than a small one. Of all the life cycle stages, this is the one most typically ignored or downplayed.

The reasons for deemphasizing the adaptation stage is the general feeling that if the system does not totally fulfill the intended need, something must have gone wrong during development. The formalized methodologies have concentrated on honing all previous stages to ensure that no adaptation is required. However, there has always been an adaptation period, regardless of how much it is ignored. This stage occurs because it is nearly impossible to predict how a system will operate in an active, production environment until it is actually on line.

The adaptation stage consists of filling project requests without routing them through project queues and without requiring cost/benefit analyses. Service sequences are established at the discretion of the user and are handled by members of the original system development team. Much of the steady-state oriented management processes are either bypassed or simplified in order to maximize the flow of adaptive modifications before the stage ends.

The adaptation stage must have a specific preagreed upon completion date. The length of this stage should be set in advance (during planning) based upon the size and scope of the project. Any unfilled requests become normal development project requests and pass through the queueing mechanisms as any request would. The completion of the adaptation stage does not necessarily imply that the system is fully adapted to its operational environment. However, without a specific end date, it will last forever, in order to avoid the discipline of the formalized work flow procedures.

The overriding danger of the adaptation stage is that major considerations may be deferred until after implementation with the rationalization that "We'll worry about that during adaptation; it's too difficult to deal with until we see the system in operation." This is an easy way to avoid thinking and planning, not a rational business decision. With this type of thinking, the adaptation stage becomes a period of making the system run, not adapting it to a production environment. Extending a life cycle is no substitute for careful, diligent planning.

Table 3–9 outlines the key characteristics of the adaptation stage.

The Postmortem Stage. The postmortem stage in the support life cycle has already been discussed. There is little difference between that postmortem and this one. Its goal is to understand the situations which occurred during any one project cycle, interpret them relative to the overall development cycle, and seek ways to improve performance.

Formalized postmortems are imperative. Without review and analysis, the development process cannot be improved. The postmortem allows care-

Table 3–9. Key Characteristics of the Adaptation Stage

PERCENTAGE OF PROJECT LIFE	10%
TIME CONTRIBUTION BY AREA	
Development	80%
Management	5%
Analysis	20%
Programming	60%
Quality control	15%
Users	20%
Management	20%
Line personnel	80%

MAJOR RISKS

- Adaptation will be used to implement nonjustified components of the original design rather than those needed for smooth operation.
- Key personnel will be reassigned to other projects before the stage is complete.
- Management's involvement will end before the stage is complete.

GOALS

- To make the system maximally operational.
- To preprocess a number of follow-up requests.
- To allow line personnel to influence the system directly.

REQUIREMENTS

- Normal implementation requirements.

ful, objective evaluation which creates the opportunity to change the process in concert with the company. Many of the problems in development occur because the attitude and philosophy of the company are not synchronized with the priorities and goals of the development cycle. Postmortem allows those issues to surface and be dealt with.

Table 3-10 outlines the key characteristics of the postmortem stage.

CONCLUSION

As mentioned earlier, project management is crucial to the successful management of a systems development staff. The development manager in a large organization may be considerably removed from the day-to-day management of any single project. However, he or she is responsible for the development life cycle, which is the key to managing the flow of work out of the project queues and into production. By allowing this cycle to support rather than limit the flow of new systems into the organization, the devel-

Table 3–10. Key Characteristics of the Postmortem Stage

PERCENTAGE OF PROJECT LIFE <1%

TIME CONTRIBUTION BY AREA	
Development	90%
Management	20%
Analysis	30%
Programming	20%
Quality control	30%
Users	10%
Management	30%
Line personnel	70%

MAJOR RISKS

- If not properly handled, this stage can become an opportunity to place blame for less than successful projects.
- Without proper attention to the process, little improvement of future projects can be anticipated.
- If the exercise is not conducted *immediately* after the project is completed, the results are substantially compromised.

GOALS

- To determine necessary changes in the development process based on experience.
- To evaluate the effectiveness of estimating mechanisms and formula distributions.
- To evaluate the impact of new implementations on enhanced or existing systems.
- To recommend changes in nondevelopment procedures (e.g., management, approvals, clerical procedures).

REQUIREMENTS

Since the postmortem is the closing activity for a project, there are no gating mechanisms to be followed. However, to ensure that the stage is complete, the postmortem evaluation comments should be a required component of the portfolio update. This ensures that a project is not considered closed until the review is complete.

---

opment manager can fulfill his or her responsibilities to the organization and direct its evolution.

The management of projects and their life cycles depends largely on the ability to identify extraordinary circumstances and adapt the processes accordingly. The life cycle (regardless of how formalized it is) is not adaptable to every situation. Different classes of work rely on different stages of the life cycle in varying degrees. Table 3–11 shows how these classes can vary within the cycle.

There is nothing magical about the development life cycle discussed here. Its definition has been kept broad because there are many environments

Table 3-11. Variations in the Life Cycle by Class of Work

STAGE/CLASS OF WORK	PRODUCTION SUPPORT	CONSULTING SUPPORT	MAINTENANCE	ENHANCEMENTS	NEW DEVELOPMENT
ANALYSIS					
User involvement	Lower	Higher	Higher	Lower	Equal
Time allocation	Higher	Higher	Higher	Lower	Equal
Criticality	Higher	Higher	Higher	Lower	Equal
Level of overlap	N/A	Higher	Lower	Lower	Equal
Formality	Lower	Lower	Equal	Lower	Equal
PLANNING					
User involvement	Lower	Higher	Higher	Lower	Equal
Time allocation	Lower	Lower	Higher	Lower	Equal
Criticality	Lower	Lower	Lower	Lower	Equal
Level of overlap	N/A	Higher	Lower	Lower	Equal
Formality	Lower	Lower	Lower	Lower	Equal
DESIGN					
User involvement	Lower	Higher	Lower	Equal	Equal
Time allocation	Higher	Lower	Lower	Equal	Equal
Criticality	Higher	Lower	Lower	Higher	Equal
Level of overlap	N/A	Higher	Lower	Equal	Equal
Formality	Higher	Lower	Lower	Higher	Equal
CONSTRUCTION					
User involvement	Lower	Higher	Higher	Higher	Equal
Time allocation	Lower	Higher	Equal	Higher	Equal
Criticality	Higher	Lower	Equal	Equal	Equal
Level of overlap	Lower	Higher	Lower	Lower	Equal
Formality	Higher	Lower	Equal	Equal	Equal
IMPLEMENTATION					
User involvement	Higher	Equal	Higher	Equal	Equal
Time allocation	Higher	Higher	Higher	Equal	Equal
Criticality	Lower	Higher	Higher	Equal	Equal
Level of overlap	N/A	Equal	N/A	Equal	Equal
Formality	Lower	Higher	Higher	Higher	Equal
ADAPTION					
User involvement	N/A	Higher	N/A	Lower	Equal
Time allocation	N/A	Higher	N/A	Lower	Equal
Criticality	N/A	Lower	N/A	Equal	Equal
Level of overlap	N/A	Higher	N/A	Equal	Equal
Formality	N/A	Equal	N/A	Equal	Equal
POSTMORTEM					
User involvement	Lower	Lower	Higher	Equal	Equal
Time allocation	Higher	N/A	Equal	Lower	Equal
Criticality	Higher	Lower	Equal	Equal	Equal
Level of overlap	N/A	N/A	N/A	N/A	Equal
Formality	Higher	Higher	Higher	Lower	Equal

All factors are either lower or higher than the sample life cycle figures.

User involvement is the level that involvement must occur.

Time allocation is general for the class of work.

"Criticality" refers to the severity of the damage resulting from suboptimal results.

Level of overlap is the tendency for the stage to repeat and overlap with one or more subsequent stages.

Formality is either higher or lower than that found in a full development effort.

where a more standard definition is appropriate. A great deal of work has been done to define the life cycle, and the pragmatic development manager should take full advantage of it. However, whatever method is chosen, the emphasis must be on adaptation to the specific environment. This method will also evolve over time until it bears only a vague relationship to the original product. In this way, it becomes the life cycle best suited to *your* organization.

4

ORGANIZATION

A department's organization has a major impact on its ability to meet its responsibilities and move work smoothly. Good organization is especially important in systems development, with its inherent transience due to the project orientation of its personnel. A stable, well-conceived structure holds the development department together through the ebb and flow of projects. The larger a department becomes and the broader its scope, the more important its organization becomes to the manager, who is increasingly removed from the department's actual work.

Establishing the department and guiding its evolution is the primary responsibility of the manager. Understanding the responsibilities of the entire department, structuring the group to meet those responsibilities, and changing it in response to outside forces can only be accomplished by the manager. Evolution is a critical component. MIS and development have earned a reputation for constant and chronic reorganization. This situation makes long-term management extremely difficult. For this reason, it is essential to carefully consider both the obvious and subtle aspects of organization on an ongoing basis and in preparation for reorganizing.

The explosion of technology and the sharpening of competition in nearly every industry have made it difficult to maintain a stable organizational structure. Each new spurt of technology seems to require a specialization which is most easily provided by creating a unique internal structure. Then, as the new technology is accepted, that uniqueness is no longer necessary and the specialized area must be absorbed or eliminated. Sharpening competition creates a need to focus attention in specific business areas, with dramatic shifts to other areas when a competitor introduces a new service. All too often, development must react to these shifts with organizational adjustments—creating additional confusion.

This chapter discusses organization as it applies to the effective management of the development process. Although the characteristics of development groups vary widely, they tend to follow a few general patterns. The first part of this chapter discusses two fairly common variations and one example of a hybrid. The most important features of these organizational types are reviewed, as well as the advantages and disadvantages of each.

The second part of the chapter deals with the factors which govern organization formation. Some of these factors can be internally controlled, while others are influenced primarily by outside forces. In either case, the development manager must consider these influences in order to avoid painful false starts and the trauma that mismatched organizations create.

The development manager must plan the organization well and function within its framework. In a basically unstable process, the ability to provide a stable working environment is essential to continued success. A dynamic environment is good, but not when it reaches the point of confusion. All too often, we excuse poor organizational planning by blaming business or technological change.

ORGANIZATIONAL FORMS

While the organization of the development department, like that of any corporate department, is governed somewhat by the diversity of corporate structures, certain forms tend to be more common than others. In many cases, the reason is that the group has always been organized in that way—at least broadly. This is probably not the best rationale for an organizational structure, given the dramatic changes in technology and methodology that have occurred over the past several years. However, continuity in itself can be good. People are often most comfortable with familiar things, and having that comfort can be advantageous.

The organization of MIS can be traced to its original placement in the financial area. This happened either because of convenience or because most of the early computer applications focused around accounting. Many MIS departments still report to accounting or finance even though they are used by all types of departments throughout the company.

This does not imply that no other reporting line is successful. In fact, many MIS organizations owe their success to the fact that the financial department has extended its scope by the innovative use of information technology. This has provided the anchor of stability for an inherently unstable discipline.

The advent of the chief information officer (CIO) has substantially increased the status and visibility of MIS. Reporting to the chief executive officer (CEO), the CIO has significantly enhanced MIS and development's role in the long-term evolution of the company. However, only a few businesses have taken this path. Change comes slowly, and although the development manager should be organizing and building the department with that future in mind, servicing today's organization is the manager's most important duty.

Here we will discuss two common mechanisms for organizing the development department: along business area lines and by internal function. We will also describe a hybrid of the two which combines some of the strong points of each. The advantages and disadvantages of each form are also reviewed so that the development manager can understand the challenges they create.

Organization by Business Area

Figure 4–1 depicts an MIS organization which parallels the basic operations of the company. It provides a reporting wing for each of the major business segments, and these areas are mainly responsible for servicing the departments associated with those business areas. There may be a dotted-line reporting relationship, as in matrix organizations, so that the business area directs the work of each wing, or the separation may be purely internal. Figure 4–1 and the following discussion are related to a manufacturing company that sells a product (or products) which it has developed and manufactures. The structure is also typical of that of a banking, service, or any other enterprise. Only the functional names are different.

Typically, this type of organization evolves in response to the entrepreneurial attitude of upper management. Everyone in the business should be a "businessman" with a fairly in-depth knowledge of how the business is run, its priorities, its products and its market. The various wings specialize in the business orientation it services, and whatever technical skills are required anywhere in the organization are expected to be provided as a secondary aspect of the business. This example shows five major wings: sales and marketing, finance, manufacturing, administration, and user services.

The sales and marketing group is responsible for providing development services for central and field sales personnel, as well as for basic marketing

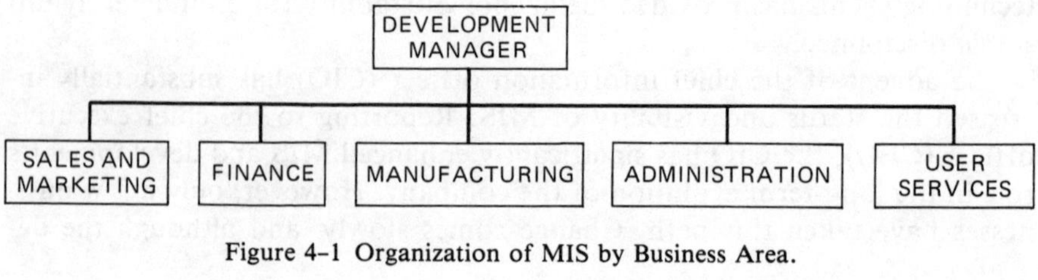

Figure 4–1 Organization of MIS by Business Area.

efforts. In many firms, this group operates at arms length from the field force simply because it is far less disciplined than most other organizational units. Of all the components of the modern company, this group most epitomizes the information aspect of the business, since much of the competitive intelligence needed to survive in today's business world centers on sales and marketing.

The responsibilities of the finance group vary widely from company to company. Most textbook descriptions of the life cycle of the typical business indicate that the mature enterprise is run by the financial department. Decisions are relegated to cost/benefit evaluations—much to the chagrin of the inventor. In less mature companies, finance can be a matter of satisfying the accountants of industry. It requires a commitment to discipline, detail, and procedure which exists in no other component of development. Given the trend toward micro-oriented software today, the people servicing financial groups require a fairly strong knowledge of PCs. PCs, and the challenges they bring, generally occur first in the financial wing of the company.

U.S. manufacturing companies are under extraordinary pressure from other countries. The response to lower-priced imports has resulted in the growth of robotics, automated factories and a host of computer-assisted products. The manufacturing wing of development often comes into direct conflict with the engineering department and finds itself developing substantial systems simply to integrate engineering applications with information systems. Often a separate development department is established just to service engineering.

The administration wing is more often part of the development department and is sometimes involved in efforts to automate the development function itself. Since all other other areas service independent departments, the steps necessary to improve the development function are difficult to push through the priority queues without an independent, unattached group. In companies which do not provide a planning and administrative department, these activities are often shifted to development administration. It is a handy place to house nonaligned activities.

User services encompasses all of the activities involving end-user computing or decision support systems. This group is usually small. However, as the use of automation grows, the user services group increases proportionately. This includes the information center, as well as efforts surrounding PCs, decision support tools, dispersed processing and nearly everything about which the end user might have questions or needs related to information processing.

Development organizations of this type have certain common characteristics. Each area aligned with a business area provides nearly all functional needs, from management through programming and support. Project queues are serviced independently by area, and specialization tends to vary depending on the level of automation by business area. For the package-oriented MIS strategy, organizing by business area tends to be most supportive, since there is more emphasis on business analysis than on technological expertise.

Advantages. There is no particular reason to organize development by business area. However, this structure has some distinct advantages which the development manager should consider carefully before making any changes.

Organizing by business area provides a direct, tangible relationship between the enterprise and development. This relationship is seen in the ongoing interpersonal relations between staff members and user management. For example, the director of marketing has, from his perspective, a captive resource pool for projects. These resources can be used for marketing projects without undue conflict with peer executives. Except on the largest projects, where adequate resources may not be available within the individual group, few formalities are necessary to establish personal priorities.

From the user's perspective, organization of development by business area is easy to understand. Within the financial group, for instance, there is probably an accounting subgroup, a financial analysis subgroup, and so on, which mirrors the group being serviced. Anyone in the user department knows where his or her service will be provided without understanding development's particular organizational needs. All users need do is to understand their own structure, and that of development becomes obvious.

Strategic planning, budgets and components of major business events, such as acquisitions, are easy to trace through the direct relationship between the user and the development department. Resource needs, trade-offs inherent in many of these events and positioning of employees are directly related to these events. The user manager can essentially isolate himself from any explicit knowledge of technology for the future simply because the development person will cover his needs.

Organization by business area has the advantage of maximizing expertise in the business areas, and specialization can focus on special needs such as robotics in manufacturing. In the more complex industries such as high technology, communications and specialized services, this orientation is almost essential simply because no pool of external resources exists. The more expertise the company can draw on, even if it is not within the intended function, the better from a competitive viewpoint.

Finally, organization by business area allows the company to keep abreast of business trends. These opportunities arise in many ways, and a multidisciplinary view of emerging directions will often highlight them more rapidly than a single perception. Organizations which concentrate on internal issues do not read the same publications, attend the same meetings, and socialize with the same people as they do when they consider themselves accountants (for example) first and developers second.

Disadvantages. With organization by business area, it is often very difficult to shift resources rapidly from one area to another. User managers quickly realize that their ability to take advantage of technical solutions is related almost directly to the number of people in their development group. In spite of shifting business directions, they are reluctant to surrender those resources for seemingly higher-priority efforts. Therefore, additional resource needs must be gained by increased staff size, outside services or a political struggle among executives for in-house development resources. This invariably creates difficulties for the development manager, who seldom has the luxury of maintaining objective neutrality.

This organizational style also creates a tendency to lose touch with technological orientations. And this is basically what development means—technological solutions to business problems. With an overriding concentration on business aspects, senior personnel within the subgroups tend to lose technological expertise. One cannot concentrate on everything at once, and technology is not an area in which it is easy to make up lost ground.

In the organization structured by business areas, it is easier to become dependent on a single person or a small number of people. The marketing development manager, for instance, becomes so ingrained in the application of technology to this area that the department cannot get along without this person. Depending on one employee is inevitable because high performers are not easy to find. But when the skills that make them high performers are not development skills, the replacement pool can be quite shallow. If an expert in SQL (IBM's relational database) is difficult to find, it will be even more difficult to find an expert in ABC Corporation's strategic planning process.

Loyalties can easily become blurred when the orientation to the business area is over emphasized. All too often, the managers or leaders of subgroups consider themselves accountants first and members of development second. Under normal circumstances this is not a serious problem, but if political friction develops, the development manager may be hard pressed to determine what side the accountant/developer is on. Such a situation is very difficult to manage and can lead to a great deal of trouble.

Finally, and again in terms of loyalty, having a business orientation as the key criterion can cause a development to respond to power plays rather than to the company's needs. This can result in a situation where weaker executives are left only with token resources rather than an amicable balance of priorities. This inevitably reduces the company's ability to compete in the marketplace.

Table 4–1 summarizes the advantages and disadvantages of organizing by business area.

Organization by Function

Figure 4–2 decribes a development group organized by function. It is for a financial services firm, but it could represent nearly any type of company. Its primary purpose is to focus the organization of the department on the skills and common approaches that unify the various functions of development. In other words, it is designed to maximize the efficency of the development process.

There are six wings to the group, most of them self-explanatory.

The systems analysis group is composed of the various levels of analysts and concentrates on performing studies, developing system specifications,

Table 4–1. Organization by Business Area

ADVANTAGES

- DIRECT RELATIONSHIP WITH BUSINESS ORGANIZATION
  - Allows a clear understanding within the user community
- A WELL ALIGNED WITH BUSINESS EVENTS
  - Tends to isolate impact of major events
- EXPERTISE IN BUSINESS FUNCTIONS INCREASED
  - Development of highly specialized business analysts
- EARLY EVALUATION OF BUSINESS TRENDS
  - Identification with the business community increases interest and independent evaluation

DISADVANTAGES

- DIFFICULTY IN SHIFTING RESOURCES WITHOUT HIGH VISIBILITY
  - Executives tend to be possessive of identified resources
- LOSS OF TECHNOLOGICAL EXPERTISE
  - Concentration on business implies less concentration on technology
- DEPENDENCE ON A SMALL NUMBER OF PERSONS
  - Concentration of expertise breeds high dependence
- BLURRED LOYALTIES
  - Is the analyst an accountant or a developer?
- SUSCEPTIBILITY TO EXECUTIVE POWER POLITICS
  - Identification of development by executives often used for political purposes

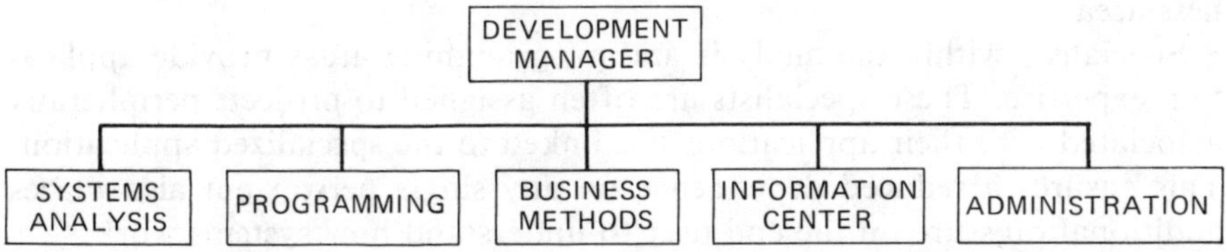

Figure 4-2 Organization of MIS by Internal Function.

assisting users and working with user departments to develop strategies and tactics for reaching their goals.

The programming group consists of systems designers and developers, who concentrate primarily on internal issues of development. They may assist the user directly, since their programming skills run the full gamut of applied languages—from assembler language to 4GLs. While they must follow standards, procedures and methodologies specific to design and programming, when a large project takes place, they report to the analysts, who function as project leaders.

The support group provides both consulting and production system support. They work on exceptional problems which endanger the system functions or are called upon when the other groups cannot adequately support the user. When systems are initially implemented, one or more individuals from the development project will be temporarily assigned to this group.

The business methods group deals in procedures, paper flow, and process-oriented activities for any requesting department. They produce no actual systems and tend to act more as facilitators. They are the specialists in applications and their operation in the live environment.

The information center is the result of a recognition of end-user computing. The center's personnel provide training on 4GL products, review developed applications, administer the certification process, review new technologies relative to end-user activities, and answer questions.

The administrative group coordinates the various development activities. They coordinate the budget process, handle expense accounting for development, verify conformity to standards, maintain all administrative control systems and measure department performance. Essentially, they represent overhead, so they are often used as the department head's special forces to solve the problems of the development department itself.

Requests are received at a central point and distributed to the appropriate groups. The organization is predominately project driven, so the centralization of this activity ensures that the project flow is smooth, controlled, and represents the direction of the company rather than of any single business area.

Specialists within the analysis and programming areas provide application expertise. These specialists are often assigned to projects peripherally associated with their applications but linked to the specialized application. This ensures a reduced dependence on any single person but also places additional pressure on the end user to understand how systems work.

Advantages. Organization by internal function is very different from organization by business area. The difference is mainly one of perspective. In the former, the specifics of MIS and development predominate, where in the latter, the emphasis is on the business orientation. As with the previous orientation, there are distinct advantages to organizing by function which the development manager should understand.

The first major advantage is that organizing by function represents a concentration on the technological aspect of development. Personnel stay abreast of the latest technological issues, have a commitment to their craft, and deal with other computer professionals. This orientation fully supports a technical role within the organization and allows the business areas to provide the business expertise. Staff members must certainly understand the business, but not in the detail required for organization by business area.

It is also reasonably simple to maintain and police standards and procedures, since these receive constant attention. This happens because the standards and procedures are the hallmark of development's identity. It is therefore in the best interest of all staff members to ensure that they are followed and expanded. They are not by-products, but rather the framework of the development group.

The expertise in any one application tends to be shared by several staff members. In a financial services organization, for example, people in analysis, programming, support, and the information center have a moderate knowledge of personal trust applications simply because each group touches that area in its normal flow of work. That knowledge may not be comprehensive or universal, but would certainly be found in more than the single expert often found in the business area organization. This has the additional benefit of reducing the company's dependence on any one individual.

Organization by internal function tends to foster development professionals who excel in the more technical processes of development. The professional project leader or analyst often has extensive experience in the discipline and can discover technical solutions more rapidly than the business-oriented professional. This assumes that the business expert does in fact exist, but one should expect to find that expertise in every user department.

Finally, organization by function provides much greater flexibility than is seen in a business area orientation. User managers have a much more limited sense of ownership of the development group (possibly one or two specialists), with the bulk of the resources existing in a pool of analysts and programmers. As priorities change, it is therefore far easier to shift internal resources accordingly.

Disadvantages. From the viewpoint of users, the most serious deficiency in organizing by function is that the perceived association between development and their own area can become blurred. Because a major wing of the development department is not specifically called Finance, for example, users may feel that finance is not adequately represented. The fact that an application specialist is specifically positioned to service their needs does not have the same impact.

Another disadvantage is that the localized level of expertise is somewhat lowered. It was previously noted that the spread of expertise is considered a major benefit. That is certainly true internally but may not seem so to users. This is especially true in a company where development is the sole source of computer expertise. In any company, there is a middle ground between any two departments where a superficial knowledge of each other's area is expected. If development has historically covered all the middle ground in dealing with user departments, organizing by function may leave uncovered gaps.

In the development department, functional organization can breed discomfort by making the staff feel isolated from the rest of the company. This is due primarily to their technical orientation and their disalignment with other departments. One's picture of business tends to develop along conventional lines. MIS is a relatively new discipline and is somewhat alien to conventional business pictures. This perception affects both users and development personnel.

Disalignment with the business structure can create an atmosphere of isolation and insulation. Career paths seem stilted, social relationships confined, and MIS personnel feel cut off from the mainstream. With the preeminence of information technology in business strategy, this isolation is now diminishing. However, it is still a problem, and the successful development manager must consider it now as well as in the future.

Table 4–2 summarizes the advantages and disadvantages of organizing by internal function.

The Hybrid Organization

The two organization structures, by function and by business area, have one thing in common: they both have singular perspectives. The functional organization is oriented to effective management of the development proc-

Table 4-2. Organization by Internal Function

ADVANTAGES
CONCENTRATION ON TECHNOLOGY Functional orientation breeds a higher level of interest in technology itself
STRONG ADHERENCE TO STANDARDS AND METHODOLOGIES These components are a major part of identity
DISSEMINATION OF BUSINESS EXPERTISE People in each group are exposed to all applications
FOSTERING OF DEVELOPMENT PROFESSIONALISM Involvement in professional groups, reading and seminars
HIGHLY FLEXIBLE ORGANIZATION Resources easily shifted to accommodate business priorities
DISADVANTAGES
DIFFICULT FOR USERS TO ASSOCIATE WITH Users must understand development as an entity
LOWER LEVEL OF EXPERTISE IN ANY SINGLE INDIVIDUAL Mix of business and technology reduces concentration on business issues
ISOLATED FROM THE GENERAL BUSINESS ENVIRONMENT Identification of development with business components can seem limited
CAREER ISOLATION FROM THE CORPORATE COMMUNITY Career paths are less obvious for developers today

ess, while the business area organization is oriented to reacting effectively to the business by being structured similarly. Most real-life organizations represent a hybrid of these two orientations, with an emphasis on one or the other.

Figure 4-3 describes one such hybrid organization which has the benefit of maximizing the development department's efficiency while retaining much of the organization's flavor, at least from the users' perspective. It is organized into four wings.

The first wing, application support, is the area most commonly involved with users. It consists of specialists in each of the applications serviced who tend to operate as business analysts. Their role is somewhat analogous to that of the marketing representative who calls on customers and is their prime contact. While others may work temporarily with the customer, the expert understanding of the customer's environment lies with the marketing person, who facilitates the work and coordinates support requirements.

Application support can be divided further into production and consulting support. These retain their organization by area and provide a relatively self-contained resource pool to service particular applications. Expertise is

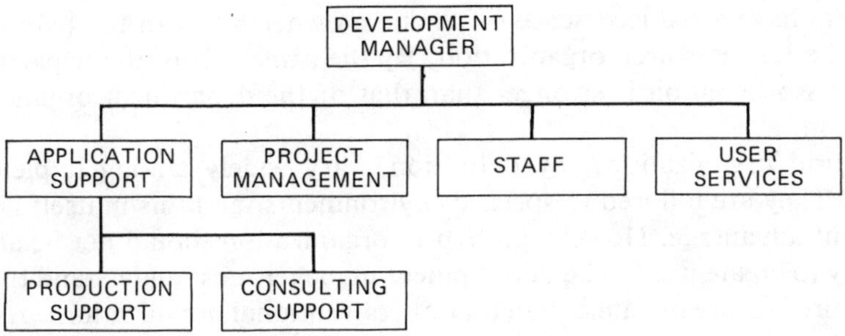

Figure 4–3 Hybrid Organization.

consolidated and users perceive a complete organization to service their functional areas.

The project management wing consists of project specialists (with some application knowledge) who are assigned personnel to handle projects large enough to justify the overhead for the area. The permanent staff in this wing is quite small—just enough to service the project. Project analysts and programmers come from the staff group. Project managers are experts in organizing, planning, staffing and controlling projects. Their existence recognizes the development department's project orientation, which was discussed in Chapter 3. This group may be responsible for the project life cycle during development, but they interact heavily with the application support group, which is responsible for dealing with users.

The staff wing consists of programmers and anaysts who are assigned to projects. It is the largest wing in the department and ranges in seniority from entry-level programmers to the super-technologist who enjoys programming and analysis but does not feel compelled to lead. The existence of the independent staff group allows a strong concentration on the methodologies and tools that the group will use. There is little interference from project managers or application specialists in the use of these tools, and many subgroups are responsible for creating the methodologies, processes and procedures associated with system construction.

User services, the final group, has the same responsibilities we saw in the business area organization. It aids users, tracks progress and fulfills any technological needs not specifically covered by the other wings. It also includes the information center.

Advantages and Disadvantages. In a hybrid organizational structure weaknesses and strengths depend on the departments' emphasis—business area or functional. Since the hybrid is midway between them, the strengths and weaknesses of each will be somewhat diluted.

Users have a reduced sense of resource ownership with the hybrid than with the business area organization. By the same token, the department's business orientation is stronger than that of the department organized by function.

Hybrid organizations, by definition, vary widely among implementations. They are tailored to specific environments, and this in itself is a significant advantage. However, a hybrid organization should not be allowed merely to create itself. The development manager must understand that this structure is more dynamic than that of conventional organizations. As mentioned earlier, one person's dynamics are another person's confusion. Any organization structure should be the product of careful consideration, not only for today's needs but also for those of the future.

Table 4-3 summarizes the principal advantages and disadvantages of the hybrid organization.

FACTORS GOVERNING ORGANIZATIONS

The development manager seeks to establish and mold an organization which fills the company's needs both today and tomorrow. The skills of staff members must be honed and applied to advantage. Acceptable service levels must be established and service commitments met as consistently as

Table 4-3. Hybrid Organization

ADVANTAGES

- COMINES THE BENEFITS OF FUNCTIONAL AND BUSINESS AREA ORGANIZATIONS
  - Technology served as well as a business orientation to less computer-literate business areas
- ADAPTABLE TO CHANGING POLITICAL FORTUNES
  - Small application group can be shifted easily
- CONCENTRATION OF TECHNICAL SKILLS
  - Allows both technological and process expertise
- USER PERSPECTIVE OF BUSINESS CONCENTRATION
  - Application support group has a business orientation and perspective

DISADVANTAGES

- CAN BE DIFFICULT TO SELL TO MANAGEMENT
  - Divergence from business and seeming complexity can make it difficult to convince executives of the usefulness of this organization
- HIGHLY DYNAMIC
  - Ability and tendency for intradepartment movement can produce confusion about reporting lines

possible. The manager must also create an organization in step with corporate directions, especially when technology is a major component of corporate strategy.

Unfortunately, the establishment of an organization is influenced by many outside forces. These conditions do not require organization adjustments, but they must be recognized and often are more important than objective analysis, in determining how the organization evolves. For example, these factors may slow the manager's movement to a favored structure, or they may even prevent achievement of that goal. Business is a world of compromise, and the manager who recognizes the need for compromise is far more likely to achieve overall success than one who always attempts to "do things the way they should be done."

Equally important in accepting compromise is the need to understand precisely what compromise will accomplish. All too often, changes are made in response to immediate requirements, with little evaluation of their impact on the company. Such ad hoc decisions tend to accrue until the resulting organizational structure has no relationship to plan or efficiency. Once this happens, efficiency drops, turnover increases, service levels deteriorate, and eventually a new manager is brought in to solve the problem.

Limitations on Choice

Table 4–4 outlines some of the factors which limit the choices development managers face in creating or changing an organization. These factors are described objectively but are seldom obvious in any given situation. Unfortunately, great experience is often required to understand them fully.

Any senior-level experience in the field provides the skills to recognize that such influences exist. Unfortunately, departments, like persons, are individuals. It is foolhardy for new managers to think that they have carte blanche authority to structure the department as they see fit. By the same token, the manager who is rising through the ranks may think that the answers are obvious, but they have not yet absorbed the point of view of their new peers or recognized the pressures operating at higher management levels. Different forces are at work and, although pervasive, are seldom obvious.

The intelligent manager operates within the existing organization as long as necessary before considering major changes. Changes may not even be needed, but if they are, understanding the way the current organization functions is more useful than intuition or the management committee's rhetoric. This period of analysis also gives the manager time to assess his or her own limitations and options in making changes.

With this information in hand, the probability of establishing a stable

Table 4-4. Factors Which Limit Organizational Choices

DIRECTIVES OF UPPER MANAGEMENT
Management exerts its influence by directing organizations—at least to some degree. They seek to match a corporate organization to their own philosophy or even their competitors' organizations. Changing this concept can be difficult, if not impossible. Slow, deliberate change based on performance is the most viable solution.
INERTIA OF THE ECONOMY
Bull markets require dynamic organizational characteristics; bear markets a concentration on business areas. Many of a development organization's characteristics are based on which market existed when it was formed or changed.
CONSERVATIVE INDUSTRIES
A conservative industry is typically filled with long-term employees who tend to resist changes or unconventional ideas. Organizations that differ from the norm are viewed with concern.
INDUSTRY TYPE
High-technology industries require maximum flexibility, while industries with an engineering bent require a specialized wing oriented to the engineering group. Financial industries are in a period of transition where technological innovation requires great technical expertise. Insurance companies place a high priority on understanding the industry. One must understand and react to the "personality" of the industry.

organization is high. Although departmental personnel as well as senior management will change, the necessary flexibility can be provided so that these changes will not cause serious problems.

Special Situations

Like limitations in options, special situations in a company influence the development department's organization. Table 4–5 outlines some of these situations and describes how their effect is perceived.

Trying to ignore factors such as a decentralized environment is fruitless. Regardless of the difficulties of managing a remote development effort, if this is the situation, the manager must satisfy the company's demands. Trying to exert control in a situation which requires minimal control will create nothing but friction. The manager would be far better served, and would far better serve the company, by establishing the checks and balances necessary to create an effective operation.

These situations can be cyclic, although the cycles are usually long lasting for years rather than months. The classic example is the tendency for business to fluctuate between centralized and decentralized management. This has been going on for years and is likely to continue. Therefore, the development manager should structure the department so that control, if not

Table 4–5. Special Situations in Companies

TYPE OF PRODUCT SERVICED

A company oriented primarily to package implementation requires significantly less technological expertise than a highly individualized company. When PC development is emphasized, the need for technological expertise rises. The frequent use of contract services implies a need for strong project management skills and an organization which supports that specialization.

DECENTRALIZED ENVIRONMENT

When a portion of development is remote from its management, a group is needed to maintain and police adherence to standards. It is also essential to provide support for applications at various levels so that problems are localized when necessary and addressed universally when appropriate. A development manager's need for administrators is increased.

INDEPENDENCE OF FUNCTIONS

When a company creates an organization which emphasizes the independence of individual functions (such as financial services and commercial banking), it is necessary either to define development as an equally independent entity or to provide all development services to each functional unit separately. In that way, separate businesses can be treated as such. With separation, a very loose set of controls must be applied, optimally at the corporate staff level.

DYNAMICS OF CHANGE

In an extremely dynamic industry or one that is changing rapidly, development organizations are under constant pressure from each business component. The development manager can best react to this situation by adapting a limited external view with maximum internal flexibility. This way, current demands can be satisfied while leaving the long-term evolution of the department to continue coherently.

personnel, can constantly shift from remote to direct management. Not a simple task, certainly, but an inevitable one.

Special situations are much easier to interpret than subtle limitations of choice. A company with many branches or divisions will inevitably shift from a centralized to a decentralized mode. The development manager should structure the department with this fact in mind. Knowing that this change will occur does not make the process easier, but it is certainly less traumatic to be prepared. The possibilities of change should be formally reviewed with key second-level managers. It is important to have as much information as possible in preparing for such contingencies, and a variety of perspectives can provide better solutions.

Political Imperatives

In a corporate environment, political sensitivity may be the most important factor in spelling the difference between success and failure. The ability to provide a perception of progress is nearly as important as the actual progress itself. Of course, to succeed over the long term, both are necessary, but in the short term, political imperatives are of paramount importance.

Understanding those imperatives has a pervasive effect on the department's organization. Its structure reveals where the department places its priorities and whom it favors. It is also a subject for gossip, since nothing is more political than talking about politics.

The first imperative concerns new development manager hired from outside the company or brought in from another division. This person is taking over from someone who was moved up or out. The development department is in trouble, and the new manager is expected to improve it. Since most executives favor organizational change, the expectation, whether voiced or not, is that the department will be reorganized.

In fact, however, the organization may not be the problem at all. It may simply be process problems, personnel, personality clashes, or any number of other potential situations, including the unrealistic expectations of upper management. However, even though management may give the new person ample time to understand the situation, they fully expect a sweeping organizational change to be made.

Although it may be disturbing for an analytical manager who finds no organizational problems, the best course—and the only realistic one—is to change the organization in some way. The changes may be artificial, but they must be made. It is foolish to buck the tide.

The second imperative is to satisfy those with political power. There is always a hidden as well as a published organization chart. The two may bear no relationship to each other, but they do exist. For example, if the financial services group is the pride of the bank in which the development group operates, that group's vice president should be satisfied. This may be a simple matter of tailoring a component of the application support group to that individual's preference, or it may be necessary to establish a separate, minimally staffed wing to service his or her pet interests.

The final imperative is to maintain flexibility. Political fortunes shift with the economy, with personality, and with age. Today's rising star may be tomorrow's burnt-out cinder. Given the development department's nonaligned position in the company, it is important to be sensitive to these shifts and prepared to react to them. Some of these changes are predictable. In fact, most corporate executives who succeed have the ability to judge these shifts and prepare for them. The development manager's distance from the executive wing may dilute this ability somewhat, but that judgment must take place. The manager must be ready and willing to change. Otherwise, yesterday's political protector may quickly become tomorrow's political liability.

CONCLUSION

In managing a functional unit of a business, it is important to create and nurture the organization which will service that function. Successful management goes well beyond intervention in response to problems or strength of will and intuition. It includes the ability to provide a framework to accomplish the tasks. Building a sound organization and structuring it properly are vital to this endeavor.

Although various organizational patterns can be followed, for a relatively new function such as development, no one form is necessarily correct or satisfactory. The establishment of an organization involves detailed analysis, political sensitivity and long-term planning. Shortcuts will not work.

Establishing organizational structures requires trade-offs, probably more so in development than in any other function today. The use of technology is quickly becoming recognized as the only legitimate way for most large companies to succeed. However, while most executives know this, they do not understand how it operates, and they feel lost when they try to learn. Such an atmosphere creates opportunities for fumbling and uneasy interference. For most executives, the organizational perspective is the easiest. They understand business and they understand organizations. Inevitably, structuring the department to match business lines appears to be the most attractive solution.

However, although this solution is best in some cases, in others it may be only a necessary temporary step. However, one key element that the development manager should keep in mind while devising an organization is that system development is not a business. It is a function which, together with other corporate functions, produces profits and fosters continued corporate growth. The best organization is the one which fulfills those needs.

5

PERFORMANCE MEASUREMENT

Nothing exists in a vacuum, especially an entity such as systems development, which is rapidly becoming one of the key components of the competitive company. Years ago, most senior executives were concerned only with the satisfaction of user department managers. That attitude either no longer exists or is rapidly changing. Management is beginning to require the same judgments from its development staff that are required of other operational units. Management is seeking ways to determine if the development staff will show continued improvement, assist in improving its competitive posture and maintain efficiency. This heightened awareness provides an excellent opportunity to increase development's visibility and its role in determining corporate strategic directions.

This increased awareness brings challenges as well. The development manager must establish the necessary measures to satisfy management's needs or see them established by others. The opportunity to define one's own measurement criteria should not be wasted.

User satisfaction is still a viable measure of the success of development. However, satisfaction can be simply a measure of comparison with yesterday, the euphoria of a recent success or ignorance of what could have been achieved. Therefore satisfaction, while important, is a less quantitative measure than that appropriate for either development or management. If measures are properly established and met, user satisfaction will be a natural by-product.

With a function such as systems development, two components must be measured: the *product* and the *process*. Measuring the product (systems produced, documentation, state-of-the-art level, etc.) focuses on how well the development department is creating a technologically superior environment for the business. Measuring the process focuses on how efficiently the department produces that product, as well as how effectively it meets service commitments to keep the product, and the people who use it, productive.

In this chapter we deal with four components of performance measurement. First, the terms of measurement are reviewed—that is, what we are trying to measure. Both product and process measures are discussed. Next, we consider how those measures vary by class of work. Third, the mechanisms used to gather measurement information are discussed, emphasizing the key elements to consider when establishing these mechanisms. Finally, the principal elements of reporting performance are reviewed.

TERMS OF MEASUREMENT

The first step in establishing performance measures is to determine, in broad terms, what is to be measured. While any given situation may contain many critical elements, two principal ones are considered here—product and process. Not all measures are quantitative. Some are qualitative, such as how the company ranks competitively and how development has supported that ranking. One should seek quantitative ways to describe this contribution, but that is not always possible.

In establishing meaningful measures, it is most important to achieve agreement between the departmental manager and upper management. As with the development department's charter discussed in Chapter 1, establishing reasonable measures should be a cooperative effort.

Measuring Product

A comprehensive review of the performance of development must include the effectiveness of the product. The product, after all, is the primary reason the process exists and is being managed—to produce and support application systems more effectively. If the systems do not work well, impressive process improvements are unimportant.

Two components of product measurement are considered—the applications portfolio and operational performance.

Applications Portfolio. An applications portfolio is a description of all of the systems and tools used by the company. It provides an inventory of all components of its information technology. Systems development is responsible for enhancing this inventory, and its worth and dissemination throughout the company is an appropriate measure of development.

The applications portfolio consists of the components needed to provide a clear picture of operational products. It is used in devising strategies, determining where current technology can provide a competitive advantage in unintended areas, where weaknesses occur, and where obsolescence exists.

The information gathered for the application portfolio depends on the development department's organization and the business. However, there are certain common elements which are crucial to an adequate portfolio, making it integral to the company and ensuring its currency. These elements are outlined in Table 5–1. The key issues in establishing a portfolio are discussed next.

The portfolio must be established as a separate project, not as an adjunct to everyday events. A significant amount of data must be gathered, much of it from users. This effort requires time and resource dedication. Attempting to accomplish this as a by-product activity may result in a second-rate product. This is an extremely important exercise and deserves the attention of a funded project.

A very effective tool for establishing the applications portfolio is the information modeling process. Although generally used for strategic planning, this process gathers nearly all of the necessary information.

The portfolio should be database resident, accessible through interactive terminals and developed with fourth-generation technology. This ensures the continued evolution of the portfolio, easy access, and a tailored presentation. It also lowers the cost of producing the portfolio and makes at least part of it available for the user early.

Data on the value, performance traits, component profile, and dynamic

Table 5–1. Elements of an Applications Portfolio

APPLICATION TITLE/MNEMONIC

The title of the application, such as Demand Deposit Accounting, together with the most common abbreviations and acronyms such as DDA or Demand.

DEPARTMENT/FUNCTION SERVICED

All departments which are directly involved with the application, with rankings of primacy.

BRIEF DESCRIPTION

A one- to two-paragraph description of the application.

SUBSYSTEM DESCRIPTION

A description of all subsystems associated with the application such as capture, posting, and reporting. Should include rankings and descriptive information relative to processing characteristics.

CYCLE DESCRIPTION

A description of key cycle periods and how they relate to the application as a whole, often in flowchart form.

KEY CHARACTERISTICS

Those characteristics which are important aspects of the application, such as volume sensitivity, amount of information produced, and so on.

ORIGINAL IMPLEMENTATION AND REASON

When the original implementation occurred and the reason for it. This can have a major bearing on the use of the product for future purposes.

Table 5-1. (Continued)

GROWTH
How the system has grown since the original implementation in terms of transaction volume, number of programs, number of users, and major changes in technological approach.

ORIGINAL COST
The original cost of the system in response to its original purpose.

ONGOING COST
The cost of operating, maintaining and enhancing the system.

SIZE
The current size of the system in both technical terms (e.g., program data requirements) and administrative terms (e.g., number of users serviced, external systems interfaced).

ENHANCEMENT LEVEL
The typical level of enhancement in terms of number of requests, time to service and cost.

MAINTENANCE LEVEL
Same as for enhancements.

SUPPORT LEVEL
Typical level of support required, as well as measures such as time to repair and so on.

FAILURE TREND
How often the system fails and the impact of failure.

VOLUME TREND
How volumes have increased over time and how sensitive the system has been to these increases.

INTEGRATION CHARACTERISTICS
How many systems feed this application, how many it feeds and how often.

TECHNOLOGY
The technological characteristics of the application—interactive, batch driven, languages used, database constructs, hardware constraints, 4GL capabilities and so on.

REPORTING PROFILE
How reporting is done and how well.

PERFORMANCE CHARACTERISTICS
Figures on performance from the operational reporting systems.

characteristics of the applications should be part of the database. All data provided by users should be gathered as a by-product of normal operational activities such as change management, project management, or job accounting activities. This makes the portfolio integral to the operation of MIS and the business, as well as broadening its usefulness.

Product Performance. In today's business environment, with decreasing prices and increasing performance, little emphasis is placed on the performance characteristics of systems. While improved price/performance ratios have dramatically changed the requirements for system efficiency, product performance remains an important aspect of systems development.

How well an application performs has a direct bearing on its worth. As an example, most on-line systems today have major components which run during off hours in a batch mode. If those components are not successfully completed, the interactive portion of the system cannot run the next day. A good contingency planning rule is that there should be adequate time available to run the off-hour work twice from the beginning up to the point where the interactive portion is initiated.

If the off-hour period is from 6 PM to 7 AM (11 hours) and single-thread backups require 2 hours cumulatively, the critical off-hour run time should not exceed 5.5 hours (half of the 11 available hours). This ensures that a failure at the end of the process which requires a complete rerun will still allow the user-sensitive portion of the system to be available on time.

Extraordinary events such as high volumes, extended days, and cyclic demands may strain the system even further. In any event, performance is important when considering the nonflexibility of time. Performance issues may not involve the counting of internal processor cycles, as they did 20 years ago, but as a function of product availability, they are as important as ever.

Table 5–2 outlines some of the more important performance measures for applications products. They are not comprehensive, nor are they necessarily applicable in every environment. However, they are representative of the types of product measures a development staff should seek and report.

These performance characteristics should be gathered at the lowest level of the system and combined to form profiles of the application. When gathered as a component of the Application Portfolio, factors such as run cost can be compared with clerical and market benefits to describe the productivity of an application in a competitive environment. These profiles can reveal significant trends as well.

As an example, if a bank intends to install automated tellers, it would be wise to evaluate the performance of its transaction posting application as a function of volume. Automated teller machines (ATMs) tend to cause a dramatic rise in the volume of transactions. If the application shows an increase in cycle time out of proportion to the volume increase curve, it may be necessary to replace or retune the application while the ATMs are being planned rather than waiting for the system to become saturated in production. The condition of the system may even cause a delay in marketing the product or result in the decision not to install it at all. In any case, the availability of such information in the applications portfolio is vital in formulating strategy.

Table 5-2. Performance Measures for Applications Products

SYSTEM RUN TIMES
The actual amount of time needed to run major components of the system. Includes interactive time available, clock time for major cycles, ratios of clock time to internal time, and so on.

RESPONSE TIMES
For interactive components, the typical response time at the terminal across various classes such as inquiries, updates, and report requests. Stated in a variety of statistical terms such as average, variation, and so on.

OPERATIONAL COSTS
The cost at the charge-back rate to run the various components of the system.

RERUN COST
The cost, in terms of operational figures, for reruns.

PERCENTAGE OF RESOURCE USED
What portion of the available computing resource the application typically uses.

EXECUTION PROFILES
The profile of the application's execution in terms of cycles used, memory expended, and time required throughout the monthly cycle by subsystem.

DECISION SUPPORT PROFILES
Execution profiles for ancillary decision support facilities.

TRANSACTION PROFILES
How the transactions perform in terms of response time, resources expended, system saturation, and so on.

REPORTING PROFILES
Lines of print produced, number of pages, cost of reporting, and so on.

Concise application profiles are invaluable in a competitive environment. A competitor's introduction of a new service can dramatically reduce a company's market share if it responds too slowly. With an application portfolio which shows the conditions of the application in performance terms, an organization can respond quickly to this challenge by knowing precisely how viable its applications are. Ours is an information age, and the effectiveness and adaptability of all applications in the portfolio are crucial to success. The constant gathering of performance information on operational systems makes the portfolio an integral part of the company's strategic planning.

Measuring Process

Just as important as a high-performance, widely penetrating product is the development department's ability to extend, enhance and support it. Measuring the effectiveness of these processes should be a major concern of upper management and therefore of the development manager.

When establishing the measures for the development process, it is important to understand the company's goals as well as the process elements to be measured. The company's development goals can be achieved by a cooperative effort in establishing these measures. Those goals will evolve over time as a function of the business environment, as well the emphasis placed on the company's information capability. Process measures must evolve in step. Table 5.3 presents the principal elements of the development process to be measured. This table, like Tables 5.1 and 5.2 is not inclusive; it should be expanded or reduced based on the individual environment. The

Table 5–3. Principal Elements of Development Measures

MANAGEMENT OF PROJECT QUEUES
A measure of the movement of projects through the various queues. Figures such as average time in queue, profile by time in queue, number of new projects, and number serviced measure the effectiveness of queue management.

LIFE CYCLE MEASUREMENT
A cross section of the development life cycle, depicting the time, resources and cost of each cycle period.

SERVICE-LEVEL COMMITMENTS
How well the department meets its service-commitments by class of work.

PROJECTS COMPLETED AND STARTED
The number of projects in each of these categories, as well as the schedule based on the time estimate for each project and in composite.

TIME SPENT ACROSS APPLICATIONS
The amount of time given each application for all classes of work and in composite.

TIME SPENT BY DEPARTMENT
The amount of time given each user department for all classes of work and in composite.

COST OF SERVICE
The cost, at standard rates, for applications and classes of work.

BENEFIT OF SERVICE
As with cost, the benefit projected as per justification processes. A cost/benefit ratio as well.

RESOURCE USE BY CLASS OF WORK
How the available resource pool was divided by class of work.

PLANNED VERSUS UNPLANNED TIME
A comparison of resource utilization as budgeted or planned versus the usage beyond the planning cycle.

most important thing is to understand what is to be measured. What is chosen as a measure determines how the department will be judged. A cavalier approach in defining these measures will produce an erroneous picture of the development group which may take years to erase.

Life cycle management is one of the principal elements of any development function to be measured. It describes the effectiveness of the various stages of the life cycle, the cost of each portion, the time required for each, and how these components vary based on application, user function, resources applied and a variety of outside conditions. If there is one aspect of the development function which the manager must control and improve, it is the effectiveness of the life cycle. Therefore, this should be the element most carefully monitored and evaluated.

Queue management is a measure of how long projects wait to be addressed, in what sequence they were handled, what characteristics caused them to be serviced quickly or slowly and which area is being favored in providing service. With a limited resource pool to draw upon, development can utilize its queue servicing performance to match management's directives to concentrate on specific business units. Queue management also depicts the work flow through the department, which, all things being equal, should describe development's service capability.

Service-level performance is a measure of how well the development department provides service or attention to users. Often this element is inseparable from queue or life cycle management, since both of these elements represent part of the service commitment. This measure is a key element for two reasons. First, since development is a service department, meeting service commitments is tantamount to succeeding. Second, service commitments are generally tied to budgeted personnel for the budgeting period (given 12 analysts, all requests will be reviewed in 24 hours; given 6 analysts, the level is reduced, etc.).

The other elements outlined in Table 5-3 can be equally critical to the judgment of the development department's success.

A key characteristic of these measurement terms is improvement versus continuity. In general, most elements within the development process should show steady improvement—perhaps not dramatically, but improvement nonetheless. It is the manager's responsibility to introduce new methods and mechanisms to ensure that this improvement continues. An example of continuity, by contrast, is meeting service-level commitments. Often, showing improvement may even create negative perceptions, especially when tied to factors such as staff size. The intelligent manager should understand the perception being created before introducing these measures. Proving, in quantitative terms, that the smaller the staff, the higher the service level may produce some unwanted reactions from management.

MEASUREMENT BY CLASS OF WORK

In Chapter 2, the four basic classes of development work were described. Each was discussed separately, with independent work queues and management mechanisms. The differences between these classes is pervasive, with each requiring independent measurement criteria. Although some of the measures may be expressed the same way across several classes, the importance of each varies with the interpretation of its impact.

Often maximum performance is not achievable across all classes of work in any specific measurement period. For example, there may be a need to emphasize support over development because hardware/software problems required the dedication of additional resources to that class. The acquisition of a new company may require the entire staff to focus on its needs. This would increase maintenance servicing at the expense of other classes.

These situations occur regularly and often. In a dynamic environment, they can represent the rule rather than the exception. While this can be a continually valid situation, it is important to present it in such a way that it does not represent a complete compromise of the measurement system. Otherwise, both management and development department members become conditioned to not meeting their goals. At that point, measurement becomes counterproductive.

This problem can be overcome by a two-step process. First, the resources allocated to the various classes are expressed as a percentage basis, in contrast to a plan or a description of a trend. Second, taking these variations with the plan, each of the reported performance figures for each class can be factored by the variation to produce weighted numbers. This effectively removes the nonplanned variances from the lower-level class measures.

Having the trend figures for allocation by class of work allows management to interpret and adjust its priorities and staffing levels. Development staff may be adjusted, strategies reevaluated or temporary staff added to ensure that proper allocation is achievable despite external events.

The next part of this chapter describes the establishment of measures for each class of work. Support is divided into two parts, consulting support and production support, since they are somewhat independent. Tables 5-4 through 5-9 present some suggested measures. It must be emphasized that no measure is inherently valuable or useless. It is of interest only when it supports both company and development goals.

Production Support

Production support depends primarily on events, so that any measures established for it must reflect time-oriented elements. Time to solve a problem and time to recognize a problem are typical examples. Table 5-4 presents measures for a production support group, stressing the emphasis on time.

Table 5-4. Production Support Measures

TIME TO IDENTIFICATION
The time spent to identify both the severity of a problem and the individual responsible. Always represented by a short period such as minutes or quarter hours, since until identification takes place, the problem must be considered severe. Evaluated in terms of average, standard deviation, groups by time.

TIME TO REPAIR
The time from identification to repair—repair being the close of the problem report, not necessarily final correction. Time representation will vary based upon severity; very severe problems are represented in minutes while less severe problems are reported in hours and possibly days. Evaluated in terms of average, standard deviation, groups by time.

REPAIR YIELD
Measures the success of the repair process. Repairs should be effective the first time, representing 100% yield. If two attempts are required the yield is 50%. Three attempts equals a 33% yield, and so on.

COST TO REPAIR
The cost, generally in terms of man-hours times the standard billing rate for the entire support cycle. Evaluated in terms of average, standard deviation, groups by time.

NUMBER OF PROBLEMS BY SEVERITY
Total number of problems serviced by severity level, with subcategories by repair yield.

TIME TO FINAL REPAIR
Amount of time spent on problem resolution after the initial support resolution is completed. Measures the effectiveness of support's correction process. Evaluated in terms of average, percentage of total correction time, number of occurrences over the average, acceptable range.

TIME FOR RERUN
Hours spent in reruns due to problem correction. Measures, to some degree, the imaginativeness of the repair. Highlights provided for multiple corrections.

NUMBER OF PROBLEMS BY TYPE
Reported problems categorized by type of interest. Examples are problems in new systems, by complexity, and by system type.

Measures should be geared to performance of the average event. However, the user who has a severe problem cares very little about how the response will be reflected in the department's monthly average. Averages are, by definition, smoothed, often hiding significant variations in performance. It is therefore important to judge the performance of production support on the basis of standard deviations. As much as possible, production support should strive to produce steady, rapid solutions, and the measures should reflect this orientation.

However, not all problems are of equal complexity. This factor must also be accounted for, or the appearance of poor or good performance will be extremely misleading. This can best be done by categorizing problem responses during the postmortem stage of the support cycle.

Each problem that was worked on should be subjected to extensive classification and the classes indicated as the event is recorded on the performance database (this database is either integral or closely related to the application portfolio). Classifications such as complexity, severity, status of the system involved, and others outlined in Table 5-5 are appropriate for evaluating the performance of the support group.

Each of these factors has a significant impact on how the group is judged. That effect may involve the factor adjustment of an algorithm by applying weighting factors to complex problems, or it might be as simple as judging problems outside of the complex category (complex problems would then be considered an exception).

In addition to solving problems, production support must review new systems or enhancements entering the production cycle. The amount of time spent in these activities, delays caused by the review process, and the number of changes rejected or accepted are all important aspects of the support function. Such activities indicate a commitment by the development group to improve the operational environment and should be judged just as problem resolution is.

Table 5-5. Sample Classifications for Problems and Requests

AGE OF THE SYSTEM OR SUBSYSTEM
Obsolete, new, 2 years old, 3 years old, etc.

COMPLEXITY OF THE PROBLEM
Trivial, intermediate, complex. Complexity measured both technically and administratively.

SEVERITY OF THE PROBLEM
Effect on the company—from crippling to a minor irritant.

TIME OF DAY
When the failure occurred (off-hours or on-hours).

TYPE OF FAILURE
From report problems to hard crashes.

TYPE OF SYSTEM
Management information systems or operational systems.

LANGUAGE
Fourth-generation, procedural, decision support, etc.

IMPORTANCE OF SYSTEM
Importance of the system to the company's existence.

SIZE OF THE PROJECT
Large, small, or intermediate in terms of time or man-hours.

Consulting Support

Table 5-6 outlines measures for consulting support work. These measures fall into two broad categories that parallel the general types of consulting activities: ad hoc requests and project commitments.

Ad hoc requests are analogous to the events that prompt production support activities. However, with consulting support, these requests tend to require some evaluation and investigation, which may take more time. Unlike other classes of work, this investigation and analysis seldom results in the initiation of projects.

For ad hoc requests, two factors are important: satisfactory response time and the number of requests serviced. A satisfactory response can vary from the answer to a question to the initiation of a production support problem

Table 5-6. Consulting Support Measures

REQUESTS MADE BY CATEGORY

The number of requests received by category. Categories are established to match critical elements. Examples are ad hoc requests, operational systems, and user systems.

REQUESTS SERVICED AND UNSERVICED

The number of requests which were serviced (completed) during the period. Unserviced requests are those which have passed the service-level commitment.

SERVICE LEVEL

The actual service level achieved, primarily by comparison to the commitment. Expressed as the relationship between number of requests completed plus number initiated and in flight over number within the commitment window. The commitment window is the time during which a request should be serviced. In other words, if a request need not be serviced for 4 days and has been in the queue for only 3 days, it does not figure in the computation.

TIME FOR AD HOC REQUESTS

Amount of time spent servicing ad hoc requests. Also represented as a function of budget commitments for that class of work.

TIME FOR COMMITTED SUPPORT

As with ad hoc requests, the amount of time spent in comparison to project commitment levels.

TIME SPENT BY TYPE OF REQUEST

Allocation of time across important types such as fourth-generation questions or operational problems. Expressed as a percentage of the whole.

TIME UNTIL SERVICED

Amount of time a request waits to be serviced. Measured in units of time that match service-level commitments.

TIME FOR SERVICE

Amount of time spent in servicing requests. Includes only ad hoc requests. Measured in units of time which match service-level commitments.

report. In either case, consulting measures focus only on the amount of time spent until some other function of the department takes over.

Creating measures beyond this boundary can weaken the rationale for consulting—providing information expertise to users. If the judgment of consulting personnel is based on the successful resolution of the entire problem, members of this group will dedicate some of their time to continual follow-up of problems that have passed on to other groups. This inevitably removes them from the role for which they were originally intended. When establishing measures, the manager must keep one thing in mind: aggressive people will strive to achieve these measures. If the measures are improperly established, the department will also perform improperly.

Project commitments are best measured in terms of service level. Consulting time is initially allocated across different departments based upon budget commitments. Those commitments are based upon the user department's willingness to fund the resources or balancing by upper management. There is no guarantee that a development consultant will be committed to a project, only an indication that the user needs help.

The measures can be expressed in hours, number of projects reviewed, meetings attended, or project responsibilities met. In any case, little can be said about the quality of or need for the effort. The only commitment development can make is to providing the requested expertise. (Of course, there is an implied guarantee on the part of the development that the appropriate consultant will be provided and that he or she will perform as ably as possible. However, when establishing measures, one must assume that these commitments have been understood and fulfilled.)

Maintenance

Maintenance measures focus on meeting required dates. Many of these measures are presented in Table 5-7. Since users and management must provide adequate time to make changes, this factor must be taken into account when measuring the effectiveness of maintenance. Maintenance resources are generally allocated across the year based on historical precedents and anticipated events such as cycle adjustments, cost changes, and W2 form preparation. When adequate lead time is provided for requests in any of these categories, the development department can generally respond without adversely affecting other work.

When lead time is not provided, however, committed service levels and project plans suffer because more resources are required for maintenance. The prime characteristic of maintenance work is that the completion date is nearly always fixed, regardless of the start date. Therefore, maintenance can have a dramatic effect on the measures for other classes of work.

Table 5–7. Maintenance Measures

TIME TO REQUIRED START
The time from notification by the user to the implementation data minus the estimate required for the work to start. The estimate is assumed to require one resource. Expressed in units of time and as a percentage of adequate time.

TIME TO COMPLETE
Time, in both man-hours and calendar time, to complete the request. Expressed in terms of average, variation and time to required start.

PERCENTAGE COMPLETED ON TIME
Two variations are used: completed on time over total number and completed on time within estimate over total number.

PERFORMANCE TO ESTIMATE
Discrepancy between estimate and actual hours expended.

NUMBER OF REQUESTS SERVICED
Total number of requests, with subtotals by application and category (complex, simple, etc.).

ALLOCATION BY SYSTEM
Percentage of requests by system, with alternative classification by user department.

ALLOCATION BY TYPE
Percentage of requests by critical type, such as acquisitions, cycle changes, etc.

NUMBER OF FAILURES
Number and percentage of requests serviced which were not 100% successful—either late or not correct.

COST OF MAINTENANCE
Time spent in maintenance times the standard billing rate. Expressed in total and across systems and departments.

PERFORMANCE TO BUDGET
Ratio of time spent in maintenance to budgeted time for the year.

Maintenance measures should reflect this factor. In fact, the user's planning for needed maintenance should be measured as well. When the user fails to provide needed information on upcoming changes, that failure can have detrimental effects on every user's resource allocation. That fact should be highlighted for all affected users.

The rise or fall of maintenance demands for application systems reflects the health of the systems as well as of the development process. As systems age, the time spent servicing the typical request tends to rise. Therefore, the amount of time spent to maintain any application should become a component of the applications portfolio, and significant trends should be highlighted when reporting performance.

The development process should produce systems which are easily maintained and require little work by the development department. Increases in system maintenance time, even if systems are being slowly replaced, indicate a problem in the maintenance process as well. These trends should be highlighted by the measures as they are collected.

Enhancements

When dealing with enhancements, the prime measures should be oriented to project flow. How many requests are serviced by application, by category of complexity, and by cost/benefit analysis are all applicable measures of the development department's effectiveness in servicing enhancement requests. Table 5–8 presents typical measures of enhancements.

Service level can be another valuable measure of enhancement success. Once again, staff numbers and budget allocations are frequently associated with a specific service-level commitment in filling enhancement requests. These commitments can be measured in terms of raw numbers, man-hours, percentage by department or any other appropriate means. Comparing performance to commitment provides a good picture of how well the department performs.

When establishing measures for enhancements, some allowance must be made for balance across several measurement periods. Users often do not wish to be continually flooded with new products or changes. After a heavy period of change, they may request some time to stabilize their environment and absorb the changes. When this occurs, the development deparment's measurement of service level must be adjusted accordingly, since it will appear arbitrarily lower for the month in question.

New System Development

Measures for new system development should focus on two factors: the phases of the life cycle and actual-to-estimate ratios. Table 5–9 outlines some typical measures for these components.

Life cycle measurement provides a view not only of the department but of the life cycle in action as well. Life cycles are not static mechanisms. They should be changed over time as experience is gained and as performance dictates. The issues highlighted by performance measurement provide the most important rationale for making changes.

If there appears to be a general shift from one phase of the cycle to another over a period of time, this may indicate that procedures are being compromised. For an example, the analysis phase is sometimes abridged in

Table 5–8. Enhancement Measures

PROJECTS COMPLETED
Number of projects actually completed for the reporting period. Shown as a function of all projects in the queue, projects in the queue at the start of the period, projects received, etc.

PROJECTS IN QUEUE
Total projects in the queue compared to the previous period, including completed projects. New projects should be classified in terms of when they were received—those received halfway through period are half a project, etc.

NEW PROJECTS
All new projects received, whether completed or not.

SERVICE-LEVEL PERCENTAGE
Ratio of project servicing level to service level commitments. Levels should be measured in terms of both number of requests serviced and time allocated.

TIME FOR PROJECTS
Time spent on enhancements as a total and by category of project.

ALLOCATION BY CATEGORY
Allocation of total project time across categories chosen to measure service. See Table 5-5 for sample categories.

ALLOCATION BY DEPARTMENT
Allocation of total project time by requesting department.

ALLOCATION BY CLASSIFICATION
Allocation of total project time by classification, as discussed in Chapter 2.

PERFORMANCE TO BUDGET
Time spent on projects compared to the original budget.

PERFORMANCE TO ESTIMATE
Comparison of actual to estimated time, with a concentration on a standard deviation from precise accuracy.

ON-TIME PERCENTAGE
Percentage of time projects were completed on schedule. Two schedules are depicted: original and adjusted.

favor of the construction phase. Construction requires far less imagination and less dependence on user meetings, and allows far more control over resource allocation. To gain these advantages, many inexperienced analysts attempt to reach this stage as quickly as possible. However, this trade-off inevitably shows up several months later in a flood of enhancement requests, since adequate time was not provided to understand the systems need.

Table 5–9. New System Development Measures

TIME BY STAGE OF LIFE CYCLE
Time spent on each stage of the life cycle. Time among stages is compared as a percentage and tracked against successful projects and those finishing late. Also compared to enhancement and support service levels.

TIME IN QUEUE
Time projects spent in the queue before being initiated.

PERFORMANCE TO ESTIMATE
Ratio of actual time spent to original estimate. Comparisons are made by life cycle stage as well as the project as a whole.

NUMBER OF CHANGES IN ORIGINAL SCOPE
Changes in original specifications. Stated both in raw numbers and in time required for the changes.

ON-TIME PERCENTAGE
Percentage of projects on schedule, for stages as well as for entire effort.

COST/BENEFIT
Benefit and cost of projects stated as a ratio.

PROJECTS SERVICED IN AND OUT OF PLAN
Projects which appeared in the original budgeting plan compared to those which were actually initiated.

Performance measurement highlights this tendency by showing a significant variation in the analysis/construction ratio. When this is discovered, additional checks and balances can be instituted to ensure that adequate attention is paid to analysis.

Over the long term, measuring life cycle performance and comparing that performance with the application portfolio's profile of system performance will reveal strengths and weaknesses in the process. Systems which fail most often may be compared to life cycles where a minimal amount of time was spent in installation. As a result of this analysis, the gating functions of installations may be changed or scrapped.

Comparison of estimates to actual ratios is an extremely valuable measure of the development department's effectiveness. If cost/benefit is a major component of project justification, the validity of the department's estimates are obviously critical to the process of systems development. It is the major determinant in a strategy to automate functions or provide additional information systems. Poor estimating mechanisms result in choosing the wrong projects for development.

High estimates are just as bad as low estimates. The development department should produce estimates that are more or less precise. Naturally, 100% accuracy is not expected; there are far too many variables. However, if the estimate is based on that of prior projects, reasonable accuracy should be achieved.

The measures outlined here are merely examples of potential ways of measuring development's productivity. In any given company, the measures chosen will vary both with need and with the difficulty of collecting the data for measurement.

There are a number of issues to consider when establishing development measures. First, aggressive workers will try to enhance their reputation by meeting or exceeding these measures. Therefore, the manager should be certain that the results achieved are in keeping with his or her performance criteria.

Second, each class of work must be measured differently in order to indicate the basic differences in the way the work is performed. One cannot choose a single measure and expect it to adequately reflect all types of department performance.

Third, measures prove very little unless they are allowed to operate over time. Merely instituting them will either improve or worsen performance—as was proven by the famous Hawthorne Works experiment. Measures must be used for a while and then be analyzed in composite. (Time study analyses were conducted at the turn of the century at the Hawthorne plant of General Electric. The early stages of the study showed that production increased whether working conditions were improved or deteriorated. It was finally determined that the workers productivity improved simply because someone was paying attention to them.)

Fourth, and last, measures are adaptable to departments of any size. A 20-person department and a 200-person department both require measurement—the former perhaps even more than the latter. The measurements may not be as comprehensive in a small department, but they are adaptable and should be instituted.

DATA COLLECTION METHODS

Both the operational portion of the applications portfolio and the process performance statistics require extensive data gathering, at least when carried to their ultimate end. Even when a small number of factors are measured, their worth depends on the completeness of the data collected.

Characteristics associated with the measurement of production jobs are gathered using the company's job accounting package. Typically, these logs provide all the necessary data on the day-to-day functioning of applications. Once the factors to be evalauted are decided, it is only necessary to find the components of job accounting which provide the information. A program is then written to extract the appropriate data, and the database is updated.

Data collected in this fashion can be used for many purposes other than historical performance statistics. For example, a cycle's operational profile for the day can be compared to the application's normal run characteristics and exceptional conditions highlighted. This process can pinpoint problems long before those problems affect the work of users.

To ensure the best possible use of this exception highlighting, the programs which produce the data should be run before the user arrives for the work day. The problem can then be sent to an operational help desk and reporting begun before the problem becomes critical. This helps reduce negative visibility and alerts the MIS executive to the problem before it is reported by peer executives.

Gathering data about process performance is not so easy. Gating information can be produced by having a system capture the pass/fail status on a database rather than with signed forms. This way, whatever was to be entered into the system can be immediately related to all other information on the project. Any pass/fail gate, from walk-through logs to implementation sign-off, can be gathered in this fashion. Since a project has a retained identity, related information is always available in composite and can reflect the life cycle of any effort.

Gathering information about resource allocation is trickier still. Development people are notoriously poor at filling out time logs and associating time with projects. The results are generally questionable and require overhead which few development managers are willing to bear. Linking the capture of data to the terminals used for development is a viable solution.

When a programmer is working on a program, job stream or data extraction inquiry, the work can be identified with a project when it is opened, extracted or printed/executed. As long as the communication facility being used gathers data (most do), the information gathered can be associated with the project. Some massaging must occur to account for slack time and increases in figures when the programmer or analyst walks away from the terminal, but this is a fairly simple procedure.

For time away from any type of computing device, accurate reporting depends on the programmer's or analyst's diligence. However, the manager should keep in mind that when the time report finally becomes part of a performance measure and is stated for all to see, diligence tends to increase. People like to get credit for their time and work. If they know that the information they produce will be used, they tend to report it accurately.

Time information should be gathered as painlessly as possible. Most program editors allow the institution of standard programs that will execute when the editor has exited or between tasks. If this facility is available, a time-gathering screen can be presented at appropriate times with entries preformatted, such as current date, time, last project worked on, and so on, which allows for simple gathering of information. A database record can also be created whereby the analyst or programmer could preformat all needed information at project inception, at the beginning of the week, or whenever it is reasonable or comfortable to do so.

Historically, most managers have been reluctant to measure performance because of the difficulty of gathering data. However, this task need not be overwhelming if properly approached. It generally requires mechanisms to be established once and then used continually. The results are definitely worth the effort.

REPORTING

There are two final products of data collection and automated massaging and reporting: analysis by the development manager and reporting of performance to upper management. Clearly, data collection itself provides positive benefits. Analysts or programmers who carefully collect data will gain by understanding how their time is spent. This closely parallels all time management programs, where the first step is to keep a log of where all time is spent. In the case of performance data gathering, not only is a log kept, but the data can be consolidated and evaluated.

Despite this gain, the real benefit lies in final analysis of the consolidated data. Informal analysis by the development manager is generally in response to events such as the completion of a project, an extraordinary project status review, or various other factors. Since the development manager is primarily concerned with this process, those events will occur regularly.

In the case of formal reporting, generally to upper management, methods and issues must be carefully chosen. Once a reporting scheme is placed before management or used to judge staff performance, it should reflect what the development manager wants it to reflect and should be consistent for a specific period of time. Otherwise, the measures will force unanticipated changes or will be ignored.

If the development department's performance is as critical to the continued success of the company, upper management must be actively involved in ensuring its constant improvement. Passive involvement will not suffice. There must be a cooperative effort to make the department more and more efficient. The first step is to provide adequate and comprehensive reporting so that upper management feels comfortable in controlling this function.

The vehicle for reporting to upper management should be carefully chosen. It must be a careful blend of the technical and administrative aspects of development. Management should *not* be "protected" from the technical interpretation of systems development any more than they are protected from finance or manufacturing. For too many years, MIS in general has sought to create a buffer between management and its internal workings.

If technology is truly an integral part of the company, then there should be a middle ground of understanding. No benevolent shielding of upper management should occur. This does not mean that one should report on the number of bytes saved in a new database design. It does mean that management should be able to judge the benefit of reducing the time needed for the construction phase of the development life cycle. No sugar coating or parables should be used to make the point. Management must understand how development works, and the format of the report must be designed with this purpose in mind.

Most operational units in an organization report in two ways: a review-type presentation and a more detailed report, which can be evaluated as time permits. The schedules for these reviews vary from monthly to annually, but generally occur several times a year. The development department's reporting should match this schedule and should be conducted like that of any other operational unit.

The presentation should consist of a small number of charts, ideally in graphic form. Pictures command far more attention than long treatises. The presentation should focus on trends and the department's contribution to corporate goals. Trends should be presented as a continual repetition of set themes: average time to repair failures, number of requests serviced, average cost of a project, and so on. This repetition allows management to comment on the result and provides the development manager with a forum to introduce improvements.

The presentation also allows visual interpretation of how outside events affect the development process. What did the new acquisition cost in terms of project flow? How much did poorly planned end-of-year maintenance cost the company in terms of new systems development? This method allows upper management to introduce changes to allevaiate project roadblocks and improve the environment for these projects. Without providing a method by which management can make changes, it is fruitless for the development manager to expect change to occur.

The presentation should provide a measure of the development department's contribution to corporate goals. A cumulative report of project-oriented benefits achieved per month is a fine way to dramatize the department's worth. Management should not be allowed to forget that the benefits quoted by user departments through automation were provided by development. Comparing the cost of the operation with the benefit achieved can pave the way for staff changes and budgetary increases as well.

A formal report should also be produced, containing more detail than that of the presentation. The department's contributions should be highlighted so that user managers will know what "slice of the pie" they have been given. This allows user managers to establish a strategy to bring their information priorities into line with those of other departments. Organizational structures are built in an environment of competition among peers. By highlighting the department's ability to provide information services, the development manager can increase the demand for development services.

The performance report should be concise, almost terse, with a focus on the statistics. Its purpose is to involve managers intimately in the process of development. To ensure that this happens, adequate figures should be available. They allow managers to interpret the performance of development and plan their own automation strategy.

There are many statistical packages available today which depict industry performance for various aspects of technology. Although these figures may not highlight development performance specifically, they do create a more than adequate profile of the level of automation in various industries. Whenever possible, parallels should be drawn between the company's information capability and that of competitors. The development manager should always do marketing. The performance report is a fine vehicle to publicize the need for systems and provide a picture of an active, improving development effort.

CONCLUSION

If the company's future depends on its ability to use technology to its advantage, the performance of the development department is critical. Without doubt, the future *does* lie with the rapid and effective implementation of technology.

To ensure that this future meshes well with upper management's strategy, the development manager must understand the development process completely. This can only occur when the process is comprehensively measured and the department is committed to its improvement. Measures should be established intelligently and the members of the department judged accordingly.

Part II
Managing The People

6

PERSONALITIES

In the early stages of the Industrial Revolution, human beings came to be treated as interchangeable parts. They were expected to perform whatever work they were assigned, to be content that they were paid a salary, and to make whatever sacrifices were necessary to keep their jobs. Management was considered to be the thinking portion of the enterprise, responsible for establishing priorities and social mores.

Over time, it was realized that motivation and the nature of the work were major components of corporate success. Human beings are extraordinarily diverse. Although they fall into somewhat predictable patterns across social groups, they react differently to given stimuli. These tendencies are reflected in their personalities, as well as in the composite "personalities" of the social groups to which they belong.

Salespersons are different from engineers. Both are different from lawyers, laborers and cab drivers. Some of these differences are exhibited because the job or profession demands them and, through a process of natural selection, those with the appropriate personalities for the job will tend to be most successful and thereby represent the role models.

Successful management requires a clear understanding of the personalities of the individuals being managed. This understanding allows the manager to create an environment in which these people will succeed, allows them to maximize their talents, and provides some degree of predictability about how they will respond to challenges in given situations. Understanding, of course, is not enough. The successful manager respects the individual's personality and recognizes the responsibility to match those personality traits to the job requirements in order to ensure corporate growth.

Personalities are most typified by their strengths and weaknesses. For every strength there is a corresponding and equally reactive weakness. An individual who reaches a decision rapidly and acts upon it quickly and with singularity of purpose is lauded for decisiveness and drive—at least, when he or she is right most of the time. Otherwise, the individual is described as impatient, radical or closed to dissenting approaches. It is all a matter of perspective.

Development managers, like all other intelligent managers, must understand the strengths and weaknesses of their staff. They must place these people in positions where their strengths are amplified and their weaknesses minimized. Many people will find their appropriate niche in the department by gravitating toward this state of balance. Others will climb to higher levels when they can control their weaknesses and limit their display. The successful manager deals with both bypes of people, protecting those who have settled into their niche while developing those who aspire to higher levels by providing opportunities for their growth.

In this chapter, the personality types most often found in systems development are discussed and related to the jobs they occupy most often and/or most successfully. This discussion is limited to major personality profiles for development people as a social group since managers of larger departments are usually forced to deal in this level of generality. The profiles of the most common jobs are discussed next, concentrating on the traits that usually spell success. Some guidelines are then presented for matching the personalities to the job profiles.

THE GENERAL DEVELOPMENT PROFILE

Ask development persons to describe themselves and, more than likely, the term they will use is "professional." The definition of a professional is broad enough to cover nearly all disciplines. Most people associate the term with extended education, a high degree of specialized knowledge, and a well-defined social group—typically lawyers, doctors, or accountants. In almost all cases, the measure of professional achievement is a degree of certification, by which one becomes a member of the profession.

The Certificate in Data Processing (CDP) is an attempt to certify MIS professionals. Its success is still a matter of controversy, even though it has been awarded to many MIS people. It is not likely to have a major influence on the discipline of MIS and development in the near future. Corporations do not require the CDP for an entry-level position, and given the spread and vitality of MIS, they probably never will.

(The effort to certify computer professionals, through the CDP and the newly established Certificate of Computer Professional, or CSP, is a laudable attempt to establish a baseline for standard competence measurement. The requirement for constant recertification adds to their prestige. In signing a contract with consultant personnel it is a boon, since it provides some measure of the applicant's knowledge; reference checking, in contrast, is difficult with this group.)

However, most MIS and development people do not refer to the CDP when they use the term "professional." More often, they are expressing the belief that their commitment to their profession and their contribution to corporate goals merit respect and elevation in the corporate community. This is their opinion of their status in the business world. This sensitivity to status reveals much about the personality of the development professional.

Understanding general personality traits is as important for the development manager as understanding individual personalities. Development people represent a social group. With a large staff and/or intermediate managers, the development executive must be able to generalize about the people in order to interact properly with them—from a distance.

Some of these traits can be generalized on the basis of development people today. This has little to do with the fact that they are in development, merely that they are the generation that exists today. Other traits develop as these people occupy their positions due to natural selection; those who are not suited drop out.

In either case, it is imperative that the development manager understand the social group being managed. This allows the manager to provide the atmosphere necessary for progress and to match the department's personality with the natural outgrowth of the individual's personality. Table 6–1 outlines some of the traits most often seen in development people. Some of the more salient traits are then discussed.

YOUTH

Most people in systems development today are in their twenties and thirties. This is due to a number of factors, not the least of which is that the discipline itself is not very old. This fact is not particularly significant except that the people in this age group are quite different from those of previous generations in many respects.

In terms of the attitude toward the job, this generation is less concerned about conventional measures of success than previous generations and is much more pragmatic when judging the companies they work for and the positions they hold.

They have very little company loyalty. They are much more interested in the abstract and personal aspects of life. The job is probably not one of their top five priorities, and this attitude can create significant problems for the manager governed by the work ethic. Many of the time-honored principles of "carrot and stick" management simply do not work with the development staff.

This does not imply a criticism of development people. To the contrary,

Table 6-1. Traits of Development Persons

YOUTH

People in development are significantly younger, on average, than those of most departments, both absolutely and in terms of their salary and position levels. This can create significant problems in dealing with user management, and especially senior management. The values and priorities of one generation are typically very different than those of another generation.

MOBILITY

Development people are more apt to change jobs frequently and are more amenable to geographic flexibility than most other groups. With competitive job markets, this tends to result in short tenure (on average).

CRAFTSMAN APPROACH

As craftsmen, development people place a high priority on the tools they utilize and the abstract quality of the product they produce. This attitude a unique mix of the product/service orientation.

SENSITIVITY TO WORK

Development people tend to identify their own worth with the success and acceptance of the product produced. While users of the product view the system as a tool, to be criticized or praised at will, developers see that same system as an extension of their personality and a statement of their level of skill.

ISOLATION FROM CORPORATE SOCIETY

Due to a general misunderstanding of what development does and how, the corporation does not relate well to systems development personnel. This tends to place development out of the corporate mainstream and breeds a sense of isolation the corporation as a whole. The result is a notable aloofness and separatism in the personalities of the staff.

ASSOCIATION WITH ABSOLUTES

Development people (nonmanagement) tend to have a black/white approach to problem solving. The pragmatism of politics and interpersonal relations is somewhat at odds with the developer's sense of right or wrong production systems.

INTENSENESS

The intense concentration required of developers implies success for those who can concentrate by excluding outside influences. While this ability is not necessarily a personality trait of the new staff member, natural selection will cause only those who display the trait to succeed.

FLEXIBILITY

Due to the dynamic nature of the discipline, development personnel who succeed tend to display extraordinary flexibility in accepting and adapting to change.

VAGUE PROFESSIONAL GOALS

Unlike persons in most business disciplines, where historic exposure defines the characteristics, development personnel enter the field with a naive understanding of what the profession involves. With this background, career goals are developed on the job from the perspective of the discipline.

the typical development staff is a productive, goal-oriented group, less concerned with job status and more concerned with the esthetics of the work than ever before. However, they are harder to manage because they are more likely than employees of the past to question decisions. The development manager must work harder to make good decisions and must be more willing to compromise than ever before.

High Level of Mobility

Development people are more mobile than most technology-oriented professionals. They are willing to move from company to company or from one geographic area to another to achieve their goals. A 4-year period of tenure on an applicant's resumé is rare.

This mobility can be seen in a number of professions, and it is too early to judge the long-term impact of this social behavior. However, one thing is obvious: turnover is much more difficult to manage in development than in most other departments. Systems are becoming increasingly sophisticated and more attuned to individual situations. Thus, substantially longer periods of tenure are required to master the intricacies of these systems in order to make a meaningful contribution.

There are a number of steps the intelligent manager can take to ease the problems of turnover. They will be discussed in detail in Chapter 10. However, these steps are limited by company policies, management style and economic pressures. Turnover will always be a problem as long as development people have a high sense of mobility.

Craftsmen

Development people have more attributes of the skilled craftsman than any other group of professionals. Their concern for product quality is high and is more important than loyalty to and identification with the company. Development people tend to identify with the systems they produce and feel attacked when their systems are criticized.

This characteristic, when combined with the factor of mobility, contributes even further to turnover. Company loyalty or a commitment to an area or organization sustains people through the hard times any company encounters. However, when people identify with their craft, rather than with the company, and feel little hesitation about moving, they see no reason to remain when times are bad. They go where the tools and opportunities to improve their craft are provided.

Like any craftsmen, development people are very concerned with tools. They wish to use the latest technology regardless of its applicability in their situation. Obviously, this tendency must be balanced by business sense. However, despite the need to balance the developer's desire for newer and shinier tools, this trait is the greatest strength of the development person. It implies a desire to move constantly with an evolving technology rather than to resist it.

Negative Characteristics

Probably the most striking negative characteristic of development people arises from the fact that their work causes them to deal largely in absolutes. Programs are right or wrong. Systems do or do not meet specification guidelines. The system is delivered on time or it is late. When such people are involved in a political situation, they can quickly become disillusioned.

Most political situations in the company are unhealthy. However, they are a reality, and the developer's insistence on cost/benefit justification or healthy business compromises is unlikely to change the situation. This conflict between the developer's commitment to product purity and the harsh realities of politics has created a great deal of cynicism among development people.

Development people tend to be highly sensitive about their work. This trait has caused the greatest strain for managers who attempt to institute walk-through procedures as quality checks. This sensitivity and defensiveness lasts long after the system goes on-line. When the inevitable obsolescence occurs and the press for a new system increases, the original developer will still see the criticisms of the old system as a personal attack. Many development managers have been amazed to receive an analyst's resignation when that person felt unappreciated for work on a now obsolete system.

In general, development people are highly motivated and intelligent. When they are managed honestly, their negative personality traits can be deemphasized in favor of the dramatic skills and drive they bring to the corporation. If technology is the wave of the future in the drive for competitive advantage, development people are the backbone of that drive. It is therefore imperative for the manager to understand the personality traits of development people and the way these traits are expressed based on the jobs they fill.

PERSONALITIES BY JOB PROFILE

The definition of the responsibilities of a department determines the responsibilities of its members. Most often, position profiles represent sets of skills and organizational responsibilities which, when matched properly with the employee, result in a dynamic, active department.

This classification defines each position and creates promotion levels as well: senior programmer as opposed to programmer, analyst I as opposed to analyst II. The descriptions and titles of jobs vary widely from company to company. A senior programmer in one company may be performing the same work as a senior systems analyst in another company. We will discuss job titles in more depth in Chapter 8. Of concern here is the fact that job profiles define the personality required to fill the job adequately as much as quantitative skill sets.

In this chapter, five job profiles will be considered: developer, analyst, support specialist, coordinator, and administrator. Although probably no companies use these precise titles, they do cover the positions in question. Their analysis should allow the reader to match most of the position profiles in his or her department.

The Developer

Developers are the programmers or analysts involved in the internal environment of systems development. Their jobs are typified by titles such as "programmer," "analyst," and "specialist." These people labor in the trenches, so to speak, and are pictured by the outside world as technocrats.

Developers tend to concentrate on their craft. They use structured methods and are generally more loyal to their profession than to the company they service. They have an intense need to occupy the leading edge of technology and emphasize that they "do nothing but maintenance" as they move from company to company. There is a dramatic fear of being left behind their peers in an extraordinarily complex discipline.

The developer generally displays a highly organized thought process and the ability to constantly juggle the characteristics of complex systems in solving problems. Their solutions may sometimes appear convoluted to outsiders, but they are crystal clear to the developer. A complex program or system has a mathematical precision, and one must be in tune with the designer to appreciate it.

Developers operate best in a single-focus environment, and the project orientation of systems development is ideal for their creative talents. The project environment is optimal for another reason as well: it complements the developer's generally short attention span. Developers have little interest in devoting the long-term attention that a supporting role requires. They prefer to finish the problem and move on, never to see the product again. In general, this holds true until the product begins to suffer the bad press which obsolescence breeds.

At that time, the trait which often causes unexpected furor surfaces—the developer's identification with the product. It is the quality of this product which is usually intimately associated with the developer's self-image.

Finally, developers have little time for office politics. They tend to be job-oriented individuals who shy away from power plays, organizational trade-offs and other diversions from their project goals. Typically, they view politics as a negative game to be played by others, not themselves.

The Support Specialist

The support specialist, like the developer, is generally a programmer or analyst whose prime consideration is the support of implemented application systems. These people may work on small development projects, but their main focus is the maintenance of a steady state for operational systems. Their responsibilities vary widely in response to staff limitations, availability, or methodologies employed, so that they may perform in many different ways. However, their orientation to operational systems is almost universal.

Support people do not identify with products. Instead, they are concerned with the consistency and dependability of the products and their impact on a smoothly running steady-state environment. This identification extends only to the operational characteristics of the system, number of failures, resources expended, difficulty in correction, or abstract systems elegance. It does not include the utility of the system for the user. That matters very little. It is how well it runs that counts.

The support person displays intense concentration for a short period. Watching skilled support specialists correct a complex system failure is a treat. They evaluate options, discard alternatives and review correction scenarios mentally with extreme clarity. The rest of the world is shut out. This ability, coupled with the fact that most specialists will follow a problem through to conclusion over hours and days, make them the ideal workers to call when trouble arises.

Unfortunately, support specialists take the developer's dislike for politics one step further: they disdain politics, and generally the power of position as well. When the cause of the problem is identified, the support specialist attempts to solve it directly and immediately. This is fine until it is necessary to explain the situation to a senior executive. The support person generally sees little difference between the executive and the lowest clerk. This fact is one of the reasons the reviews of problem resolution discussed in Chapter 3 are instituted. Such reviews prevent unfortunate confrontations.

Support specialists are oriented almost totally to problem resolution. They complain vigorously about "how screwed up all the systems are" but actually are happiest when they have a backlog of problems to solve. They consider the resolution of problems to be everyone's primary goal and expect recognition not only for their work but for the time spent on it as well. A support person must almost be driven out of the office after spending a night solving a problem.

The company orientation of support persons is generally higher than that of developers. They tend to relate to the company's activities and benefits because their identification with any specific discipline is much lower.

The Analyst

The analyst discussed here is typically the person who is in constant contact with users. Varying in title from "business analyst" to "systems analyst," this position forms a bridge between the business environment and the development staff.

In the analyst, the understanding of political imperatives emerges. The close relationship with a business discipline allows analysts to understand the user community. They are often involved in meetings and plans where the political sensitivities of user management are highlighted, and all too often they participate in political intrigue.

Since the reports and responsibilities of analysts are directed to the more politically neutral development staff, they often find themselves at odds with the more functional system principles of development. In departments large enough to sustain independent analysis and construction groups, this dissimilarity in approach often breeds considerable conflict. The analyst wants to produce the product expediently, while the developers want to do it right. These concepts are seldom mutually exclusive. In this struggle the manager is often in the middle and must constantly seek a compromise.

Because of their affiliation with user departments, analysts tend to be less project oriented and more service oriented. This is a reasonable position if handled properly. It is a bridging mechanism, however, and what must be sought is a reasonable middle ground. Projects are the business of development and require the full attention of the analyst from start to finish.

Analysts are typically the most flexible members of the development department, at ease in nearly all environments where strong personalities are required. They work well with senior management, have good communication skills and are adaptable to new situations. Management finds their aggressiveness and their more visible ambition good indicators for advancement. In general, the analyst gives the outside world a picture of the development function. The good analyst can be the greatest help to the development manager. The poor analyst is the manager's worst problem.

Analysts are often prime candidates for blurred loyalties. This problem is caused by their closer association with the business area than with the craft of development. It is the analyst who most often states, "I'm a manufacturing person first and a development person second." Although this attitude indicates a strong identification with business, it can create significant problems when conflicts arise between the development department and a user.

The Coordinator

The profile of the coordinator is evidenced by the positions associated with projects. Titles such as "project leader" and "project manager" are most typical, with some separation reflecting the degree of personnel administration involved. Coordinators most often come from the analyst ranks because of the belief that to lead a project adequately, one must be intimately familiar with both the product and the users for whom it is intended. However, this attitude should be tempered. Familiarity is certainly required, but it does not have to be the result of constant exposure in an analytical role. If the analysts define the requirements properly, the coordinator can concentrate on managing the project, with its goals and check-offs. This is the most demanding part of the coordinator's job and, as discussed in Chapter 4, creates enough strain without requiring intimate knowledge of applications.

The coordinator must be the ultimate pragmatist, with the ability to interpret the wants and needs of users, management, and the technocrats in order to bring projects to their optimal conclusion. This is seldom achieved with total satisfaction all around, but the general level of satisfaction should be adequate. To achieve this requires compromise and the ability to subsume one's own opinion at times in favor of the final goal—implementation—without bruising one's ego.

The coordinator requires a heightened political sensitivity balanced by a thorough understanding of the responsibilities and goals of the department. Without political sensitivity, users will invariably feel that systems are being developed for their own sake, and the preconceived notion of development as a group of technical gurus will be perpetuated. Without an understanding of departmental priorities, the basic tenets of development will be compromised and adept users will quickly suborn the ability of development to meet its responsibilities.

The coordinator must be a calm, steady performer with a healthy ego. Much of the job involves marketing and sales: emphasizing the contribution development can make and providing a good impression of the development professional. The coordinator must be an excellent communicator and be comfortable in nearly any situation involving groups of people with dissenting opinions. The role is rife with situations of dissent.

Because of this role, the coordinator tends to be a loner, somewhat isolated from all of the groups serviced. Being forced to compromise lingers in the mind longer than victory, and the persons who lose generally remember who forced the compromise on them. This separation breeds a high level of independence which, while generally positive, can easily lead to awkward situations where independence borders on revolt. Managing an aggressive coordinator can prove challenging.

Just as programmers sometimes resist changes in development languages and processes, coordinators resist changes in their process tools—project management techniques and methodologies. The resistance of programmers is generally easy to detect; their work is unambiguous. Project management techniques require far more interpretation, and resistance can go undetected almost indefinitely. This has been the downfall of methodologies far more often than any inherent limitations in the methodologies themselves.

Finally, coordinators generally possess one characteristic identical to that of most development managers: an intense desire to lead. Given their project role, this trait is essential. However, management requires an understanding of the limits of one's authority. All too often, coordinators establish mini-domains which can easily move in different directions than the department. This tendency can cause a great deal of conflict. It is natural to manage a group in line with one's own personality as long as one remembers one's position in the hierarchy.

The Administrator

The role of administrator is somewhat alien to most development departments. Development people are mediocre administrators. Their project orientation and the constant technological changes they must cope with preclude the mental sets necessary for seemingly mundane administrative functions. However, these activities are essential for a smooth operation. The administrator's work is the counterbalance to corporate administrative procedures.

The administrator controls and monitors budgets, distributes and reviews procedural papers, ensures proper paperwork flow and handles the many activities endemic in the corporate environment. Full-time administrators are found only in the larger development organizations. Nevertheless, someone performs the required administrative duties, even if they are done poorly. With development's poor reputation for administration, it is surprising that more companies have not established this independent position.

Administrators are strongly process oriented. They depend on and relate to the step-by-step administrative procedures inherent in the financial and personnel growth of the company. Reveling in smooth rote procedures and striving to improve their automatic nature, they focus on ways to accomplish goals. The methodologies are generally more important than the goals themselves.

While this attitude may be a fine counterbalance to the volatility of the typical development person, it tends to alienate the administrator from the department's line personnel. Staff members often see this position as blocking their goals and doing little more than slowing down the process. Most peer managers are thankful that administrators exist to relieve their own burdens.

The profiles we have just discussed are not universal. They have the same relationship to the people who fill these positions that sociology has to psychology. It is quite possible to find an extroverted, pragmatic person who is also a good programmer. In addition, many people are content to sacrifice certain personality traits on the job to gain other advantages: travel, flexible hours, prestige and other benefits. Still others treat the job as assembly workers do—they turn their active minds off when they reach work and turn them on again when they leave.

Still, development persons, as a group, tend to display the traits we have discussed. The development manager must establish an environment and a responsibility structure which accords well with their personalities. Once this requirement is satisfied, the manager can begin to understand and enhance the personality traits displayed by the individuals who fill the jobs.

MATCHING PERSONALITIES TO JOBS

The manager lucky enough to have employees who do not care what job they fill, are open and honest about their goals and attitudes, and are willing to allow someone else to choose their jobs has an easy task. The only need is to give them the positions that match their personalities and let them work. They will undoubtedly be content, productive and fiercely loyal. Productivity will be high and the manager will have few internal worries.

Unfortunately, myriad outside influences prevent this from ever happening. People are motivated by factors ranging from a need to match their parents' achievements to an altruistic desire to better humanity. All of these factors shape people as personalities, not merely as workers. These personalities give managers the most satisfaction as well as the most problems.

All departments have defined profiles which reflect gradations of jobs, both within a work classification and across classifications. Department members are expected to move through several of these levels before reaching the position for which they are suited. These grades reflect not only enhanced experience or skills, but also the individual's approach to the job. How well the person accepts responsibility, reacts under pressure and responds to politics are typical qualifications for advancement. In many industries, especially government agencies, these skills are only implicit—but they exist nonetheless.

For the manager, this means that while employees are moving toward the position where they may be most qualified and content, they will occupy interim positions where the traits which make them most effective in that final role will appear as negative qualifications. An example is the coordinator who, while serving an apprenticeship as a programmer, will care not a whit for the elegance of programs. Generally, an attentive manager can identify employees who are capable of moving up; simple counseling can prevent these interim negative traits from getting out of hand.

Certain personality traits, however, are in complete conflict with position requirements. The support specialist who refuses to work past 4:30 is a classic example. Whatever the reasons, if the individual cannot bring himself to handle odd hours, the job fit is wrong. He or she cannot be allowed to enter that position or remain in it. It is the manager's responsibility to move this person out—hopefully, to a more appropriate job in the department. The coordinator who refuses to compromise, the analyst who cannot deal with users, and the programmer who cannot concentrate on a problem for long periods cannot function well. It is foolish for them to try.

Table 6-2 presents various personality traits and shows how they relate to the position profiles described earlier. Each trait is classified as negative (−), positive (+), or neutral (0) in relation to performance. The table depicts these traits in real-world rather than clinical terms.

If an individual is working as a developer, his or her traits can be mapped across the table to see how effective the match is. When conflicts arise, it is important to understand how crucial they are—for instance, if the developer, in this case, is unable to work without close supervision. However, referring to Table 6-2, that trait is classified as neutral weighting, indicating that although little need for supervision is normally a positive trait, it is not significant one way or the other. Therefore, this problem should not limit the developer's performance as long as he or she is not constantly thrown into situations where close, prolonged supervision and feedback are required.

The effective manager ensures that staff members are not constantly exposed to situations where their weaknesses are highlighted. Potentially, a career path exists where problematic characteristics are incidental. If this is the case, avoiding exposure of the weakness is a temporary situation and can result in the retention of a valuable employee.

If the employee wants to remain in the position where the weakness will eventually cause difficulty, a method must be found to reduce the impact of the trait. The manager should keep in mind that personality traits cannot

Table 6–2. Personality Profiles by Position

TRAIT	IMPACT				
	DEVELOPER	SUPPORT PERSON	ANALYST	COORDINATOR	ADMINISTRATOR
EXTENDED CONCENTRATION SPAN	+	+	0	0	0
ABILITY TO BALANCE PRIORITIES	+	+	0	+	0
ATTENTION TO DETAIL	+	+	–	+	+
ABILITY TO COMPROMISE	0	–	0	+	–
CONCEPTUALIZATION SKILLS	+	0	+	+	0
INTENSE CONCENTRATION	0	+	0	0	–
NEED FOR STABLE WORK HOURS	0	–	0	0	–
FLEXIBILITY FOR WORK HOURS	0	+	0	0	0
ABILITY TO TAKE DETAIL DIRECTION	+	0	–	–	0
COMBATIVENESS	0	0	–	–	+
CREATIVITY	0	0	+	0	–
INDEPENDENT ACTION	0	0	+	+	0
AGGRESSIVENESS	0	–	+	+	+
DECISIVENESS	0	+	+	+	0
MAKES DECISIONS WITH MINIMAL FACTS	–	–	0	+	–
ACCEPTS CRITICISM	+	+	+	0	+
ACCEPTS REJECTION	+	0	+	+	+
ACCEPTS DYNAMICALLY CHANGING ENVIRONMENT	0	0	+	0	0
COMMITMENT TO CRAFT	+	0	0	–	–
COMMITMENT TO COMPANY	0	+	0	+	+
GREGARIOUS	+	–	0	–	–
INTROVERTED	0	+	0	–	+
EXTROVERTED	0	0	0	+	–
POLITICALLY SENSITIVE	0	–	+	+	+
POLITICALLY STIMULATED	–	–	+	–	–
NEED FOR CLOSE SUPERVISION/FEEDBACK	0	0	0	–	0
SHORT ATTENTION SPAN	–	–	0	0	0
DISCIPLINED THOUGHT PATTERNS	+	+	0	+	+
REACTIVE	–	+	–	+	+
ENJOYS CLOSE WORKING ENVIRONMENT	+	–	–	–	–
STRONG EGO	+	+	+	+	+
DOMINANT PERSONALITY	–	+	0	–	+
DEALS IN RIGHT/WRONG PROBLEM SOLUTIONS	+	+	–	–	+
PRAGMATIC	0	0	+	+	0
GETS THE JOB DONE	–	+	0	+	+

Table 6–2. (Continued)

CONSERVATIVE	+	+	0	0	+
DRIVEN FROM THE OUTSIDE	−	−	−	−	0
DRIVEN FROM THE INSIDE	+	+	+	+	0
CHALLENGE DRIVEN	0	+	0	+	0
JOB ORIENTATION	0	+	0	−	0
CAREER ORIENTATION	0	−	+	+	0

PART B: ANALYSIS OF TRAITS

Personality traits are expressed in behavior. While behavior characteristics are influenced by variety of forces, over time they describe tendencies which are consistent. The traits expressed here represent behaviors in terms in which they are most likely to be perceived in a day-to-day working environment.

EXTENDED CONCENTRATION SPAN
: Ability and tendency to focus on a single problem for an extended period—days to weeks—to the exclusion of outside stimuli

ABILITY TO BALANCE PRIORITIES
: Ability to maintain control of and perspective on many issues of varying importance

ATTENTION TO DETAIL
: Tendency and need to understand all or most aspects of the problem

ABILITY TO COMPROMISE
: Ability to compromise on issues which are important to the person in the interest of progress; implies the ability to judge what should and should not be compromised

CONCEPTUALIZATION SKILLS
: Ability to understand the idea behind an issue, as well as how it can be made operational

INTENSE CONCENTRATION
: Ability to concentrate on a problem and keep all of its aspects in mind, regardless of outside pressures, typically for hours

NEED FOR STABLE WORK HOURS
: Tendency to compartmentalize work and leisure time to the point where nonstandard hours are significantly disturbing

FLEXIBILITY FOR WORK HOURS
: Tendency to prefer nonstandard work hours—not simply long hours but unpredictable work patterns

ABILITY TO TAKE DETAIL DIRECTION
: Ability to accept specific directives without developing a sense of being personally constrained

COMBATIVENESS
: Tendency to react to conflict situations by strongly defending positions until a win situation results or equalized sacrifices are achieved on the specific issue

CREATIVITY
: Ability to take a proposed idea and develop the concept with little direct practical exposure

(cont.)

Table 6–2. (Continued)

PART B: ANALYSIS OF TRAITS

INDEPENDENT ACTION
Ability to perform with little direct supervision or reinforcement about to propriety

AGGRESSIVENESS
Tendency to seek out opportunities beyond the scope of assignments, at times without knowledge of the strategies at higher management

DECISIVENESS
Ability to reach a decision on an issue in good time

MAKE DECISIONS WITH MINIMAL FACTS
Tendency to make decisions on the basis of few facts, at times without the knowledge needed to avoid risk

ACCEPT CRITICISM
Ability to take criticism without emotional involvement or rash reactions

ACCEPT REJECTION
Ability to accept rejection of an idea or plan even when the reason for rejection is inconsistent with the facts

ACCEPT DYNAMICALLY CHANGING ENVIRONMENT
Ability to function at a peak level despite instability in the environment, either positive or negative

COMMITMENT TO CRAFT
Tendency to dedicate oneself to one's profession rather than to the company

COMMITMENT TO COMPANY
Dedication to the company rather than to the discipline practiced

GREGARIOUS
Need to be part of a group and identification with the group itself; the group can be as broad as the company or as narrow as a project team

INTROVERTED
Being predominately concerned with one's own interests; does not preclude the ability to be concerned about others

EXTROVERTED
An active concern with others beyond the needs of the function, at times to the sacrifice of one's own interests

POLITICALLY SENSITIVE
Ability to perceive the influences of political interests in a situation and to understand how they affect the job

POLITICALLY STIMULATED
Actively pursuing political situations and placing political aspects above technical considerations in most cases

NEED FOR CLOSE SUPERVISION/FEEDBACK
A continual need for reinforcement regarding performance, coupled with a desire to be closely supervised

Table 6–2. (Continued)

SHORT ATTENTION SPAN
Inability to concentrate on a single subject for an extended period

DISCIPLINED THOUGHT PATTERNS
Ability to order things coupled with a need to have them ordered before operating

REACTIVE
Tendency to act only when prompted by explicit outside stimuli

ENJOYS CLOSE WORKING ENVIRONMENT
Operating best in a close interpersonal situation; needing steady peer involvement

STRONG EGO
Ability to separate aspects of the job from personal worth

DOMINANT PERSONALITY
Possessing a manner or attitude which tends to stifle discussion by others

DEALS IN RIGHT/WRONG PROBLEM SOLUTIONS
Mental set which seeks absolutes (right or wrong) and is uncomfortable with results or decisions which represent a compromise

PRAGMATIC
Tendency to allow the situation or need to define the correctness of a path taken

GETS THE JOB DONE
Concentration on completion of the effort or project; tendency to place this above quality or comprehensiveness

CONSERVATIVE
Desire to study an issue extensively until the risks are minimal to nonexistent

DRIVEN FROM THE OUTSIDE
Requires outside influences to perform at peak levels

DRIVEN FROM THE INSIDE
Sets levels of performance based on personal criteria and places these above outside performance criteria

CHALLENGE DRIVEN
Seeks and requires challenging situations to operate at peak levels

JOB ORIENTATION
View the work as a job, not as an important measure of success

CAREER ORIENTATION
Regards work as an important measure of success and strives to constantly enhance the role, primarily through promotion

PART C: PROFILE DEFINITIONS

DEVELOPER
Usually a programmer or analyst, predominately in the internal role of Systems Development. This person is concerned primarily with the production of the product, not with its applicability to the environment.

(cont.)

Table 6–2. (Continued)

PART C: PROFILE DEFINITIONS

SUPPORT PERSON
A person who supports operational systems. Dealings with the world outside of development are sporadic and focus on the solution of a specific problem.

ANALYST
Concerned primarily with the business application of an automated system. This person typically provides a bridge between the user and the developer. He or she tends to specialize in business discipline such as finance or manufacturing, as opposed to technical skills.

COORDINATOR
A person most often in charge of projects requiring heavy interface between the business environment and development. This person strives to complete a project within predefined limits.

ADMINISTRATOR
The person who handles administrative duties such as budgeting, facilities, and the myriad internal process control activities of any department. This role is not substantially different from that of any other department beyond an ability to understand technical issues and technicians.

be reduced to strengths and weaknesses which can be improved or overcome at will. Personality traits make people what they are. Some cannot and should not be eliminated or reversed—simply controlled and dealt with. When they represent conditions which have a temporary impact on the department, such as the eruption of political furor involving a support specialist, they are best avoided until the situation changes.

The classifications used in this chapter are broad, and Table 6-2 is representative. The preparation of such a table for the department can be extremely valuable for the manager. The table will indicate how well personnel fit to job profiles, what problems can be anticipated in personnel movement, and how effective the department will be.

Of course, the relative merits described are subjective. The definitions of positive traits are far from absolute; they vary across industry types, style of management and personal preference. However, these traits do exist, and they define how a person is likely to perform in a given environment.

CONCLUSION

Most successful departments are a well-blended group of personalities. They work well simply because their members complement each other. Managers should seek specific personality traits for each position and attempt to build project teams which include complementary characteristics. They must keep in mind that such traits seldom exist in any one person. In fact, many are mutually exclusive.

People reach their optimum productivity when their personalities match the profile characteristics necessary for the job. Programmers are most happy when their responsbilities involve close attention to detail and well-defined measures for correct and incorrect results. Analysts are most comfortable when the requirement is for somewhat unstructured reactions to user needs. However, not all programmers fill programmer positions and not all analyst types are analysts.

Typically, people gravitate to the roles for which they are most suited. They then find satisfaction and contentment, and are high producers as well as excellent employees. Unfortunately, outside influences such as peer pressure, salary and other factors cause mismatches to occur at almost all levels. When this happens, productivity drops, affecting not only the employees in question but their co-workers as well.

Managers are not directly responsible for their employees' happiness. Short of psychological counseling, there is no way that a manager can be expected to provide jobs which satisfy everyone. The manager is responsible for creating an atmosphere where, given the maturity of the employee, job satisfaction is possible.

Understanding the traits required to fill various positions and staffing these positions with appropriate candidates is the most important consideration in managing various types of personalities. This is done not only through counseling but in hiring as well. As will be seen in Chapter 7, attaining a suitable match between the person and the position is far more important than hiring abstract technical skills. That fit can be achieved only if the manager distributes the personalities throughout the department to match the needs and attributes of various jobs.

The manager of a development staff faces more challenges in matching personality styles to jobs than exist in most disciplines. Historical precedence has defined the personality traits for accountants, salespeople, factory floor supervisors, and nearly all other disciplines since people gravitating towards these positions do so because there is a universal understanding of what those roles entail. Development is not afforded that luxury.

People enter the development field because it provides upward mobility and an open job market, or because it is "the way to go." There is simply no history to predict who is most appropriate for development positions. That will remain true for many years to come. This fact places a greater burden on the manager to understand who will produce at an optimum level and why.

The manager's technical or project skills are of little avail in managing personalities. Managers are in leadership roles primarily because some aspect of their personality separates them from the balance of the staff. They can succeed only with hard, painstaking work and attention to the personalities of their staff and by effectively matching these personalities to the traits required for the positions. When this match is achieved, the staff will be happy and productive and the responsibilities of the organization will be met.

7
ESTABLISHING A DEPARTMENT PERSONALITY

A successful department develops a personality of its own. This personality colors everything the department does and is as descriptive of the group as it is on the individual level. That group personality represents more than the amalgamation of all the individuals in the group. It is an example of the whole being greater than the sum of its parts.

Much of the typical department's personality is defined by precedent and convention. For example, all of the groups in a company know that the accounting department will act and react in a certain way. The same is true of manufacturing, marketing and any other department, simply because they have existed for a long time, their responsibilities have evolved slowly, and their members naturally fit in with the department's personality.

Quite often, however, the personality does not become successfully entrenched or deteriorates. When this occurs, the department may continue to produce, but not with the same drive and effectiveness as before. The spirit needed to produce and succeed is lost. It is supplanted by individual goals and priorities, and while intermittent periods of productivity occur, they are governed by a single individual's stength, not by the cohesiveness of the department. When that individual moves on, the department once again languishes.

Establishing and maintaining a department personality is important for any manager, but especially for the manager of systems development. Unlike other disciplines, this function has few historical precedents. This fact places additional pressure on the manager, as discussed in other contents in previous chapter subjects. The manager must work explicitly to accelerate the natural progression.

While team approaches often develop into general traits in development, this usually happens in response to projects rather than as part of the normal everyday set of activities. When the project ends, this personality development disappears. It is incumbent on the manager to foster this group atmosphere beyond the life of the project. Without the manager's efforts, it will not continue indefinitely.

Because of the project orientation of development, the establishment of a department personality is even more important than it is for most other groups. Projects ebb and flow, leaving people with a great deal of uncertainty. In this unstable work environment, an effective group personality provides continuity and stability despite the transient nature of the work.

In this chapter, we discuss the various aspects of a department personality, considering how the manager can foster a naturally developed situation or establish it explicitly. The key elements of a department personality are discussed, since it is a combination of these elements that the manager seeks to establish—not an abstract concept. The typical elements of a naturally developed group personality are reviewed so that this process can be recognized and enhanced. Finally, practical methods which can foster and nourish the developing department personality are discussed.

In Chapter 6, we stated that the key to managing individuals is to understand their personality traits and motivations. Management of a department is precisely the same, albeit somewhat more difficult. A department with a clear identity or personality will operate without strong, continual supervision and still fulfill the goals and responsibilities of its charter. This allows the manager to concentrate on the evolution of the department for the future.

KEY ELEMENTS OF A DEPARTMENT PERSONALITY

The manager cannot merely say, "Our department will display this personality, style, or philosophy" and expect significant changes to occur. Regardless of how well conceived or expressed, that approach will bring results only in rare cases, and only when that personality already exists. The manager must take concrete, visible steps either to establish that personality and style or at least to foster one which already is taking shape.

Before establishing or nurturing a group personality, the manager must understand the key elements which indicate that it is developing. When it is not developing naturally, he must understand what attitudes and mental sets are necessary to establish it. Like individual personalities, a group personality is not expressed or stated in abstract terms. It is an amalgamation of elements expressed in performance, attitude, and behavior.

The elements of a group personality to be discussed deal primarily with understanding—that is, understanding by staff members. Understanding does not imply total agreement or acceptance. It does imply a realization that the elements are realistic and reasonable in the specific environment.

Identification with Team Goals

Most management development programs involve setting of objectives, measuring progress and fulfilling the responsibilities of the job. This generally represents a mixture of personal growth goals and programs designed to benefit the company (increased sales, improved operating efficiency, etc.). Success in achieving these objectives becomes the measure of career success and the principal criterion for salary increases and promotions.

The viability of the method and its benefit to the corporation depends largely on how effectively these goals are set. Do they parallel the strategy of the company? Are they in keeping with the scope and responsibilities of the department being serviced? Do they represent a significant stretching of the individual's capabilities so that more is being accomplished today than yesterday? If the answer is yes, the exercise will ensure an aggressive, evolutionary group posture.

Like individuals, departments must have goals and objectives which are well grounded, well understood and coordinated with those of the corporation. They should have specific measures, and progress should be visible and should represent a significant effort to achieve. As with most management programs, the goals and objectives should be formal, agreed upon, and form the basis for departmental measures of success.

Departmental goals cannot be developed in a vacuum. If they are to be achieved, not merely perceived, the staff must identify with them. With this identification comes identification with group dynamics; they cannot be achieved without the efforts of each member of the group. The importance of achieving the goals will cause group members to make sacrifices to ensure that they are met. For example, they may assume responsibilities not strictly their own when another member falls behind, without the consideration of personal gain.

The manager's efforts to gain the group's identification with goals cannot be half-hearted. The staff will pay careful attention to such an attempt, considering what it means to them and the depth of the manager's commitment. Failures are committed to memory, and the second try will be received with far more skepticism than the first. The manager's efforts must be equal to the staff's responsibility to make the program work. There are several factors which should be kept in mind when establishing departmental goals.

First, the goals must be real and must be recognized as such by both upper management and the staff. The surest way to ensure noncompliance is to have a key manager say, "The goals are nice but they make no real difference." Second, the goals must be achievable. If failure is certain, people will take steps to make sure that, in the face of departmental failure, they at least have personally met their objectives.

Third, there should be group rewards for success. Just as individual success provides personal benefits, group success should result in group benefits. This may take the form of increased, company paid educational opportunities, relaxed working conditions, availability of more sophisticated tools or any benefit that can be used by any or all staff members.

Lastly, the goals must be rational and must stand up under questions by the staff.

Understanding How the Department Works

As important as knowing what the department is trying to accomplish is understanding how the work is done. This is accompanied by an understanding of how these two elements work together. Each member of the group has a clear picture of how the other members do their portion of the job.

This knowledge implies an understanding of the charter, procedures and policies of the department. It allows the charter and other mechanisms to be organic and directive for day-to-day activities. The larger and more specialized a department becomes, the more important this factor is. In a large department, responsibilities there are inevitably divided to the point where no solution is achieved by any one person. Without an understanding of the flow of work, subgroups or individuals tend to meet the "letter of the law" for each segment of the job. This is certainly not the intent of charters or procedures. The spirit is more important than the letter, and only when the group perceives the flow of work to be sensible and obvious will the overall goals be accomplished.

Few development groups understand how their own group operates from the beginning of a job to the end. They tend to view activities as reaching a gating point and being turned over to another group, which performs some mysterious verification or adjustment. There is no sense of what is being done or why it is important. With a small group, this is never the case, since all aspects of the job are visible and obvious. In order for the larger group to function with this same efficiency and camaraderie, the internal operations must be equally obvious, visible and natural.

This is the expressed purpose of formal policies and procedures. The importance and preparation of these documents is discussed in Chapter 12. In terms of the department's personality, the importance of those procedures is that they be understood by all staff members. If they are not ingrained, representative of the way the group operates, and followed as part of the normal operation, this is worse than having no procedures at all. In this case, procedures become a means of protecting individuals from their departmental responsibilities by hiding behind unproductive rules.

To ensure a clear understanding of how the department works, the manager must establish procedures intelligently and follow them personally. It is important to remember that, as discussed in Chapter 6, development personnel are intelligent, perceptive individuals who focus as much on the way things work as on the final outcome. For them to concern themselves with the way the group operates, that operation must be sensible and consistent. Creating a procedure to satisfy an obscure requirement is not adequate. The mode of operation must be real and supported.

Understanding Outsiders' Perceptions and Concerns

It is not enough to produce and maintain systems or take a positive approach to accomplishing departmental goals. It is equally essential to promote the department's accomplishments and attitudes to the outside world. When a productive departmental personality is displayed, staff members are as concerned with the outside world's view of the group as they are with their own perceived contributions.

Regardless of how well a department functions, failures will occur. Schedules will not be met, adequate support will not be provided or the product will have shortcomings. If team members are sensitive to how those failures are perceived by the outside world, they can not only help to prevent them but can significantly reduce their impact and visibility as well. It is not a matter of covering up problems. Rather, it is an attempt to solve the problems internally without needless publicity.

The manager must tell the staff what group personality is being displayed to the outside world. Is it a "customer is always right" philosophy or a conservative, in-depth, evaluative approach? Will the users expect a rapid, dynamic response to any and all problems, or will they anticipate a dependable, steady response cycle based on problem evaluation? Many different philosophies are viable. The style displayed by the department needs to be consistent regardless of who is placed before the public.

Understanding the Group's Evolution and Growth

In a team environment, all members should understand where the group's future lies. They must perceive how the group's role will change and what part each team member is likely to play in the future. With this knowledge, all members of the department will pull in the same direction. The individuals create that future with their day-to-day response to situations. Without a unified approach, individual priorities will inevitably stifle and suborn that direction in favor of personal goals.

This process is analogous to an individual's perception of career plans.

Individuals function far more effectively if they know where they are going. Few professionals are satisfied to come in in the morning, do their work and leave, and forget the job at night. How their daily work will meld into tomorrow's organization or environment is extremely important to them. The department operates the same way. Each member develops along with the group. This evolution of the group provides a way of dealing with short-term trepidations as that future unfolds.

This process cannot occur without a real and agreed upon understanding of how that evolution will take place. Development of that understanding places a heavy burden on the manager. The manager must develop and promote a strategy for the evolution of the department which goes well beyond the conventional strategic plan for applications. That plan always exists, in general on an informal basis, but all too often is poorly publicized.

The department which has a plan adequately presented and understood by the entire staff will operate to ensure the plan's success. Without that understanding, individuals will act independently to ensure their own future. Often this activity is a response to one's unknown status in the future. An example is that of COBOL programmers who see the influx of 4GL. If these programmers have a clear understanding of their future role in the department, they will facilitate that trend. If not, they may spend most of their time job hunting rather than aiding the process. An atmosphere may also be created in which they attempt to impede progress in order to protect themselves.

Understanding the Group's Contribution

When a departmental personality exists, the staff has a clear picture of its contribution to the company's success. This goes beyond the individual's understanding of his or her contribution to the department. When project stress arises or significant problems occur, the department will pull together and commit itself to fulfilling its responsibilities. Group members understand the company's dependence on their efforts and feel that they are part of the general strategy.

The feeling that the department's responsibilities are being met, and the group's judgment of their success or failure, are crucial to a group personality. The efforts of the entire group will be focused on the goals of the department's charter. Just as individuals require this focus, so do departments. Without it, a spirit of protectionism rather than contribution exists.

This group ethos is manifested most visibly in the department's pride in itself. There is a tendency to state performance in terms of "we" rather than "I." The manager must encourage this response to success by congratulating the group as a whole, rather than singling out individual performers for recognition. It is equally important to recognize suboptimal group performance. In an environment where group personalities are prevalent, the department will handle poor individual performers socially. The manager should react to the group's decisions on performance rather than exerting direct control.

RECOGNIZING NATURAL GROUP PERSONALITY DEVELOPMENT

All development departments sometimes experience a period when a group personality surfaces naturally. In most cases, the development of that personality is related to a specific project and the team assigned to service it. It occurs regardless of the previous condition of the department. That is, whether the department works well together or not, the dedication of the small team will create precisely those characteristics which are desired for the group personality. Understanding this natural group personality development and fostering the atmosphere it creates allows that growth to continue and spread.

The timing of this development cannot be precisely predicted. It may not begin with the manager's efforts to develop a department personality. The manager can create the proper environment, but these conditions must be allowed to grow naturally. The key is to recognize that this process is occurring and to build upon it.

The Special Project

As was discussed in Chapter 3, most of the activity in systems development is focused on projects. People move into and out of projects, dedicate themselves to their successful completion, and then begin another project. In many cases, the department itself bears a resemblance to a huge project, with actual project teams representing the tasks and activities within the general environment. A department cannot be effectively managed in this fashion, but most new ideas and attitudes flow directly from important and concentrated project efforts. For this reason, the development of a department personality generally flows from special projects.

Generally, these projects occur in response to a specific need or a goal to be met. They are seldom intended to do anything more than meet the user's needs. Therefore, there is no sense, at least initially, of a goal continuing beyond the normal target date. Projects develop on an ad hoc basis, just as the business responds to competitive and technological pressures as they arise.

In most cases, special projects have a significant impact on the company. This creates high departmental visibility and an environment where established procedures are bypassed to a degree. Organizational boundaries become somewhat blurred, engendering the sense that the project team is a self-contained department—a microcosm of the department as a whole.

This atmosphere can sometimes be created artificially, based on the degree of flexibility provided for the team. However, the project itself, and its goals, must be real. They must exist in response to a tangible business need which is recognized as critical not only by the development staff but by corporate management as well. That recognition alone creates the sense that the project requires carte blanche.

The existence of a "department within a department" can cause friction among the staff, especially with those members who are comfortable in their current roles and seek no change in the status quo. While some degree of resistance involves nothing more than protectionism, some of it is valid and must be recognized by the manager. With the positive atmosphere created by the concentrated, intense project structure, it is easy to forget that the day-to-day running of a department also depends upon the effective management of mundane functions. That atmosphere should then be infused into the balance of the department without destroying the positive attributes which already exist.

The characteristics of special projects are fairly universal. When they exist, one quickly senses the development of a group personality. That personality is not always positive. It is shaped by a number of outside forces, not the least of which is the makeup of the team. However, by recognizing these characteristics, the manager can watch the team's development and, when a positive personality develops, can take a hand to guide the team in useful directions.

Challenge. For a group personality to emerge in a project team, there must be a significant challenge involved. It should be primarily a business challenge, as opposed to a purely technical one, to promote a sense of contributing to the company rather than simply fostering professional growth. The team must see itself as meeting that challenge against certain odds. While those odds generally consist of time constraints, they can also represent organizational issues, availability of resources or competitive pressures. However that challenge is expressed, it is real and visible.

To meet the challenge, the group must make sacrifices. These sacrifices should go beyond working long hours to include subordinating personal ideas, assuming extra responsibilities or resolving problems which require help from other team members. This implies a reliance on other team members for success. There is little sense of position or power—merely doing what is necessary for the group to succeed.

The challenge, and meeting it, become all-consuming. For the project to be successful, the sacrifices should not be great enough to seriously affect the personal lives of those involved. Otherwise, the motivation will be to finish the project rather than to produce a quality product. The group must feel that the challenge can be met and that success is possible. However, the effort always requires stretching one's capabilities and sacrificing certain personal goals.

Newness. The project will include a new and unused methodology or technology for the department. This requires team members to learn quickly and "on the fly." Many mistakes will be made, and some retrenching is required. This forces the team to make hard judgments and reduces the individual's identification with the project. The identification shifts to the group.

Due to the rapid rate of technological change, the newness of the product or process generally involves technical issues—the database, interactive applications or state-of-the-art hardware or software. However, this is not always the case. Instead, the innovation may consist of the introduction of new business lines or techniques, which involves not only learning new technology but developing a new business strategy as well.

The newness of the product usually causes some difficulty in integrating it into the current environment. This requires the team to develop new techniques which may cross current procedural boundaries. As mentioned previously, not all techniques will be appropriate for a well-run department. Some will, however, and can cause a significant departmental evolution beyond the completion of the project.

The charting of new ground increases the interest of the rest of the department in the project. Often nonteam members become involved on their own simply to gain experience with the new technology or process. This expanded interest makes it significantly easier to integrate the results and gains after the project is completed.

Personal Chemistry. When a group personality develops from a project, it is usually because the team members work well together. Their personalities are cooperative and symbiotic. This allows them to focus on meeting the challenge and adapting the new technology and process without wasting time protecting their egos. This chemistry can seldom be predicted. It seems to occur naturally and strengthens with success.

The idea of chemistry governing the success of a project is often overstated. There is no single good mix which exists in a department, to the exclusion of others. The chemistry is created as much by the challenge and newness of the effort as by natural attraction. However, that chemistry always develops in a project of this type and will exist after the project has ended.

Loss of Group Personality

Projects such as the one just described occur regularly. The group personality develops, challenges are met, a good working atmosphere develops, and a strongly positive reaction to development's capability spreads throughout the company. It is equally true that a departmental personality exists in only a small number of companies. While these two facts seem somewhat at odds, there are certain factors which cause the group personality to disappear after the project is over.

In most cases, the group personality is lost because no attempt is made to capitalize on it. Either the concentration is centered on the project goals and the product or the characteristics displayed during the project are misinterpreted as representing an amalgamation of skills. In either case, after completion of the project, the members return to their original groups, or form new ones, and the singularity of purpose and camaraderie are lost. They linger on of their own volition for a while but, without an explicit effort to integrate them into the staff, they eventually dissipate.

In order to foster and strengthen this atmosphere, the intelligent manager must incorporate the improved processes developed during the project in the daily environment and must take certain practical steps. These steps, which are outlined in the balance of this chapter, do not require much money or time. Their benefits are more abstract than those provided by implementation of new systems, and are difficult to appreciate on the bottom line. Nevertheless, these benefits are well worth the effort.

PRACTICAL METHODS FOR MAINTAINING A DEPARTMENT PERSONALITY

Analysis of the characteristics and processes which cause the natural development of a group personality leads to several conclusions. First, the development of that personality is one of the primary factors in project success. Second, much of that development takes place in response to external stimuli and is seen as filling needs rather than as a plan in itself. Close communication, individual sacrifices and commitment to a goal all occur initially because those things must be done. Afterward the group begins to benefit from the steps themselves and furthers their use because they promote a more satisfying work environment.

The manager is left with the task of duplicating those steps, and thereby the environment, in the department as a whole. Once those steps are taken and the department's personality develops, it is self-perpetuating and requires only the heightened sensitivity of the manager to ensure its continuance. It is essential to establish that personality on a *department* basis because the department represents continuity in the face of the constant change and upheaval of projects. Allowing that personality to exist only during projects becomes counterproductive because little common direction or culture is created. The social environment becomes too narrow, and instead of a department personality, one sees the department of cliques.

There are certain practical methods that the manager can employ to foster a group personality. The combined result of these methods is a sense of camaraderie and a unity of purpose which will bridge even the most difficult economic times. Naturally, these steps require a receptive group. Generally, one does exist, since people are social creatures and tend to gravitate to structured social environments. Work represents a significant portion of the average person's life, and there is a strong desire to make it as pleasant as possible. This requires some effort on the part of the manager, but the results are not only far more productive for the department but provide a much more pleasant experience for all concerned—including the manager.

Communications

During the 1960s, communication was stressed as the primary management tool for ensuring productivity. A wealth of material was published, seminars were held and encounter groups were established to aid management in improving communication with the staff. While communication is probably not the complete answer to successful management, it does foster unity for people who operate in groups.

Effective communication is based on an attitude largely contradictory to the "need to know" approach seen in many of today's corporations. Essentially, it means telling the staff as much as possible. This practice keeps the staff involved in all aspects of department life and prevents much of the compartmentalization which develops when communication does not exist. While it does not prevent rumors from developing, it does provide a way of getting real answers rather than being forced to rely on second-, or third-hand stories.

In communicating effectively with a development staff, there are some key considerations:

- Recognize the intelligence of the group. They are not likely to be easily fooled with half-truths or outright lies.
- Recognize the difference between formal and informal communication.

They are quite different and are interpreted in different ways. With formal communication, the manager is the boss. With informal communication, there is a peer relationship.
- Timing is important. If a major event is taking place, communicate it before it rises through the rumor mill. (The author was once involved in a situation where the development staff learned that their company's data processing department was being moved to a new location through the Sunday paper. It was formally announced to the staff first thing Monday morning. Needless to say, this did not engender great faith in management's communication ability.)
- Address all issues raised by the staff. Some may not be important to the manager but may be of great concern to the department.
- Saying "I don't know" is far better than making up an answer. Few managers are omnipotent, and employees generally do not expect them to be.

In small departments, everyone knows a great deal about what is going on. Small departments also display group personalities more readily than large ones, partially because they are better informed. Therefore, in larger groups, one of the most important ways of combatting the loss of the small group's personality is by addressing communications to the group as a group—not to isolated individuals or smaller groups.

Working Committees

One of the primary ways of establishing a group personality is to allow the department members to control as much of their destiny as possible. Granted, one of the responsibilities of management is to chart the department's future and ensure that the proper tools and environment exist to bring the plans to fruition. However, many of these tools and plans can be implemented in various ways. If these issues are left to the staff, given appropriate parameters, they will display far greater commitment to their success than if the plans are simply presented.

By establishing working staff committees—those expected to carry out the plans—the commitment to success can be achieved. Missions and parameters are established with the committee before they begin their work, and progress is reported regularly to department management. The key to success is to draw the committee members from the department—not from management. In fact, management should not be associated with the committees in any way, with the exception of the formalized review process.

Committees are generally of two types: research and maintenance. Research committees deal with new methodologies, technologies and procedures. An example is the selection of a development methodology. Who, after all, is more qualified to investigate and choose the methodology for developing systems than those who will actually use it? The committee is given management's requirements, which may include statements on the simplicity or complexity of the method, costs, integation capabilities with current products, response characteristics and limitations. The committee is also given a charter which defines its scope, responsibilities, completion date and the allocation of the members' time to the effort. With this in hand, the committee utilizes the experience of the group, existing project control and reporting mechanisms, and whatever facilities are normally used to accomplish the task.

The second type of committee provides periodic, scheduled maintenance activities. These include standards reviews, productivity issues, application performance reviews or any other issues which can be controlled by the staff itself. Staff members make proposals for changes in existing structures using a formal system, and the proposals are acted on by the committee. If they receive approval, the committee's recommendation for implementation is then taken to management for final approval.

This method is quite similar in concept to the quality circle, which is increasing in popularity in the business world. It creates a sense of control on the part of the staff and develops the attitude that the department is the *employee's* department, rather than simply a workplace. It increases the sense of unity that is the hallmark of a group personality.

The manager's role in establishing these committees is twofold. First, the manager must provide the initial impetus to get them established. The committees must understand that they are doing something meaningful and of benefit. The more autocratic the department has been in the past, the more difficult this process will be. Second, the manager must respect the work of the committees. Too many vetoes of recommendations will endanger the process and breed cynicism among committee members. The committees must be provided the time and guidance necessary to make the process work—not just lip service.

Staff Meetings

Full-scale meetings are a major event for department personnel. They make employees feel that management is including them in its plans. These meetings should be formal and regular, with an open forum for discussion and responses to employee concerns. The important point is that the responses are made to the group, not to individuals.

Staff meetings should be utilized to communicate the findings of the committees to the balance of the staff. They then become true "staff" meetings, where communications run both ways: from manager to staff and from staff to manager. Managers presenting information to the staff should be aware that the meetings are important and formal. Preparation should be made and unresolved issues followed up in a formal manner.

The Library/Lounge

Establishing a library, where all periodicals and publications are stored and where adequate facilities are available for the staff to read them, creates an atmosphere of both learning and group gatherings. The opportunity arises, in a professional environment, for members of the staff to discuss technical issues and debate future technological implications. This promotes a sharing of ideas independent of the project orientation that exists at the work station.

A group personality cannot develop when members of the group operate in isolation. This is especially true when conceptual issues are at stake. When inividuals feel that they are less well prepared than their peers, they will either strive to catch up by themselves or retreat from new issues. In either case, there is a sense of being threatened. Although the existence of a library/lounge does not prevent this from happening, it does provide a nonthreatening environment in which people can gather. Before the advent of complete work stations, development people gathered outside the computer room to pick up reports. While this process was inefficient, it did provide a meeting place, at a nonresident location, where they could share ideas. That sharing may not have always resulted in obvious work improvement, but it did allow for a melding of personalities through osmosis. The library/lounge achieves the same result, and in a more professional manner.

The Manager's Presence

In the book *In Search of Excellence,* the concept of managing by observation (MBO) was proposed. This concept states, essentially, that an effective manager operates best when immersed periodically in the environment where the actual work is done. Wandering through the offices and cubicles where development is actually occurring provides a firsthand perception of morale, productivity and progress far beyond what can be achieved in management meetings.

This activity also helps to foster a department personality. A department always reflects, to some degree, the personality of its leader. It is through the dictates and strategy of the department manager that this personality is displayed. When intermediate managers are involved, the communication of that personality will inevitably be diluted. MBO provides an opportunity for the manager to assure the department that the desire for a close, in-control staff is real and that their feelings are understood and respected.

Without this assurance, the staff can easily develop the sense that the concept of a department personality is just another way to keep the troops at bay. Once this attitude takes hold, it is nearly impossible to dispell. The manager must take whatever steps are necessary to keep the momentum going. A department personality is far more frail than an individual personality and requires management's sensitivity to be maintained.

Sharing of Resources

Development departments tend to separate staff members along application lines. The objective is to ensure a competent response to users' requests and rapid correction of problems. While there is some controversy as to how efficient this arrangement is, there is no doubt that it creates significant problems in establishing a general department personality.

Rather than unifying the staff, this separation creates a competitive atmosphere between the application groups. Although competition can be healthy, the type that prevails in development here seldom remains healthy for long.

If there must be segregation along application lines, the department's integration and personality can be protected by sharing the resources among applications on a planned basis. Developers should move from one application area to another in order to ensure that the department personality remains intact and counterbalances any isolation that might develop. As a side benefit, increased support is provided for each application area due to a wider exposure to all applications.

CONCLUSION

The idea of a department personality should not be interpreted as an Orwellian threat to individualism. It is simply a common direction and set of goals and culture which rules the actions of the group as a whole. A department that does not have a common personality presents a disjointed view to the outside world and inevitably finds itself pursuing divergent paths. Formalized strategies and directives cannot substitute for a healthy department personality. There are simply too many choices and interpretations to ensure progress toward a common goal unless the group intimately understands its culture and strategy. The group personality must be ingrained and universally understood.

People are social animals. When they are organized into a department, they inevitably develop a personality. If the manager does not effectively nurture and direct that development in positive ways, the results can be catastrophic. The resulting problems are subtle rather than dramatic: lowered productivity, higher turnover and friction among staff members.

Fostering positive department personality development, understanding the tendencies for its development and taking positive steps using practical methods to maintain it will ensure evolution of the group and provide a productive atmosphere. With the daily pressure to produce systems of high quality and at ever-accelerating rates, the subtle aspects of a department's social environment are often ignored. However, it is precisely these subleties which often govern continued success and effectiveness.

8
HIRING AND CAREER PATHING

As any good development manager knows, the success of the department depends upon the success of its members. Therefore, the acquisition and retention of productive, dedicated people is one of the managers major concerns. The dynamics of the profession make this factor even more critical in development than in other business functions because the technical talents required to perform at peak levels are constantly changing.

Many companies have responded by actively seeking out, in recruiting programs, individuals who possess the technical skills necessary for new software/hardware products being installed. For a new operating system, for example, "experts" in the system are hired to ensure success. When a database system is needed, the first step is to seek employees experienced in that technology.

While this approach does fill technical voids, it unfortunately does not increase the department's portfolio of business expertise. Nor does it ensure an adequate melding of the new individual with a department personality which may have taken years to create and nurture. In fact, the new person, with his or her narrow technical focus, can have a negative effect on the working environment. Alternatively, of course, a person with new talents and attitudes can have a positive effect by infusing new ideas into a group which may be becoming so ingrained in a single approach that their insights are growing stale.

The development manager is constantly faced with this dilemma when replacing people, expanding the department or moving promising people into new areas, either up the ladder or laterally. Often the manager has little choice. There may be a requirement for specific technical expertise to accomplish the task, with no option but to hire from the outside. Conversely, the manager may know that a valuable employee may be lost if he or she has no opportunity to move into a vacated or newly created position. At these times, the manager must be sensitive to the risks inherent in the situation and prepared to take steps to resolve it.

Although departments are made up of people, they are not and cannot be designed specifically for people. They are organized to meet business goals productively and efficiently. Effective managers establish organizational structures to meet those goals and place people in positions where they complement each other and maximize their talents. Organizational matters were discussed in Chapter 4. In this chapter, the issues involved in bringing people into the established environment are dealt with, as well as the means to ensure adequate career pathing within the department.

We begin by discussing the establiment of an overall goal for the department's organization in relation to the people who will make it operate. This creates an atmosphere in which the manager can hire and promote people with a plan in mind, rather than merely reacting to changing needs. We then consider the use of position profiles and their counterpart, position descriptions. In the first case, people are moved into positions; in the second, positions are created for people. With this background information in mind, the primary subjects of creating career paths within the department, as well as recruiting issues, will be covered.

ESTABLISHING AN OVERALL GOAL

Although the manager is sometimes forced to deal with specific and obvious departmental needs, personnel issues should not be reactive—at least, not as a standard mode of operation. The manager must constantly build the department for the future. That future may be dim, perhaps, and transient situations may require departures from the plan, but nonetheless, an effective long-range plan should exist. Without such a plan, the manger has no way of molding the diverse talents within the department into a dynamic force for the company's use. The department will then degenerate into a succession of projects, each with a search for personnel and the problems of where to go when the project is done. This does not breed continuity or efficiency.

Technological change obviously makes planning somewhat difficult. The development of new mechanisms and tools often requires restructuring in the early stages of technology use. This difficulty is less acute than it appears to be, however. Many of the influences can be predicted by experience. Effort and thought are needed to understand the implications, but it can be done.

Just as technology has an impact on planning, so do transient business situations. Economic downturns, major acquisitions and changes in upper management's philosophy can all have a critical influence on the people recruited and the priorities for moving them into new positions. However, even with all of these inescapable situations, effective organizational and personnel planning can be done.

Picture of the Department

Establishing an overall goal for career pathing and recruiting begins with describing the department in terms that aid in meeting the goals. This includes a picture of what the department looks like today, as well as how it will have to change in order to service the company adequately. Two components are necessary for this exercise: the organization and the people needed to fill it.

The Organization. Development departments are predominantly driven by emerging technologies and the tools which allow these technologies to be used. The organization is established to give the company the skills needed to maximize the emerging technologies. The manager must try to determine which technologies will be utilized and how the organization can best present them.

An example of how a manager establishes the organization for emerging technologies can be seen with the advent of the information center. The information center generally develops from the use, by the end user, of PCs and/or decision support software. If the development manager foresees the influx of these products, he or she can predict, to a degree, what role development will play in their use. If it is a consulting role, it may be necessary to hire or train staff to understand the use of these tools and their applications.

A consulting role may not easily fit into the current organizational structure, especially if the department is structured around applications. It may then be necessary to train or hire an individual dedicated to information center issues in one of the groups not allied with a specific application, such as support. Since the manager feels that this individual will eventually form the nucleus of an independent group, the person chosen to fill the role might be one slated to fill a managerial role. Thus, the individual is given an opportunity to gain technical expertise in the initial stages of the operation while providing the managerial talent needed for future expansion.

This process involves more than simply designating an application technician from a particular application group, who has displayed no managerial talent, to handle information center questions. Conflicts arise not only across application areas, because the individual chosen will always favor his or her own user base in the initial stages, but with persons who feel that they are next in line for management when the unit expands.

The People. Just as important as the organization's structure is understanding what people will be necessary to fill the company's future needs. With an idea of how the department will evolve, the manager must ask, "What skills must people possess to make this department work?" When dealing with current needs, the answers and actions are fairly simple—either hire or train. When dealing with the future, the issues are a little more obscure.

In the case of the information center, for example, one cannot simply hire a PC expert to fill perceived need. This person will be either frustrated or underutilized until the concept gains momentum. This can result not only in disruption but also in a compromise of goals as the new employee strives to push the issue faster than the company is capable of absorbing it.

In order to bring the necessary talent into the department, it is far better to seek an individual with an appropriate background who possesses other skills that can be utilized in the interim. In the case of the information center, a staff analyst to fill a support role who tinkers with PCs as a hobby is an appropriate choice. Alternatively, a new programmer or analyst hired from a company with extensive PC or 4GL usage would provide the needed expertise. This allows the individual to grow at the company's pace.

In any case, for the department to grow, both in terms of people and of scope, the manager must have a picture of the department's future organization. This includes the mechanical arrangement of functional units as well as the personnel skills necessary to fulfill these functions. The picture should be clear in the manager's mind and communicated to the staff. This allows continual mapping of current skills and needs in the department's career pathing and hiring.

Picture of the Company

Just as important as a picture of the department is a picture of where the company is headed. Obviously, this is required to ensure adequate product and service coverage but, equally important, it allows the department to keep in step with personnel needs. Corporate evolution can be felt in ways both subtle and obvious.

The general trend from a product to a service orientation is a prime example of subtle effects on personnel development and hiring. People oriented to the production of a product alone are primarily concerned with efficiency and scheduling elegance. They stress the building of systems and the justification of projects on a purely cost/benefit basis. Departments with a predominantly batch processing emphasis mirror this approach when resource usage is scheduled to bring utilization as close as possible to an even, nonvarying level.

A department with a service orientation is considerably different. The primary concern is to give the user or customer information on demand, regardless of utilization impacts. This involves a fundamental change in attitudes and requires a considerable effort on the part of the development manager to bring it about.

Some changes are more obvious, but the personnel action required can be equally complex. The movement of an organization from a centralized to a decentralized or distributed arrangement is not uncommon, nor is the reverse. When distributing the development function, the manager is typically faced with the problem of providing managerial talent at external locations. Without preplanning, this talent is not likely to be available. In addition, when application exposure has been limited to specific groups of employees, the manager finds it difficult to provide the external site with a well-rounded individual. Therefore, when the company appears to be moving toward distribution or decentralization, the manager must take steps to ensure that supporting talent exists. That cannot be done overnight.

All companies, regardless of how staid or conservative they are, evolve. In order for development to support that evolution, it must ensure that its talent pool is in step. Only by constantly monitoring the subtle signals and strategies of the corporation can the manager hope to have the necessary talent ready when the company needs it.

Skill Inventories

With a clear picture of the department's needs and the company's direction, the manager must provide the necessary skills. At any point in time, some of these skills may seen extraneous. But, given the rapid changes that can occur, these skills may have a dramatic impact on the department's ability to react to future situations.

Few managers can keep all of these skills in mind in any but the smallest departments. A formal inventory of skills is required, prepared initially by questionnaire, and updated on an ongoing basis. Optimally, this inventory is automated to the point where it is possible to index the data on a composite basis when the need arises. Table 8–1 shows a typical skills inventory portfolio for an individual. Figure 8–1 shows some sample composite data pulled form a fairly large development staff.

An extensive skills inventory not only allows the manager to identify specific available skills but also shows which necessary talents are lacking in the staff. For example, if the strategy being developed indicates a general movement to database technology, the manager can determine if any staff members have been exposed to that technology. If not, the next person hired may be required to have database experience even though no such

Table 8-1. Sample Individual Skills Inventory

NAME: John Q. Smith CURRENT POSITION: Analyst—Level 2

ORGANIZATIONAL UNIT: New Systems Development

PREVIOUS ORGANIZATIONAL UNITS: Production Support

MANAGEMENT EXPERIENCE: Project Management (Medium Scale) Outside Remote Site Support Internal—Akron Plant

DATABASE EXPERIENCE: PRODUCT/MONTHS

IDMS	12	ADABASE	4	ENVIRON		OVERALL	32
IMS		DATACOM/DB		IMAGE	16	OTHER:	
DL1		DMS		PC BASED	9		

COMMUNICATIONS EXPERIENCE: PRODUCT/MONTHS

CICS	12	NOMAD		OTHER:	OVERALL	12
DATACOM/DB		SRI				
TSO	6	PC BASED	9			

FILE/DATA STRUCTURES: PRODUCT/MONTHS

SEQUENTIAL	42	ISAM		CHAINING	6	INDEXING	12
DIRECT	12	QSAM	09	LIST		OTHER:	
HASHING	6	VSAM		LINK		OVERALL:	48

OPERATING SYSTEMS: PRODUCT/MONTHS

MVS	18	VS 1/2		MCP	9	DOS	
VSE	12	VM	9	UNIX		OTHER	

SOFTWARE PRODCUTS: PRODUCTS/MONTHS

SAS		SPF		SYSTEM2000		JARS	
FOCUS		ROSCOE		LISP		SIM3270	
RAMIS		SCRIPT		OSCAR			

APPLICATION EXPERIENCE: SYSTEM/MONTHS

DEMAND DEPOSIT:	9	CURR EXCHANGE	3	PROOF/TRANSIT	
INSTALL LOAN:	12	PERSONNEL	08	MIS	
PERSONAL TRUST	4	GEN LEDGER	7	OTHER:	
CORP TRUST		ACCTS PAYABLE	12		

Note: For brevity, the categories and entries for this skills inventory example were limited. In the typical medium-sized to large organization, one may find twenty to thirty entries for any one category and categories ranging from the specific (graphics, robotics, etc.) to the very general (languages). Additionally, categories and products should be periodically purged as they become obsolete or obscure.

knowledge is immediately needed. It is also possible that a skills inventory may be the deciding factor in determining which database management system is chosen, given abundant exposure to one product over another.

In any case, the inventory of skills represents the available talents and capabilities at the manager's disposal. When matched with the picture of where the department and the company are going, they form the backbone

SELECTION CRITIERIA: Database Experience
Product = Image·
Secondary Level = 36 Months Any Database
Tertiary Level = Project Management = Medium

STAFF PROFILE: 300 Potential

MEET ALL CRITERIA: 4

John Doe Jane Smith Ernest Gamble Georgine Barefoot

STAFF COMPOSITE:

DATABASE EXPERIENCE:
0 months = 50 (17%)
6 months = 60 (20%)
12 months = 100 (33%)
>12 months = 90 (30%)

IMAGE EXPERIENCE:
0 months = 250 (83%)
6 months = 10 (3%)
12 months = 36 (12%)
>12 months = 4 (2%)

PROJECT MANAGEMENT:
0 months = 200 (67%)
6 months = 25 (8%)
12 months = 50 (17%)
>12 months = 25 (8%)

Note: Obviously, a skills inventory search capability yields considerable benefit in many areas of the organization. It is of particular value for systems development due to the wide range of potential product and application needs as well as the dynamics of product usage and experience priority.

Figure 8-1. Sample skills inventory query.

in establishing a rational career pathing and recruiting strategy. Neither issue can be effectively addressed without an intimate knowledge of the base upon which the manager is building.

An overall goal contains all of the components that the manager considers important when building a department for the future. In includes a view of where the company is going and how the department can best serve it in the future. Since technology will be a major part of that future, and since the development manager is, by definition, an expert in technology, he or she must lead the way in planning technological services. Understanding what people are needed and in what roles is the key to achieving that goal. It begins with the picture of the future, is augmented by an understanding of the skills available today, and is accomplished by career pathing and effective recruiting.

PROFILES AND POSITION DESCRIPTIONS

In Chapter 3, the subject of organization was discussed with an emphasis on understanding the responsibilities of each component of the department. It is extremely important for the manager to understand, from both a conceptual and a practical point of view, how the department operates. That operation must be understood in terms of the work of each subgroup, as well as the interdependencies that exist among them.

In order to ensure that departmental commitments are met, the responsibilities of each individual and position must be carefully defined. These individual responsibilities, and the skills necessary to meet them, represent the group and the department. When the descriptions and profiles of the staff members do not match the charters of the department and/or subgroups, the overall responsibilities of the department will not be met. A department may operate effectively for a time without profiles and descriptions, but eventually, as new people come in or new positions are occupied, the unwritten responsibilities will be open to interpretation. And not all staff members will interpret them as the manager intended.

The purpose of position descriptions and job profiles is twofold. First, as discussed, they ensure that the responsibilities of the department are fully met. They are one of the ways the manager tailors a department, even though every individual cannot be directly supervised. Second, they provide the framework for career pathing and the criteria for hiring. While descriptions and profiles will evolve along with the department, they represent a level of stability which allows employees to plan long-term futures and take the steps necessary to execute those plans.

Job Profiles

A job profile describes the duties and skills necessary to meet responsibilities, with gradient levels, within the department. They tend to be generic and are based on general skills applicable to several subgroups within the department. In order to be adequately translated into specific day-to-day responsibilities, they must be used in concert with the charter of the group.

Figure 8–2 is a sample job profile for an analyst's position. It can be seen that the skills and responsibilities match several groups within the organizations described in Chapter 3. Regardless of whether the individual works in the database area, new systems development, or support, the responsibilities and skills presented here do not change. However, when viewed in concert with the charters of the group, it can be seen that in one area the individual is judged on an ability to define and maintain data integrity and in another area on the ability to translate user needs into operable project definitions.

POSITION TITLE: Analyst III

ORGANIZATION UNIT: MIS—Systems Development

SCOPE

- Works independently on complex information systems projects and supervises junior analysts on less complex projects.
- Provides technical expertise to non-systems development personnel for supported and approved system products.

PRIME RESPONSIBILITIES

- Performs systems analysis in accordance with accepted policies, procedures and current techniques on all approved projects.
- Ensures that developed systems meet all design and performance criteria as outlined in policies and standards.
- Evaluates impact of potential systems or enhancements on the operating environment maintained by MIS.
- Evaluates end user developed systems to ensure that the integrity of corporate information is maintained.
- Cooperates with the supported user base to develop plans for information usage and potential new applications to service business needs.
- Develops specifications for construction of applications and/or databases for use by development staff and end users.

DECISION-MAKING AUTHORITY

- Recommends certification of end user developed systems based upon integrity, performance and operating standards.
- Approves specifications developed by junior analysts.
- Approves design documents prepared by programmers and data analysts.
- Certifies that systems to be implemented have met all end user requirements.

SKILL REQUIREMENTS

- In-depth knowledge of generic applications in use by serviced business units.
- Exposure to design and operating characteristics of database, communications and systems software employed in serviced applications.
- Working knowledge of current techniques and methodologies of the development department.
- Ability to solve complex business problems through the use of accepted methodologies.
- Well-developed communication skills, both oral and written, with an emphasis on presentation techniques at the senior management level.

REPORTING RELATIONSHIPS

- Reports administratively to the first-level manager in systems development
- Reports to the project manager during specific project assignments.
- Has no functional reporting responsibilities beyond those stated.

(cont.)

Figure 8-2. Sample position profile.

CAREER PATH

- ENTRY: Analyst II, Recruiting, Technical specialist II
- UPWARD: Project manager, mid-level technical services, first-level manager of computer operations

RECRUITING GUIDELINES

- University degree in computer science or a related business curriculum
- Seven years' experience in MIS, at least three in analysis
- Four years' experience in insurance field
- At least one years' experience with supported database management system, communications system and operating systems

Figure 8-2. (Continued)

The gradient levels would be equally generic. A variety of experience is generally the primary criterion for advancement. Regardless of the area serviced, this continues to be the most important factor. Increasing technical proficiency is not the criterion for advancement, but rather for performance evaluation. The profiles represent an increasing set of responsibilities rather than an increased capability in performing specific duties.

Profiles are drawn with long-term growth as the primary consideration. Like organization charts, profiles are drawn *before* names are filled in. They represent an abstract picture of the department, without consideration of the talent pool available to fill the responsibilities. In all likelihood, after preparing the profiles, the manager will find that significant gaps exist, that is, that the personnel within the department do not have all the skills required to fill the profiles.

These gaps are as important to the manager as the places where the needs of the positions are completely filled. They form the basis for training, establishment of careeer paths, and criteria for future recruitment. As these gaps are filled, a comprehensive department will arise which is more than capable of fulfilling the responsibilities of the company.

Position Descriptions

Position descriptions represent interim roles and are generally tied to specific events. In general, they are linked to personnel as they are drawn up. As such, they can be seen to represent rewards or the authority and skills necessary to accomplish specific tasks. They do not depict long-term career pathing goals, but they can be the most effective vehicle for recruiting needed skills in a start-up situation.

Figure 8-3 is a typical job description, in this case tied to a mainframe conversion requiring extensive decision-making authority. It is not intended

POSITION TITLE: Manager—Mainframe Conversion

ORGANIZATION UNIT: MIS—Systems Development

SCOPE

- Plans, directs and executes conversion of hardware and software from installed mainframe computer systems to new generation of equipment.
- Develops, recommends and implements new or enhanced procedures, policies and standards necessary to reflect maximum use of new equipment.

KEY RESPONSIBILITIES

- Development of strategic and tactical plans for the migration of old hardware and software to new generation of equipment.
- Presentation of status, schedule and budget to senior management on a bimonthly basis and MIS management on a monthly basis.
- Recruiting of necessary external staff to augment hardware/software expertise within development.
- Provision of education and experience for all MIS staff members to maximize efficiency by project completion date.
- Selection and installation of necessary systems software to utilize new equipment efficiently.

DECISION-MAKING AUTHORITY

- Authority over allocation and scheduling of interim equipment not used for production applications.
- Work assignment for all personnel temporarily transferred to conversion project.
- Negotiation of contracts for temporary personnel services.

FINANCIAL RESPONSIBILITY

- Budget responsibility for Cost Center 86–253 through conversion life

ESTIMATED TIME PERIOD OF POSITION

- Three years from project initiation

RECRUITING GUIDELINES

- Candidate is incumbent staff member—no back-fill involved

Figure 8-3. Sample position description.

to represent any responsibility beyond the end of the project, but it is necessary to legitimatize the responsibilities needed for that period. (In this example, the period was three years—a career in many MIS organizations.)

Descriptions in a department are nearly always needed because the rapid evolution of development requires extraordinary approaches to specific needs. Specialized technical needs can often burst in on a department despite all of the planning involved. The manager may not be able to envision how the required skills will fit into the long-term department picture, but the need must be filled nonetheless. In this case, a position description is the optimum means of identifying the responsibilities and skills required for the new position. It does not disturb the continuity of the normal career pathing and allows the new function to blend in with the department naturally. When the new role has stabilized and been absorbed, it can be worked into the normal profile scheme.

Salary considerations are another primary reason for establishing descriptions. The acquisition of a new skill or recognition of expanded scope, however temporary, may require a salary beyond what is defined by the general profile scheme. In this case, the description is an appropriate way to accommodate the need.

The principal problem with job descriptions is that, while they are intended for an interim situation, they live on long afterward. The result is a hodgepodge of job titles and overlapping responsibilities where career paths are vague at best. (The author was once involved in a company with over forty job descriptions, all active, for a department of twenty people. The descriptions were used almost exclusively for salary adjustment. If a higher salary was required, the individual was "promoted" from analyst/programmer to programmer/analyst. The differences in responsibilities and scope were purely cosmetic. The individual's real job underwent no change.)

It is important that descriptions and profiles remain separate and distinct in the minds of the staff or the individuals filling those roles. Profiles represent long-term career paths and ensure the department's ability to fulfill its charter. Descriptions represent interim steps to accomplish specific goals.

Developing Profiles and Descriptions

The responsibility for establishing a well-rounded set of profiles and job descriptions falls on the development manager. The manager may not actually do the work, but he or she must provide the criteria and give final approval. This is the manager's mechanism for establishing the department's direction.

Figure 8–4 outlines the steps generally followed in establishing profiles and descriptions. No differentiation is made between those needed for a description or a profile. The steps do not change, only the content.

The human resources department must be intimately involved in the effort. They can provide the expertise necessary to speed the change and are most capable of tying the resulting profiles and descriptions to salary ranges. The salary ranges are extremely important in finding and keeping qualified people. Profiles and descriptions must result in a salary structure which allows the department to compete in the salary market. If one cannot draw the people to fill the resulting profiles, the elegance and effectiveness of these profiles will be a moot point.

The following are the typical steps used to develop profiles and descriptions.

1. ESTABLISH DEPARTMENTAL RESPONSIBILITIES
   The source of these responsibilities is the department charter. It represents a composite of all responsibilities within development and, where applicable, those shared among groups.

2. IDENTIFY BROAD PROCESS STEPS NEEDED TO MEET FUNCTIONAL RESPONSIBILITIES
   The result is a list, within each functional activity, of the tasks needed to complete the process. (For example, to construct a system, needs must be analyzed, specifications developed, programs written and tested, etc.)

3. IDENTIFY WHICH STEPS SHOULD BE PERFORMED BY SEPARATE GROUPS
   This ties the steps to organizational units and shows when specific profiles are needed.

4. IDENTIFY THE SKILLS NECESSARY TO ACCOMPLISH THE TASKS
   Provides the technical and administrative skills required by the department.

5. RELATE THE SKILL AND PROCESS STEPS TO INDUSTRY STANDARDS
   When developing profiles, it is important to relate them clearly to the titles, scope, and responsibilities most often seen in the industry. This allows more effective recruiting and ensures that the resultant descriptions can be appropriately tied to technology.

6. ADAPT SKILL REQUIREMENTS TO LOCAL STANDARDS
   Endemic educational profiles and available backgrounds should be a component of job profiles. It is fruitless to require a background which cannot be found locally across the entire staff.

7. CREATE REASONABLE GRADIENT LEVELS FOR EACH PROFILE
   Gradient levels (junior, senior, etc.) are best established by breaking down either total years of experience or scope of responsibility into manageable steps. This allows promotion within a discipline over a number of years. Generally, three levels within a position are adequate.

8. APPLY SALARY SCALES TO POSITIONS
   This is generally a two-step process. First the human resources department applies salary grades based on whatever formula is in use. The results are generally reworked based on local standards.

9. MIGRATE TO THE NEW PROFILES
   People should be moved into the new profiles over a period of time. Optimally, this movement coincides with their upcoming review. Extending the period allows new positions to be absorbed rather than providing a traumatic change.

Figure 8-4. Typical steps in developing profiles and descriptions.

The realities of technology may also require some profiles to be more specific than usual. For example, if the department emphasizes the database analyst, the application or support analyst, it may have to develop independent profiles for this position. There is nothing inherently wrong with this type of trade-off as long as the manager fully understands the implications.

CAREER PATHING

Career pathing is the production of a road map through the department, and potentially into and out of the department, by which employees can take steps to advance their careers. This road map is tied to the skills the employee must develop and refine, the responsibilities which must be accepted and satisfied, and the challenges involved in each successive position occupied. Merely presenting the road map to the staff is not an acceptable career pathing process. What is also needed is active participation by the manager and the employee in the process, as well as a thorough understanding of its goals.

With the increased education required of the typical development staff member, a visible career path has taken on added importance. Employees are thinking beyond the challenges of today and placing major importance on how their goals will be met in the future. This heightened concern has outstripped the ability of most departments to provide a clear picture of the future, which is one of the major reasons for development's chronically high turnover rates. Employees will find a way to satisfy their advancement goals—if not with the current employer, then with another.

For the company and the department, a well-founded career pathing mechanism reaps enormous benefits. It allows the positions to be filled internally, avoiding considerable recruiting and training costs. It avoids the loss of time incurred in immersing new employees in the corporate culture to make them productive. Most importantly, it allows planning to deal with fewer variables. It is much easier to plan programs if the talent to make those programs work is either available in-house or will be with some training and exposure.

Career Pathing Mechanisms

The primary ingredient in successful career pathing is well-established job profiles. These profiles must state specifically what an employee must do to move from one level to another or change directions—for instance, from applications to database. The total job profile package should be available to all department employees, complete with salary ranges. This allows employees some latitude in planning their careers and gives them responsibility for managing their own careers rather than deferring that responsibility to their manager.

The staff should understand the profile mechanism and be able to relate it to the strategy of the department. If programmers are rated lower than analysts because the department plans to move from internal to purchased software, the employees must understand the rationale. They can then make their own career choices. If they wish to remain programmers, they need to reconcile themselves to the lower end of the department scale or seek opportunities elsewhere. If they seek further advancement, they can begin to focus on analytical skills. In either case, they will be dealing with facts rather than rumors.

The second major factor in career pathing relates to the maintenance of the program. This responsibility falls on two groups: development and human resources. Each group's involvement will vary from company to company, based primarily on the influence exerted by human resources. However, each group must provide the input associated with its own expertise.

Development must include the new issues of technology in the profiles and responsibilities. These issues, such as the introduction of fourth-generation capabilities, can dramatically alter skill requirements and career paths. Human resources must maintain salary parity across job levels in order to remain in a healthy competitive position. Optimally, human resources is also the contact point for employees who are planning career steps because this department offers a more objective perspective than development itself.

Career Planning

Career planning consists of counseling in which employee and manager match the employee's career goals with the department's opportunities. The employee's perception of goals may be somewhat blurred and subject to change. The profile of the department's opportunities is also subject to change as new technologies and methods evolve. Therefore, career planning is a continuing process.

The primary goal of career planning is to establish a plan by which employees are exposed to needed skills and develop those skills by their own efforts. Employees then see the department as meeting their career plans instead of seeking satisfaction elsewhere. The department must allow employees to fulfill these goals by providing positions and opportunities for the employee to display the acquired skills. If a plan is followed by the employee and no result is achieved, a planning program will produce more negative than positive results.

For larger departments, an individual other than the manager should be designated to maintain plans and assist in career planning. This eliminates the employees concern that his or her plans may not be congruent with the manager's perception of what the employee should desire. Often employees state their goals in terms that will be approved by their managers. This ensures that merit increases and good project assignments will occur.

However, a career plan must further the individual's goals, and the individual should feel free to express these goals without fear. The objective facilitator of these goals is far more likely to aid the employee than the subjective views of the manager. Confidence in the confidentiality of the counseling sessions is equally important. The individual chosen to coordinate these plans should cooperate with the individual's manager, but not to the point of revealing the discussions conducted to develop the plan.

Benefits of Career Pathing

Formal career pathing mechanisms and the planning activities that support them provide obvious benefits to employees. They gain the perspective of long-term goal satisfaction, along with a commitment by the corporation to help them succeed. They also understand the options available if their career plans change. Left to themselves, most people do not establish a formal plan for their career. The company-backed pathing and planning provides the help needed to create that plan.

The benefits of career pathing achieved by the corporation help justify the expense and effort involved. These benefits also justify the efforts of the development manager even when the program does not receive active support by upper management.

First and foremost, career pathing tends to reduce turnover—at least the factors directly associated with salary levels and perceived career gains. People generally dislike changing jobs. If they feel that their career can be advanced by their current employer, they are far more likely to stay. When career pathing is first employed, some initial turnover may result from the publicizing of future plans and relative scaling of positions. For example, the programmer in a department that deemphasizes in-house development may quickly seek other employment. This is generally a temporary situation, however, and the department is merely losing an individual who would have left anyway when the strategy became apparent.

Second, career pathing increases the probability that employees will gravitate to the positions they are most capable of filling. They will not move to analysis, for example, simply because of the title or of what the term means in their neighbor's department. Therefore, the people filling analysis positions are more likely to be those who wish to perform analytical tasks. This ensures increased productivity over time.

Third, career pathing emphasizes the matching of skills to positions. This means that when individuals move to higher levels in the department, they will already have spent time honing the skills necessary for the new role. Programmers will develop senior programmer skills before they fill that role rather than afterward.

Fourth, career pathing implies cooperation between management and the employee. It makes employees resonsible for deciding what they want from their career rather than drifting until they decide that they should be somewhere else. There is nothing more disturbing for a manager than to promote one individual and have three others state that they wanted the position when the manager had no idea that they were actively interested in it.

Salary Considerations

Surveys over the past several years have indicated that, for the typical professional, salary is not among the top four or five motivators. Factors, such as challenge and job satisfaction tend to rank higher. However, even if salary is not an important goal, it does represent a basic statement of the employee's stature and importance to the company. Therefore, regardless of survey results, salary is a major component of career pathing.

When job profiles are established and grade levels are set, salary ranges are established for each position. Most often these ranges are set by persons outside of the development department using obscure formulas to translate responsibilities and skills into salary midpoints. The criteria used may range from the number of persons managed to a complex combination of action-verbs. However they are derived, the development manager, working with the human resources department, must ensure that the levels are rational and competitive.

If salaries are not competitive, the department is likely to become a training ground for other companies, regardless of the logic of the career pathing. If they are not rational, people will move to positions they are not truly interested in simply to secure the salary they want. The manager must ensure that the salary provided across the employee's career plan represents only one factor and not the primary motive.

RECRUITING

Despite the attention paid to career pathing, the development manager always needs to recruit new personnel. External recruiting will be discussed here. Internal recruiting generally is subject to corporate policies and procedures (job-posting guidelines, etc.), and once the applicants are identified, the process closely follows that of external recruiting. Some preference is certainly paid to internal applicants, but the process is similar.

Recruiting is a risky proposition. Decisions on applicants must be based upon relatively short exposure, perceptions are often based on the image the applicant presents, and an unknown element is being injected into a department which may be operating extremely well. Therefore, the process should be undertaken with considerable care and planning.

Like career pathing, recruiting begins with the establishment of job profiles and organizational planning. Although recruiting may not be the prime concern when those profiles were developed, they do define the guidelines for the individuals who will eventually be hired. Except for temporary needs, which are accommodated by job descriptions, the profiles should be the basis for the recruiting program.

Reasons for Recruiting

Given an established department, there are two reasons why a recruiting program should be undertaken: to fill gaps resulting from turnover or reassignment within the department, and in response to the department's expansion. Even with these reasons, however, the first priority is to provide opportunities to staff members. Employees hired from the outside must be exposed to company policies and attitudes, which can require anywhere from three to twelve months. It is far better to make this effort with junior rather than senior people.

Filling Departmental Gaps. Regardless of the attempts to determine how new technology will influence the company, it will sometimes be necessary to recruit experts from the outside rather than to train them internally. At times, this need can be so acute that there is no opportunity to utilize internal personnel.

The principal difficulty in recruiting from the outside is that there is little knowledge within the department with which to judge the applicant's capability. The manager can sometimes ask the vendor to aid in the interview process, either by providing a list of questions or by participating directly. Often, however, policies preclude the vendor's active participation, and the manager is left to his own devices. Competent external recruiters can fill the gap at times, but they are often more difficult to find than competent technicians.

Without adequate help in the recruitment process, the manager is left with background checking to satisfy his needs. While background checks tend to yield subjective evaluations, when coupled with a knowledge of the department's sophistication, they can fill the gap. In any case, every avenue should be followed to ensure the applicant's technical competence when his or her capability cannot be judged by those within the department.

Generally, some departmental expertise does exist. If so, the manager should include the most competent staff person in the interview process. As will be seen later in this section, technical competence is not the prime ingredient in a prospective employee. However, there is no reason why the necessary expertise cannot be acquired.

Hiring managers is somewhat more risky. While it should be avoided if possible, there are times when it is necessary. Since management requires a far more subtle combination of skills and attitudes, the techniques used to hire technicians do not often work. However, the risk in hiring a manager can be significantly reduced if the following three guidelines are used.

First, search for a leadership background rather than technical expertise. There is a tendency in systems development to be overly impressed with strong technical skills.

Second, try to determine the applicant's views on critical company personality issues. It can take a great deal of time to find out that a manager is out of sync with company and department cultures. Much damage can be done during that time.

Third, understand what background attributes are important. Is industry experience the predominant consideration, or is exposure to a certain scale of operation more important? One cannot always choose backgrounds, but it is important to know what the *key* elements are.

Departmental Expansion. Departmental expansions which occur in response to increased automation can easily be handled by normal career pathing. Recruiting may be necessary to back-fill the open positions resulting from promotion and transfer, but this can be accomplished utilizing university and/or trade schools as a source of applicants. Extensive background reviews are seldom necessary and the flexibility of graduating students generally precludes the introduction of negative habits into the department.

However, at times, the expansion of a department can be more traumatic, as in a decentralization program, a corporate acquisition or expansion of functional responsibilties. When these and other dramatic events occur, the manager must often hire many new employees, at all levels, from outside the company. The principal drawback of this situation is that during the recruitment and integration of the new people, the numbers involved precludes the concentrated attention given a single new employee. Hence, the impact of new people, for better or worse, is difficult to judge.

The manager should approach this influx of new people precisely the same way as he does in setting up a new staff. It is necessary to return to the profiles, charters and strategies to ensure that the new employees fit the department profile. There is a tendency to hire a certain number of people who are the most impressive. Inevitably, this practice breeds conflict within the incumbent staff as well as among the new employees.

Recruiting Guidelines

It is nearly impossible to remove all emotion from the recruiting process. Since the process involves human beings, emotions should always play some part. However, they should become a factor only after sound, sensible judgment takes place. The following guidelines provide a framework to judge potential employees.

Matching the Technical Need. Before beginning the recruiting process, determine what technical skills are being sought. Extend the list to include the skills and background which complement the plans of the department as well as providing cross-function support. For each item on the list, define what substitutes can be made when precise matches are not possible. For instance, it may be desirable to find an individual with a specific database background, such as IMS (IBM's prime database). However, if this experience is not available, exposure to any formal database management system may suffice.

Once these required skill sets are established, adhere to them. It is easy to be impressed with alternate skills and consider reshuffling the staff to take advantage of them. This can easily result in a severe morale problem and involves the additional risk of reducing support in precisely the area where it is needed. If the organizational structure is sound and the recruiting plan is sensible, do not risk compromising either of them.

Melding with the Department. Although technical expertise is essential in fulfilling the development department's responsibilities, it is far more important to hire an individual who fits in with the department personality. Technical skills can be developed through training and exposure, but personality traits are difficult to alter. A highly skilled technician who does not meld well with the department will quickly become frustrated and will not live up to his or her potential.

Injecting new blood into a department can produce positive results. Whenever a new employee is hired, both this person and the incumbent staff require some adjustment. However, too dramatic an adjustment will not work, and the carefully nurtured department personality can be jeopardized. It is therefore critical to judge the applicant on the basis of how well he or she will fit in.

Melding with the Company. The concept of a corporate culture has become a clarion call of most coporations today. Even when not explicitly defined, some culture is evident in a company or, often, an industry. Insurance companies are generally conservative, while high-technology companies tend to be dynamic. These characteristics are pervasive and must be a consideration when recruiting.

Job applicants should be judged on the basis of how well they will fit into the company culture. While some staff members will operate entirely within the department, many will deal with other departments at some time.

How well their recommendations and efforts are received often depends more on how they are presented than on their inherent quality. When there is a dramatic mismatch between the employee and the company, it is very difficult for that individual to be productive.

Involving the Staff. Applicants should be interviewed by as many people as possible, including not only managers but a few staff members as well. This provides the manager with the widest variety of opinions before making a decision and allows the applicant to meet potential co-workers. Thus, there should be no surprises for either party on the first day on the job. A wide range of interviewers reduces that risk.

Involving the staff also strengthens the concept of a department personality. If this idea is truly important to the manager, the members of the staff should be involved. It makes the hiring decision more of a group activity than a management choice.

Final Decision Criteria. When departmental involvement occurs, the manager should exercise veto power over any hiring decision but should not hire anyone to whom the group is opposed. The manager can cast the deciding vote, but it is extremely unwise to proceed contrary to the wishes of the larger group for several reasons. First, the reversal of the group's decision puts the entire process in question. Second, the manager should understand that the new employee would join the department bearing a stigma—no one wanted him but the boss. Third, the staff has a far better picture than the manager of how the department operates and reacts to personalities. They may not be able to vocalize their opinion as well or as objectively, but their understanding is implicit.

Using Professional Recruiters. In most cases, the use of a professional recruiter can significantly ease the hiring process. The recruiter provides an additional screen and, hopefully, brings in applicants who have a high probability of matching the manager's needs. However, there are good recruiters and bad, and the difference can be very difficult to discern. There are two main rules to remember when dealing with recruiters.

First, avoid recruiters who "shotgun" resumes. They are obviously not doing much screening process, and it is highly unlikely that any one recruiter or firm can quickly find a large number of good applicants in their back-files.

Second, before any recruiting begins, the recruiter should spend a day in the department to understand what is being done, what the plans are, and what type of people fill the staff. Realistically, it is impossible to present people for consideration without understanding the environment in which the potential employee will operate.

CONCLUSION

One of the key ingredients in keeping employees long enough to become productive is the opportunity to pursue their careers within the company. People generally dislike changing jobs and will avoid it if they perceive a future with their current employer.

An effective career pathing program can provide that perception and opportunity. In addition, it allows the manager to focus attention on what the department should look like regardless of the people currently filling the roles. While it is true that people make departments successful, organizations are not established for the employees. They are established to fill a business function, and it is the manager's responsibility to ensure that this purpose is not compromised.

Regardless of how effective career pathing is, there is always a need to recruit new people. Recruiting programs, whether dealing with one new person or many, should not be approached cavalierly. Successful programs are based upon a clear understanding of what skills and personality types are being sought. Proceeding without a clear plan and hiring on the basis of an emotional response can have a traumatic impact on the entire department's productivity.

Successful career pathing and recruiting are inseparable components of effective department growth. With a good career pathing program, people tend to stay with the company longer, grow with the enterprise, and increase their contribution to the corporate goal. With such a program in place, the manager is able to control and conduct recruiting programs with specific, well-focused goals in mind. As a vice-president for a large northeastern bank once stated, effective career pathing allows him to "recruit for the bottom" of his organization. This provides maximum flexibility and the widest possible choice of candidates. It is not always possible to have this luxury, but it should be one of the goals in building a department for long-term growth.

9

POLITICS, PRESSURE AND STRESS

Recent studies have indicated that MIS is one of the ten most pressure-filled disciplines. That, comes as no surprise to most professionals who have been in the field for more than a few years. This pressure is exerted for a number of reasons and from a number of sources.

Pressure is a normal part of life. It is, in fact, one of the forces which brings individuals to the height of their capabilities. However, individuals have different thresholds for pressure. When that threshold is crossed, the result is stress. Stress is an unhealthy condition which breeds discontent and creates an atmosphere ripe for staff dissent. It can affect the individual emotionally as well as physically.

There are numerous seminars and books on the subject of dealing with stress, both personally and in business. The real difficulty in dealing with pressure and stress is that it is quite difficult to distinguish between them. Most often, the problem becomes acute before any steps are taken to overcome it.

Social pressures affect us as well. People in a pressured environment are expected to operate well under pressure. This factor is often of primary importance in many performance reviews. In many cases, individuals are assigned to high-pressure projects as part of their development. With this type of conditioning, is it any wonder that a person who is beginning to feel the impact of pressure is loathe to communicate that fact to the manager?

In MIS, and thus systems development, a high-pressure environment is a fact of life. Whether this situation is fair or healthy is, pragmatically speaking, irrelevant. People who wish to pursue a career in the field must accept it and deal with it. However, as we saw in Chapter 6, a wide range of personalities exist in development. The fact that some of them function better under pressure than others does not mean that those with a low threshold for pressure cannot make significant contributions. If the manager is to maintain an effective department and utilize all staff members fully, there must be an understanding of when to shield people from pressure and when pressure exerted on the manager can be directly transmitted to the staff.

Politics are one of the prime causes of pressure and stress in systems development. In negative terms, politics is the imposition of one's will on others for personal gain. In positive terms, it represents normal human interactions with compromises and priorities. What separates these two types of politics is the motivation behind them. If the result for the corporation is positive, it can be considered good, albeit unpleasant for some at times. If it is purely for personal aggrandizement, any gain for the corporation is merely a by-product. That type of political pressure has little place in a healthy management. Unfortunately, it is all too common today and must be dealt with.

This chapter deals with pressure, stress and politics in the everyday activities of systems development. First, we discuss the reasons why development is so vulnerable to these factors. With the constant changes in the discipline, it is important to understand these reasons if the manager is to deal with them intelligently. Second, we discuss the influence of these factors on the development process itself. Next, we analyze the situations in which the manager should or should not shield the staff from political pressures. Finally, how pressure and stress affect the manager's decision-making process closes the chapter.

This chapter is not a comprehensive treatise on the psychological effects of stress and pressure on the individual. That is better left to professional psychologists. Dealing with pressure and stress is important to all of us in coping with our fast-paced society. This chapter highlights what the manager may expect in leading a group of diverse individuals in a high-pressure discipline. In steering the development process, the manager must make trade-offs in order to make the process palatable and successful in the corporation. This requires an understanding of the effects of stress and political pressure.

VULNERABILITY OF SYSTEMS DEVELOPMENT TO PRESSURE

All corporate departments receive their share of pressure and are affected in some way by office politics. While pressure, especially the political variety, is generally exerted on the department manager, some of it is transmitted directly to the staff. The level of pressure each department feels, or its share, is generally governed by the style of the company. In financially driven enterprises, most of the pressure is turned on the finance department. On the positive side, however, this department is invariably given the tools to meet that challenge.

One of those tools is power. In this example, the finance department is able to exert a great deal of power over the other units of the company. Regardless of the style of the company, this pattern prevails. Unfortunately, MIS and development seldom exert such pressure. They are inevitably the recipients.

There are a number of reasons why this pressure is felt so keenly and why development is so vulnerable to it. Pressure results from both internal and external causes.

Internal Causes

Individuals often create and intensify the pressures they feel because of their personality traits. Unimportant projects or aspects of the development process become overwhelming problems simply because these individuals see the project as crucial to their careers or are uncomfortable with some aspect of the process. This is a situation people must deal with and to which managers must be sensitive.

Some of these pressures are directly attributable, or at least more acute, because the individual is involved in systems development. This discipline is marked by constant change and staff members can seldom rely on skills developed over time. They are repeatedly forced to relearn basic aspects of their jobs because a new technology is involved. On-line systems require very different approaches to development than batch systems. Thus, experienced batch analysts or programmers find themselves relearning basic skills and being subjected to reevaluation of their worth. Of course, all wokers are subjected to these changes, but few as often or as dramatically as development personnel.

The constant changes in the company's use of development also places the individual under stress. Analysts find themselves dealing with dramatically different levels of management from project to project. During one project, for a department which considers development unimportant, the analyst deals with clerical people who care little for the effort and see it as threatening. Minimal formal communication is required and management displays little concern. The next project may involve a technologically sophisticated department, whose desire for the system creates a continual set of upper-management status meetings, pressures to take shortcuts and emphasize speed, and extensive revisions in the original design. Either scenario is acceptable if one has the experience and personality to deal with it. However, the process of shifting from one environment to another creates turmoil for the individual. The analyst is uncomfortable and frequently feels less than adequate. Stress is the typical outcome of this situation.

Finally, the fact that the posture of the development department is constantly shifting breeds stress. As these shifts occur, the staff member must learn how to deal with an immediate supervisor over and over again. A sense of discontinuity develops and the staff member finds himself constantly waiting for another change to occur. It is often said in dynamic organizations that if one is unhappy, one need only wait and things will change. This is equally true if one is happy—the likelihood is high that the situation will deteriorate when the next change occurs. Some change is always healthy. Too much change breeds chaos, resulting in lowered productivity for the department and, more critically, added stress for the employees.

External Causes

While situations internal to development can cause significant pressure, external causes can be equally significant and far more difficult for the manager to control. The more advanced the automation of the corporation, the more acute these pressures can become. Development becomes particularly vulnerable as the company shifts from a passive interest in it to an active commitment to technology. While this is an event all development managers work long and hard to create, it is probably the most stressful period a department will experience.

This stress occurs because a significant shift of gears must occur within the department. Historical precedents for dealing with projects, justifications, management reactions, and visibility have to change. Once upper management has made a commitment to development, however, the assumption is that the department will immediately react to the new priority. Another assumption is that the same personnel who operated in the earlier enviornment can and will perform equally well in the new one. Neither assumption is necessarily valid. It takes time, planning and some shifting of people to react to the new corporate posture.

In order to maintain momentum and viability in the eyes of upper management, the development manager is forced to accelerate what would normally be a deliberate, lengthy process. This acceleration is fraught with risk, not only because it may affect the department's performance but also because it increases the stress on personnel. Workers find themselves dealing with users in a dramatically different way, having little time to adjust to new situations, and being asked to take on new or expanded responsibilities for which they have little training and possibly little interest. However, while the risk exists, the manager has little choice but to accelerate the process. The intelligent manager will remain sensitive to this risk and its effects while still attempting to maintain momentum.

As a central service organization, development is constantly on the critical path for projects. Workers are either evaluating needs for justification or constructing the systems to fill those needs. For users/requestors, this role is an absolute fact—at least from their perspective. Therefore, they tend to have little understanding of development's principal contributions to the project: control, discipline and integrity. Since development personnel generally understand their central role in the process, they do attempt to accelerate it and maintain integrity. This situation creates pressure and brings little positive feedback from the developer's customer—the user.

These and other pressures are constantly being exerted on development. As long as the department's importance to the company continues to grow, the pressure will mount. In most cases, pressure itself is not the prime factor in stress. The crucial factor is the constancy of that pressure and its implications for the basic concept of the development function which causes the pressure to be mutated to stress.

IMPACT OF POLITICAL PRESSURES ON THE DEVELOPMENT PROCESS

While one tends to see the impacts of pressure and stress, whether generated by everyday work or political forces, on people and their productivity, political pressures have a pervasive influence on development itself. These pressures often have a reactionary impact on the process. Assumptions about the quality and integrity of individual process phases may be compromised. Certain phases may be bypassed completely due to time constraints which the developers cannot respond to adequately. (Invariably, the phases bypassed involve tesing or documenting—the very phases which will cause the most difficulty later.)

The compromises created by politics force the development manager to adjust to the will of the user. These compromises almost invariably involve time; the project must be completed in three months rather than six. If no additional resources are available to accelerate the schedule, the only alternative is to alter the process itself; stages must be shortened or eliminated in order to reduce the schedule. It is at this point that the process is most often placed in jeopardy.

The Basic Conflict

In a mature development department, the development of systems is based on established procedures and methodologies. As will be seen in Chapter 12, these components are generally adaptations of industry standards. All of these standard mechanisms are based on the premise that as each phase of the process is completed, its objectives are fully met. For testing phases, the systems produce specification-defined outputs and do not fail. For documentation phases, all standard documentation exists.

Since any development project includes many phases, the relationships between them become quite complex. By-product outputs from the first phase may become critical inputs to the final phase. Given the principal objectives of the first phase, these outputs may appear obvious targets for compromise, but a significant problem will occur if they are affected—a problem well out of proportion to their perceived importance. Regardless of how well the standard mechanisms are adapted to the specific company and how well they are trimmed of excess, the development process is complex and highly interdependent. These characteristics, complexity and interdependence, define the nature of the process.

Conflict arises because compromises on projects invariably involve a compression of time. When resources are available, this can be done without affecting phase outputs, at least up to a point. Unfortunately, few managers have the luxury of an unaligned resource pool. Therefore, the options are generally narrowed to elimination of seemingly noncritical components of the process. However, seldom are any components truly noncritical, and the manager effectively mortgages the future by eliminating elements of the process.

The traditional reaction has been to produce estimates which allow for this eventual compression and provide a buffer zone in which to compromise. The theory, of course, is that the manager will be able to compromise away the time which was never really necessary, leaving enough time to complete the project following the normal process. In some cases, this inflation of estimates is a conscious step based on historical precedents: if management typically insists that the systems be produced in 80% of the estimated time, the first estimate is inflated to 125% of the actual requirement. At other times this inflation is nearly subconscious, typically reflected in the use of nonrepresentative estimating methodologies which the manager knows will yield high estimates. In either case, the result is the same—the manager has leeway in order to compromise.

The problem with this approach is that eventually the manager is taken to task. The most common way is for management to reduce the first-phase estimate automatically by a factor and then begin the compromise process. Another way is to accept the estimate as is and simply defer projects because the cost is too high. Deferring projects that are otherwise justifiable reduces the manager's market. The customer base shrinks, along with the department's importance to the company.

The avoidance of unreasonable compromise in the development process varies dramatically from company to company. There is nothing like a good performance track record in allowing the development manager to stand firm on estimates and time frames. Without it compromise is inevitable, and until that track record can be built up, the manager is left to determine what can be compromised without causing undue pain later on.

The most reasonable approach for the manager attempting to respond to political demands while establishing a track record is to compromise on the scope of the project rather than on the process itself. In this fashion, the user is given a quality product even though it may not be the total product desired—at least in its initial implementation. Subsequent phases may expand the system out to the point where it meets all of the user's needs. This has the added benefit of lowering phase risks simply because less is being attempted at each phase.

When phase activities must be sacrificed, they should be as visible as possible, so that they are least likely to be forgotten by both the requestor and the developer. For example, rather than produce minimal documentation, produce none. Eventually, development will be allowed to complete that aspect of the process because the end user and management will be maximally affected by the results of the compromise. Never reduce those activities which are invisible to the outside world or which help development to perform well. Those components will never receive priority, and development will be the only department to pay the price.

When political pressure is exerted, the development manager must always remember that development is a highly complex, interrelated process. Sacrificing components of that process may yield short-term advantages when dealing with politically powerful executives. Processes do not tire or complain when they are compromised, as people do. However, the results of such sacrifices are pervasive and often cumulative. Any alternative to compromising the process once it is well tuned and responsive, should be considered. If the process must be altered in response to outside pressure, this should be done with a thorough understanding of the implications and never done quietly.

DEALING WITH IMPACTS ON PERSONNEL

The vulnerability of development to exteral and internal pressure not only places the process in jeopardy but also has a major impact on personnel. The morale and productivity of the staff often suffer. Not all people handle pressure equally well, and all too often, managers tend to equate failure with an inability to handle this pressure.

However, the ability to maintain high productivity under pressure is not the only criterion of success. The effective manager uses all the skills of the staff to reach the department's goals. In order to take maximum advantage of those skills, the manager understands when to shield the staff from pressure and when that pressure can be most advantageously transmitted. Much of the manager's success is attributed to this ability to transmit pressure selectively to the staff. That selectiveness must take into account both the situation and the capabilities and limits of staff members. This is not easy to accomplish.

Perspectives on Pressure

One of the factors that make managers successful is their ability to handle pressure. Development's centralized service role, as discussed earlier, creates pressure from a variety of sources in the company. The manager of development who wishes to succeed must be able to contend with this pressure on a constant basis.

In some cases, a technical specialist may rise to the role of manager. While there are a few exceptions, the pure technician is, by personality, ill-equipped to handle political pressure and stress. The technician's world is black and white; gray areas tend to be upsetting. While that individual may contribute greatly to the department's growth, the day-to-day pressures and compromises required in dealing with upper management eventually spells the technician's downfall. (This situation is not universal, although it is general enough to represent the norm. The author once dealt with a development manager who considered himself a pure technician. However, his long tenure with the firm in a variety of roles had secured him a base of power and respect not usually associated with the manager of development. That fact, more than technical strength, contributed to his success.)

Therefore, the successful manager is well equipped to deal with day-to-day pressures. That ability is intuitive enough so that the manager is often unaware that pressure is being exerted. Unfortunately, this lack of awareness causes difficulty in determining how and when to shield personnel from pressure. It is a matter of perspective and mind set. Overcoming this problem requires considerable sensitivity on the part of the manager. There is a need to consider when to shield staff members from pressure and when to transmit that pressure directly.

Pressure seldom results in clear feedback that the manager can measure. Far too much emphasis has been placed on handling stress and pressure well for employees to admit to themselves, much less their manager, that pressure is beginning to affect their performance. It is for the manager to determine that fact and to blend transmission of pressure with shielding in order to achieve an effective mean.

When to Shield the Staff

It is unreasonable to expect a manager to shield employees from pressure constantly or to shield all employees. First, adapting to pressure is the only way an employee can grow in the corporate environment. It is analogous to the normal maturation of a person in the world. Second, it is unreasonable to expect managers to absorb all the pressure exerted on the department. There is just so much that any person can handle without suffering from burnout.

However, an organizational structure implies that each succeeding level absorbs some pressure as it is transmitted downward. The manager of development, and direct reporting managers, must understand their staffs well enough to determine how and when this shielding will take place. While the personality profiles, as discussed in Chapter 6, provide the basis for this judgment for individuals and job classes, there are a few situations the manager must carefully monitor.

For the new employee, especially the young one, it is important to provide nearly total protection from pressure. Adapting to a new environment or role is difficult enough without having to determine when to satisfy whom for reasons that defy concrete justification. With new employees, the objective is to teach them how things are done. Forcing them to deal with compromises too early will prevent their adaptation to the methods and procedures the department requires to achieve consistency.

For the new reporting manager or project leader, protection from pressure is equally important. This provides an atmosphere where the rising individual can learn the job and develop a relationship with the reporting staff in the most advantageous manner. At some point, new roles do require acceptance of increased pressure, but this is best accomplished slowly and deliberately. There is a temptation, especially when the new person is taking over the manager's role, to adopt a sink-or-swim approach and force that person to fill in immediately. This certainly relieves the manager of any additional burden. However, if the manager is building for a long-term future, it is wise to give the rising individual every possible opportunity for success. Shielding this person from pressure until he or she is optimally equipped to handle it is by far the best course.

Finally, employees who do not handle pressure well should be kept away, as much as possible, from situations in which they must make politically oriented decisions. They should always be made to understand the political ramifications involved, but should be asked to define the pros and cons of possible alternatives and let the manager make the final decision. The experienced employee—one who does not fit into one of the above two categories—must be made to understand when the manager's decision is motivated by political pressure.

When Not to Shield the Staff

The most obvious way in which pressure is directly transmitted is to senior people and direct managerial reports. These are the people who, like the manager, have risen to a position where adapting to pressure is expected. Their role may not be as political as that of the development manager, nonetheless, much of their performance is predicated on a pressure environment.

There remains the need for the manager to understand which pressures to transfer and which ones to absorb. Organizations are generally structured as a pyramid. This structure applies to pressure transfer just as it does to breadth of control. The assumption is that each succeeding level of the organization absorbs part of the pressure before transferring it to the next level. Without this screening activity, compromises and trade-offs are made at elementary levels where absolute attention to methods and procedures is expected.

There is probably no more difficult aspect of management than understanding how much pressure the staff can handle. It is just as risky for the manager to absorb too much pressure as not enough. The key to success is to achieve a balance whereby all members of the staff operate at their healthy limit of pressure. This requires understanding and sensitivity on the part of the development manager.

EFFECTS OF PRESSURE ON THE DECISION PROCESS

As mentioned earlier, the development process is not very adaptable to pressure. The process is complex and the phases extremely interdependent. The personnel are often expected to function in a number of roles, some of which they are not adequately equipped to handle. The centralized role of the department, with competing user/customers, discourages shifting of people among parallel efforts.

Since process complexities, shifting priorities, and competition for resources are constantly present, development managers must fill the decision-making role of management more often than the average manager. Those decision points are seldom allowed to be technically driven or to follow standard procedures. Most of the time, myriad outside factors confuse and color the issues.

One consequence of the pressures on the development process is that the manager's decisions can have negative effects that are not felt until long after the decision has been made. The opportunities for making major mistakes occur often, and the effects are well out of proportion to the potential benefits of submiting to pressure. Such situations are numerous and often subtle. The individual or department advocating the compromise seldom understands its implications. Most often, the manager must decide whether to compromise based on endemic situations. However, there are classic examples of political pressure affecting the decision process. There are also responses or approaches which are equally classic.

The most common situation, and probably the most dangerous, occurs when the manager is asked to lower the project estimates to meet cost/benefit thresholds. Acquiescing to this request most often yields immediate congratulations on the part of the user, accompanied by compliments on the manager's understanding of business priorities and his or her bottom-line attitude. It is, however, an extremely dangerous compromise.

First, it places the entire estimating process in question. If the manager—who is well removed from the process itself—can arbitrarily lower estimates, why have an estimating process at all? Second, the pressure to produce a satisfactory product, in a shorter time than estimated, falls totally on the development department. The user makes no sacrifices and takes no responsibility for failure, either in meeting the schedule or in product quality.

At times the manager must be prepared to reduce the time needed to produce a requested product. However, simply reducing the estimate should never be done. Reducing the scope of the project is by far the better alternative. It extends the responsibility for the compromise to the user as well as the developers. The user must operate in a degraded environment, and development must produce the product in less time. The pressure is shared by both parties, along with the responsibility.

Another common situation occurs when the manager is asked to permit a system implementation even though some key component is missing or has failed. Most often, the component is missing because a gate designed for internal integrity has failed. This places the entire burden on development to support and enhance a system which is clearly less suitable for support or enhancement. The pressure is obviously to implement on schedule in spite of limitations in the product.

The true danger lies in the fact that, despite assurances that the user will allocate funds for completion, the user's commitment is extremely limited. From a business perspective, the user is correct. If a new product has a higher benefit than the implemented project's retrofit, it should be worked on. This leaves development with the problem of hiding its efforts in order to finally bring the operational system into line.

At this point, the manager is faced with an ambiguous situation. On the one hand, if the system is not ready, it should not be implemented. There are certainly some negative connotations for a schedule overrun, but that is inevitable in a multiproject environment. On the other hand, the user is willing to accept the system; therefore, the manager who refuses to do so appears to have an inflexible commitment to procedure. However, although systems can and often are implemented before they are totally ready, the portions which are incomplete should be clearly visible to the outside world. The problems or limitations should be obvious enough to ensure everyone's commitment to the project's completion.

The manager may be pressured to bypass normal project mechanics and to "muscle" a system in when some expertise exists in the user area. This trend is becoming more common with the spread of PCs and 4GLs. Often a prototype system is involved, developed by either the user or an outside service as a by-product of another activity. The premise is that since something already exists or a user resource is available, the normal development process is unnecessary.

When systems are implemented by development, they are the responsibility of development. Although the idea of using previously developed systems is a good business decision, user-developed products seldom have the integrity or discipline of development systems. Therefore, the existing system will have to be substantially adapted before it is acceptable. And unfortunately, since most of the adaptation involves invisible components of the system, the user perceives little benefit from the effort. Generally, adaptation of an existing prototype or an externally developed system seldom reduces overall development time.

At this point, the develoment manager should agree that the estimate for systems completion may be reduced but should insist that schedules be quoted for a conventional development effort. All phases should be included and all gating activities should remain intact. If the user wishes to appoint an individual to improve the schedule, that individual should be temporarily transferred to the development department, not merely made available.

Understanding these situations, even understanding the correct response, does not alleviate the pressure that the development manager can expect when the situations arise. There is a need to stand by procedure and policy most of the time, but the realities of corporate life dictate the need to bend periodically to political pressure. Estimates will have to be revised downward, systems implemented before they should be, and prototypes revised rather than following normal processes. If the manager can at least cause these situations to be exceptions rather than the rule, a great deal has been accomplished.

DEALING WITH PRESSURE AND POLITICS FOR THE MANAGER

It is fine to describe the method by which the development manager absorbs the transfers pressure to the staff. The manager represents the peak of the pressure pyramid and is forced to deal with politics of all kinds. At best, the pressure can be rationalized with the attitude that the manager is part of the business and a large part of the job is to further the company's competitive position. If operating under pressure and producing a quality product directly aids the enterprise, some gratification can be achieved despite the constant stress and compromise the job requires. However, political pressure is all too often exerted for personal gain irrespective of company benefit. When that occurs, it is difficult to rationalize the resulting sleepless nights and stress.

It is a fact of life that the pressure comes with the job. And while managers, by nature, typically handle pressure better than the bulk of the staff, it can sometimes become overwhelming. It is extremely important for the development manager to deal with pressure and politics effectively. Failure to do so will not only result in significant personal problems but will lower the manager's productivity as well. Since the manager sets the example for the department, when he suffers from the effects of stress and pressure, the department suffers as well.

This chapter, as stated in the introduction, is not intended to be a comprehensive treatise on dealing with personal stress. For the manager who finds it difficult to concentrate on the work at hand, who suffers from the physical symptoms of stress or feels unable to cope with the workload, it is wise to seek help. There are many seminars, books and organizations that can provide relief.

Experience provides some comfort in dealing with politics. For most professionals, the following facts will not be particularly surprising. However, in the day-to-day struggle to balance a technical discipline with the sometimes staggering pressures exerted on development, it is easy to lose perspective on what represents the job and what represents the political game.

One of the easiest facts to forget is that development exists, at least partially, to bring discipline to a sometimes frenetic business. The assurance of integrity in systems and data is essential for the modern company. The tremendous flow of information into the company and the speed with which decisions must be made preclude the luxury of painstaking, detailed interpretation of the data. Analysis must be done by automated systems and, since the massaging of the data takes place under the cover of systems, the integrity of the process used for development is paramount to the company's success.

Using political pressure to shortcut the integrity of the process is extremely dangerous, not only to development but to the company as a whole. Most senior executives understand this. They may not be totally pleased with the length of the process or its cost, but they do understand its worth. A development manager who insists on ensuring process integrity, and who can prove its worth, will seldom be forced to compromise that process beyond the breaking point.

Another fact is that development personnel, even though they may not be able to handle pressure constantly, can handle it for short periods. They understand the need for extraordinary efforts when the manager is under pressure to bring in a system ahead of schedule. They may not like the situation, but they can and will support it. The staff should be given the opportunity to understand all the implications of project scheduling. If the project must be rushed to meet political pressures, they should be told. Communication is one of the manager's most effective outlets for the pressure exerted on him and should be utilized.

Finally, development managers should not feel that they are the final protector of the company's information assets. While they may be stewards of a sort, the responsibility for information integrity is shared by everyone, just as it is for the integrity of the product and the company's image. If one member of the company is attempting to shortcut the process and violate that information integrity, it is the manager's responsibility to make that situation visible. Managers should not feel the need to stand alone against the rest of the company, screaming for discipline. This should be a shared responsibility.

CONCLUSION

Pressure, stress and politics are an inescapable part of corporate life. They are even more acute in the typical development department for a variety of reasons, ranging from the temperament and personalities of the staff to the centralized service role of the function. This places a burden on the manager of development not only to deal with pressure personally but also to understand the implications for the staff and for the development department.

The opportunities to compromise the integrity of development in response to political pressure occur frequently and in ways both subtle and obvious. In many cases, the manager has little choice but to bend. In others, the decision to bend results inevitably in major problems later on—problems well out of proportion to the issue causing the compromise. Unless he understands the interrelationships of the process, the manager will make more dangerous compromises than safety dictates.

In Chapters 6 and 7, the subject of personalities was discussed, in terms of both individuals and the overall department. People react differently to pressure. Some handle it better than others. In order to ensure continuity and progression for the department, the manager must carefully determine how much and in what way pressure will be transmitted downward in the organization. This is not a yes/no issue. Understanding and sensitivity are required to transmit the proper level of pressure without taxing the staff's capability. In addition, if the department is to function truly as a unit, its members must understand the political pressures which exist. Individuals may be shielded from pressure, but they must always understand its existence and implications. Otherwise, they can never truly be part of the overall enterprise, since political pressure is endemic to the culture and personality of the company.

Sitting atop the development pyramid, the manager bears the brunt of the pressure exerted on the department, as well as pressure exerted personally. It is unreasonable to expect any single person to absorb all of this pressure; some of it must be transferred to lower levels. This relieves the manager and allows the department to function as a whole.

The image of the development manager who personally handles whatever pressure arises tends to cause managers to accept automatically whatever comes their way. Any inability to absorb that pressure, either by the manager or the staff, is often equated with failure. This should not be the case. Everyone has limits. Understanding that pressure and knowing those limits can help enormously in dealing with what has become one of the top ten most pressure-oriented disciplines. Sensitivity to this issue can be one of the principal tools in the development manager's arsenal, promoting personal longevity as well as the stability and comfort of the staff.

10

PERKS AND BENEFITS

Why is it that some organizations are spoken of with great pride, while others are considered sweatshops? Development managers are constantly aware of the excellent companies, either explicitly, by talking with people from those companies, or implicitly, by never seeing their resumes. The definition of a "great company" goes well beyond salary. In fact, organizations often seem to have that reputation despite their low or average salaries.

In many cases, the reputation and personnel stability spring from company-oriented benefit programs. Excellent health plans, savings and stock purchase programs, or extracurricular activities are major factors in the minds of most professionals today. These programs provide personal security, which gives the employee a feeling of comfort and freedom from worry. They are financially significant in that they can easily represent up to 30 to 40% of the employee's salary. For the individual, it would be even more expensive to match this company-provided benefit level.

The levels and types of benefit packages vary substantially with industry type, geography and business success. Programs vary from basic supplemental health coverage to the exotic, including foreign vacations and sabbaticals. They represent a significant cost to the company and cannot be provided without a decent profit margin or at least the expectation of profits in the future. This remains true of the regulated industries, where, whether a quoted profit exists or not, the cost of the programs is included when allowable charges are negotiated.

Although some corporations provide extensive benefit programs for altruistic reasons, the primary motive is competition for skilled people. The programs provide an environment which draws people without the need for astronomical salaries. The classic example is the high-technology field, where competition for skilled engineers has bred benefit programs far beyond anything conceived of a few years ago.

Development managers working for a company with an extended benefit program have a major advantage over their peers. They have an advantage in competing for new people as well as a good reason to keep them. However, over time, benefit programs often become as much an expectation for the employee as competitive salaries. They can become a backdrop for the work environment rather than a motivator.

This chapter is not about standard company benefits. The typical development manager is not able to improve or extend these programs simply to court staff. This is not to say that the manager should not exert as much influence as possible to expand them. Every opportunity to improve the company's competitive position should be taken and the impacts, financially and psychological, should be brought to the attention of management. If working committees exist for program review, the manager should attempt to become a member in order to protect the company's investment in staff. Staff continuity makes life considerably easier for the development manager. Any opportunity to enhance that continuity should be seized. The expenditure of time will be repaid multifold.

The subject of this chapter is the perks and benefits the manager can provide for the development department. To a large extent, this is governed by the company's policy and procedure, as well as by its financial flexibility. In order to institute some of the benefits discussed, the manager must find imaginative ways to market them. For managers who are truly committed to making their department a great place to work, the efforts will be well rewarded.

The balance of this chapter is devoted to a discussion of seven benefits which can create a department employees will be proud to be a part of and loath to leave. For each item, the rationale and the impact on the employee's commitment to stay with the company are discussed. In most cases, the cost of these programs need not be high. If taken to their ultimate, of course, they will be correspondingly costly. But in most cases, some quantifiable benefit can be perceived, and these situations will be highlighted. The chapter begins with a discussion of the objectives of a benefit program so that success can be determined.

The development manager should keep in mind that benefit programs are an augmentation designed to create a satisfactory working environment. They should not be considered substitutes for job challenge, recognition for contributions, good employer–employee relations, or adequate salary. Such substituting of them will yield a stagnant staff of nonperformers rather than a productive group of professionals.

OBJECTIVES

Work is a major component of the typical person's life. It represents far more than a source of income. It is a means of challenging one's capabilities and growing through that challenge, a significant source of the social interaction most people need, and often a means of establishing or confirming self-worth. Most professionals want their jobs to be satisfying and enjoyable. They want to enjoy coming into the office every day and finding themselves in an environment they do not wish to leave.

One of the principal objectives in establishing a program of perks and benefits is to create just this situation and environment. The benefits are tied to the workplace itself, although in some cases the concept of the workplace is extended to the home. Managers who can create and foster this atmosphere find themselves in the enviable position of achieving dramatic productivity gains, a staff commitment to make the department successful, and a good reputation for the group. That reputation creates pride among the staff and provides a drawing card for skilled professionals when recruiting is necessary.

Development people often use professional organizations to meet with their peers. In addition, the fact that work is a major topic of discussion in a social environment provides many opportunities to compare the benefits of different departments. People who enjoy working in a department are proud to describe how satisfying their environment is. It is this sense of pride which keeps people from looking for new jobs.

The manager must understand that there is a significant difference between accepting a new job and beginning to seek one. In most cases, once an individual has made the commitment to seek employment, he or she will eventually leave. Beyond righting obvious wrongs in the treatment of the employee, making the decision to "see what the marketplace has to offer" is the key point in leaving the company. Something prompted the individual to take this step, and this is the situation the manager should be trying to avoid.

Job challenge and satisfaction are crucial in preventing an employee from taking this step. Matching the job to the employee's style and personality, keeping a department personality active and maintaining a leading-edge technological stance all contribute to this feeling. However, difficult times always exist for an employee when job satisfaction and challenge are not preeminent. It is at these times that small factors can make the difference in motivating the employee to stay with the department.

It is this objective that the development manager has in mind when establishing perks and benefits. It is not a simple matter of keeping people happy, but of making their experience with the department and the company so positive that they will not even consider looking elsewhere. Productivity gains will invariably be achieved in such an environment, the manager's principal motivation should not be productivity. The sense of commitment to the department is primary. A lowering of turnover is the most important measure of success. (In the author's experience, one situation more than any other that signals that such an environment exists. When employees complain about being bothered by calls from recruiters, the manager has succeeded. People who are happy in a department do not want the interference of outsiders trying to draw them away and forcing constant career decisions on them. Conversely, when calls must be screened to prevent people from being contacted by recruiters because of high turnover, this is a clear sign of the failure to provide a good working atmosphere.)

FLEX TIME

The concept of flex time is not new. Many corporations today utilize flex time for office employees whose duties do not require them to be available at specific times of the day. Instead, an employee is expected to work a certain number of hours per day across a number of days. If the number of hours is eight, for instance, the employee may have to be in the office for a specified period, say 10 A.M. to 2 P.M. Beyond that, the individual's work schedule may vary, so that some employees work from 6 A.M. to 2 P.M., while others work 10 A.M. to 6 P.M. All are there for a core period to facilitate staff meetings, presentations and whatever activities require full, guaranteed staff attendance.

At times, flexibility is even greater. Employees may be required to work a certain number of hours per week, but at their own discretion. At times, the schedule must be adhered to, and variations must be prescheduled with the manager's approval. In extreme cases, the honor system is used and employees can vary their schedules freely, as long as the total weekly commitment is met.

Flexible working hours provide significant benefits for both the employee and the company. For the employee, outside interests can be pursued more consistently. Involvement in children's activities, community work, and college programs is more feasible when work schedules can be altered to allow a higher and more dependable level of participation. In addition, flexibility allows the employee to schedule work around their own biological clocks. Some people are not "morning people" and would just as soon start work later in the day. They perform at a higher level and are far more comfortable with a late schedule.

The company gains the advantage of spreading out demands on company facilities and resources. Parking problems are often relieved, cafeteria services are less strained and longer hours of coverage are provided. This is often the only option for a company with both West Coast and East Coast offices, other than forced scheduling of overlapping shifts. Also, productivity is higher since employees work in tune with their schedules rather than being forced.

The benefits for the development manager are impressive. Beyond providing simple employee satisfaction, flexible hours spread computer demand for projects across a wider time range. There is also the advantage of having development personnel on site when key operational activities are taking place immediately following shift changes. This places expertise on site, with corrective documentation available, as opposed to having to call the support person's home when problems arise.

Flexibility can be a major factor in lowering turnover. After some experience with flexible hours, people commit their time to outside activities, which may take place during the standard 8–5 work day. As these activities grow in importance, employees become loath to give them up by moving to a company which does not provide flexible hours.

Because development is a service department, some concessions to flexibility must be made. Application support must be provided throughout the time an application will run. Further, development is not always in control of the timing for its interdepartment meetings. While those meetings can generally be scheduled for whatever common coverage period is involved (in the earlier example, 10 A.M. to 2 P.M.), there are exceptions and staff members must recognize the need to be flexible themselves. It may in fact be necessary to limit the number of people who can take advantage of a flexible time program.

Despite the concessions, flexible time can be feasible for most development departments given minor adjustments to conventional schedules. Typically, the flexibility allowed managers and project leaders is much less than of line personnel. However, the advantage to the staff as a whole is high, and the spread of work can dramatically increase the department's productivity.

When the company has no established flex time program, the development manager must be imaginative in initiating it. The first rule is never to refer to the program as flex time. Generally, the most successful way of introducing it is to justify spreading the load on the test computer system. While this may not be the predominant reason for such a program, it is certainly a true statement. This approach usually works well due to its bottom-line interpretation by upper management.

Obviously, this approach requires some subtlety. The department manager and the direct reporting managers must handle the necessary adjustments in day-to-day scheduling carefully. Meetings, for example, cannot be changed due to "flex time schedules." They can legitimately be rescheduled because the employee is "working early hours for the project." This approach does produce additional pressure on managers because they cannot rely on procedures that are not officially published. However, the added burden is not generally high and the benefits are well worth the extra effort.

WORKING AT HOME

Closely allied with flexible hours is the concept of allowing the employee to perform part of the work at home rather than in the office. This arrangement provides many of the same benefits of flex time: involvement in nonwork activities, working when the employee is most productive, and so on. When both spouses work, it has the added advantage of allowing easier schedules for taking care of children. That benefit itself can keep an employee committed to the company.

Much of a developer's work does not require full-time office attendance. In fact, when deep concentration is required, the office environment, with its noise and activity, may actually hinder maximum productivity. The home provides a calm atmosphere and eliminates the pressure and stress often found in the office.

From a practical point of view, working at home tends to increase the number of hours dedicated to work. Commuting to and from the office is eliminated, breaks are less formal and shorter, and since employees are available for family activities, they seldom mind working later or earlier than normal. More can be accomplished, with less stress, in the relaxed, nonthreatening environment of the home.

Since development is a service function and requires the dissemination of knowledge about emerging technologies, the typical developer cannot always work at home. There is a need for meetings, discussions, system walk-throughs and the cooperative testing that make a department work well. However, when employees understand the need to schedule their activities around a benefit such as home work, one to two days a week at home can reasonably be anticipated.

The scheduling of work at home must be done carefully. As with flexible hours, all applications must be properly covered. This means that the manager must exert control and discretion when allowing employees to work at home. The problem is not overwhelming, and if the employees understand what is at stake, there is a high probability that they will cooperate.

Ideally, staff members working at home should be given communications capabilities. A pool of working terminals or PCs, with attendant modems to support their efforts, will greatly enhance their effectiveness. However, not all of a developer's work requires communications devices. Design documents, procedural measures and initial coding efforts or analysis can be done without them. Communications certainly enhance the effort, but the gains can still be achieved even if that capability cannot be provided.

The manager can expect some resistance to such a program. In many minds, the workplace is the office and the work of the corporation is to be conducted there. PCs have negated much of that argument, but conventional ideas die hard. The manager must develop ways to prove that productivity will take place out of the office and that the program will not be abused. Realistically, this requires no more control than the project tracking mechanisms commonly used in development. However, additional measures will probably have to be designed in order to assure management that control is being maintained.

TERMINALS FOR SUPPORT

The support function produces greater pressure than other phases of development. It interferes more with employees' life at home and, more important, forces them to come into the office to solve problems—an extremely irritating situation. Employees feel tied to the office, without a life of their own. Opportunities to move to a company without constant and chronic calls at night can be very attractive for both employees and their families.

However, the development staff, with its central importance to the corporation's health, must provide constant support. Support cannot realistically be provided, long-term, over the phone. There are too many things to check, too many paths to be analyzed and too much verification to be done. In order to avoid the trip to the office, support people attempt this type of resolution, but they know it is second-rate.

Providing terminals for support people on off-hour response can alleviate much of this pressure. During the evening, they can monitor the progress of applications to the point where they can go to bed with some confidence that their sleep will not be interrupted. That in itself is a major advantage.

The cost of such a program is minimal. It involves the purchase of special terminals, probably portable computers, since the transportation of full-scale terminals would prohibit their use. The advantages of the program will more than compensate for this cost if, for no other reason, the speed of failure recovery is increased by the time required to drive to work. In a heavily automated environment, where users depend on the results of nightly runs early in the morning, delays of a few minutes can have a significant impact. Therefore, a dependable, rapid response to problems is beneficial enough to outweigh the minimal investment.

This type of program is especially advantageous when new systems are implemented and must be carefully monitored during their early operation. It allows the constant support necessary without the stress created by on-site support. While some persons will undoubtedly need to remain on-site, the number will certainly be lower than without terminal support. Support will improve, and the employee's attitude toward the job will remain positive.

WORKING COMMITTEES

In Chapter 7, the concept of working committees as a vehicle for establishing a department personality was discussed. These committees give employees some control over their future. They can generally exert pressure by making changes and enhancements in the standards, procedures and other mechanisms with which they work.

Working committees provide opportunities which do not exist for many programmers and analysts. In most medium-sized to large departments, programmers and analysts are given assignments with specific goals. Their opportunity to lead, or even act as peers, in a committee forum is limited. They deal in the practical application of tools already chosen for them.

This is an important issue for most detail-level analysts and programmers. Much of the science of development lies not with the application of methods but with theory. Anyone who has dealt with a structured discipline understands that the difference between what is taught in seminars and books and actual implementation is great. Much of the theory and conceptualization is lost in the adaptation of the discipline.

Programmers and analysts enjoy dealing directly with development theory. It gives them the sense of being true craftsmen and having a significant impact on the future of the discipline itself. The working committee allows the staff to deal with theory and adapt it to a practical purpose. Both adaptation and selection of development tools can be handled through these committees. In this way, the staff controls not only how those tools are used but also which tools are selected.

Regardless of how strong the manager's technical background is, the staff is far more qualified to choose and maintain the tools of their craft. Dealing at a distance, the manager quickly becomes isolated from the realities of developing systems and the use of tools. The belief that the manager has the ability to choose development tools is unrealistic. He certainly must give final approval, since issues such as cost, performance and resource usage are typically his domain. The manager must also initiate committee proceedings and provide the charter, which gives the manager control over the beginning and end of the process. With status reports throughout the effort, managers have as much control of committee work as of projects. That should be adequate.

As an ultimate achievement, a successful working committee can formalize its findings and present them as working papers for professional organizations. Their work may even be significant enough for presentation at seminars and conventions. This level of peer recognition and pride has few substitutes. The opportunity to be part of an organization which allows and fosters such a program is hard to beat. It represents the merging of extracurricular activities with the work environment.

The benefits to the company consist of an enhanced commitment for the department and an improvement in overall capabilities. The committee can bring the department to the leading edge of technology. The cost is minimal—principally time. The committees should be provided time during working hours; otherwise there is no commitment on the part of management. The time can be built into project estimating mechanisms, subtly, so that it simply appears as a factor in measuring resource availability.

THE WORKING ENVIRONMENT

No manager should underestimate the impact of the attractiveness and comfort of the workplace on an employee's attitude. This is a subject that invariably arises in discussions about work. One person indicates she occupies an office, has an outside window, or has new furniture. Just as the conditions of the home are a source of pride, so are the conditions of the workplace.

In the minds of overachievers and, therefore of upper management, office working conditions are often considered extraneous. Their focus is on upward movement, career challenge and specific goals. For a far greater number of workers, the office is a place where they go to do a job. The conditions there are a major determinant of how they feel about the job and the company. Over time, extremely positive conditions become an expectation rather than a motivating factor, at least on a day-to-day basis. However, when employees compare one company to another, those conditions again become a source of motivation, a reason to stay with the firm which provides them. That attitude is seldom overt, but it exists nonetheless.

Ask programmers or analysts what conditions they prefer, and the vast majority will respond in favor of private offices. However, with the premium paid for space, as well as the need for dynamic growth and rearrangement, the work environment will inevitably consist of modular furniture in a cubicle arrangement. This system is a reasonable compromise between the privacy of the offices and the chaos of an open office arrangement—the infamous bull pen.

An open office arrangement precludes the concentration required for quality development. Disruption is constant, the sense of personal space is nonexistent, and few people can engage in imaginative thought with a group of co-workers looking at them. Most work ethics equate productivity with activity. Development, however; entails quiet thought, and the work environment must allow it. An open area puts pressure on the staff to provide a picture of furious activity.

Cubicles retain the flexibility of an open arrangement. As the size of the staff changes or its conformity shifts, the cubicles can be easily rearranged to meet new needs. Easily movable furniture will optimize project assignment. As project teams are created, the furniture can be rearranged to ensure that team members are in close proximity. Some interference will occur simply because of this movement, but at least all project team members will be close by for the life of the project.

No all cubicle arrangements provide equal working conditions. When poorly arranged, they bear a resemblance to a maze, with few positive attributes apparent. When designing the initial arrangements, it is most helpful to choose an office furniture company that has some experience with development staffs. That experience can help the manager avoid the more classic mistakes made in designing furnishings. Once the manager or administrative group understands the variables involved in designing a workable arrangement, they can easily manage any rearrangements fostered by change within the department.

Cubicles should provide a degree of privacy. This allows staff members to personalize their work space without interfering with the privacy of their co-workers. High walls interspersed among the more conventional five-foot walls provide islands of privacy. The smaller the area within these islands, the better. Optimally, two to three people share one of these islands, separated from each other by the shorter walls. They can therefore engage in some social interaction without disturbing others.

Small touches such as plants, ambient lighting to ease eye strain, and access to windows make the office more pleasant. A good arrangement also includes sensible colors (let the employees choose the colors by vote), open aisles, and strategic placement of common areas for walk-throughs, meetings and social gatherings. The objective is to provide an atmosphere which creates not only a sense of ownership but also efficiency of function.

Depending on the conditions enjoyed by other departments, some development employees may require a private workplace. If users normally work in private offices, the principal project leaders or analysts may require private offices or, at least, private meeting areas which are always available. Without this arrangement, developers will always be dealing in an atmosphere where they appear to be less important than their user/customers. That sense stifles cooperative work.

Obviously, the purchase of furnishings, in whatever arrangement is chosen, involves a capital expense. The development manager must develop a budget for the purchase. If conditions preclude the purchase of furnishings for the entire department, cubicles can be bought piecemeal and the open arrangements enhanced until a more comprehensive solution is possible. The higher walls can be positioned such that the open office is subdivided into more private islands. As funds become available, the finishing touches can be provided.

EDUCATION

Development people have an almost unquenchable thirst for knowledge. Their jobs involve constant problem solving, and this fuels a desire to enhance their education. The ability to foster that educational growth, whether through formal degree programs or courses and seminars, can become an important benefit, motivating employees to stay with the company despite attractive outside offers.

Many educational opportunities are provided through standard company programs. Masters degree programs are attractive enough to either draw people or keep them under employment for several years. Optimally, employees are allowed to devote part of their normal work time to the degree program, either to attend classes or for nonclassroom work. Obviously, a sensible arrangement is necessary. The purpose of the job is to contribute primarily to the company's goals, not the employee's extracurricular activities. However, educational advancement always improves the company. This should justify the contribution of time by the company.

Degree programs such as the masters in business administration generally involve substantial screening by the company. The manager's job in this case is to make an aggressive effort on the employee's behalf. The program will yield benefits both today and in the future, so the time and effort are well spent. Conversely, failure to secure approval for the individual who is committed to such an effort generally guarantees the loss of that individual. Achievement of the degree quickly becomes a consuming desire. If it cannot be satisfied with the current employer, it will be satisfied elsewhere.

Continuing education generally requires less stringent justification. Most often it involves merely the manager's approval, indicating that the education will enhance the employee's performance. Except in the most ludicrous cases, nearly any continuing education can be viewed as enhancing the contribution of the employee. Therefore, within limits, requests for continuing education assistance should be approved.

It is important to provide opportunities for employees to demonstrate their improved capabilities. For example, the employee who has taken a writing course can provide the documentation on ensuing projects. The work should then be reviewed by the manager so that employees are confident that their efforts are recognized. Education should never be ignored. It should be fostered both because of the improvement it provides and because an atmosphere where education is respected is a good drawing card for committed employees.

Videotape programs are available from many sources for in-house education. They provide training in technical disciplines, as well as in the managerial and administrative aspects of the job. Most vendors that provide video programs will negotiate corporate contracts which provide a preset number of tape hours per month or per year at a greatly reduced rate. Given the cost of out-of-town classes, with the attendant travel and lodging, video programs provide very cost-effective education.

By providing video programs, the manager allows an employee to remain on the leading edge of technology. In a high-intensity field such as development, this arrangement provides an understanding of new technologies before the employee's performance is judged. The subject matter should be a mixture of technical and nontechnical material. This allows growth in all aspects of the job. It is wise to include some self-growth material as well, chosen by the employees themselves.

Employees should be provided time to take advantage of the program during the day, as well as off-hours. Some people simply do not have the luxury of off-hours time, or the office may be so remote from their homes that education on their own time becomes a burden on their families and interferes unduly with their personal life. The time provided should be reciprocal, however. If the company is willing to sacrifice some of its time, the employee should be willing as well.

For development people, educational opportunities and recognition for scholastic achievement can become a great source of satisfaction with a department and a company. At times, managers may find themselves training people for other employers, but this is more the exception than the rule. In most cases, it provides a significant inducement for long-term employment by creating satisfaction beyond the job itself.

SUPPORTING OUTSIDE INTERESTS

In Chapter 6, the subject of general personality profiles for development personnel was discussed. Two of the key characteristics of these workers are their high education and their search for gratification beyond the workplace. While this pattern is not particularly unusual, it is somewhat unique for a group whose careers have historically dominated their lives. The rapidly changing development environment requires an intense concentration to keep up. Yet development people, like many of their generation, do seek as much satisfaction from their nonworking lives as from work.

The intelligent development manager accepts this situation and, rather than redirecting it, uses it to tie the employee to the company. This is done by creating a situation in which the employee's outside interests are enhanced or extended by membership in the department. By doing this, the manager creates an environment where the office extends the employee's enjoyment of life. Such an environment is difficult to leave, and the employee becomes much more committed to the success of the department and the company.

Through communications lines, a mainframe computer can be made available to every member of the department. In this way, all the power of the software for the office computer can be used for home economics, financial planning, and entertainment, as well as for the enhancement of outside business activities. As long as the system's resources are not exhausted there should be no conflict with corporate goals.

The installation of personal improvement software specifically for the use of employees is not particularly expensive, and security considerations are no greater than when the employee is at the office. The employee who wishes to breach security will find it much easier to do so in the office. There are few problems that outweigh the positive impacts of such a program.

Some care must certainly be taken in deciding how the service is provided. Making system time available to members of development and not to the rest of the company will create dissent and undoubtedly doom the effort. Therefore, it must be made available to all. In general, development people will take far greater advantage of the service than other employees, so there should not be an overwhelming drain on the system as all 2000 company employees log on to computer games simultaneously. Only a small number of people will use the system because only they will be capable of doing so.

Some security arrangements must be made for employee/users. If they are using the system for budget planning, a substantial amount of personal information will be held on the system. That information must be protected and locked to their passwords. In addition, a reasonable amount of historical storage and disk usage space must be provided so as not to limit company production work. The time limits for the facilities should be scheduled away from peak production hours to ensure maximum availability for operational systems.

Even with these considerations, employees will quickly become dependent on the facilities provided. The opportunities the systems provide for simplifying their personal lives will allow greater freedom while bringing their outside interests more in line with the success of the company. They will also provide more reason to stay with the company.

CONCLUSION

Job satisfaction generally centers on intellectual challenge, a comfortable, competitive salary, and recognition for accomplishments. These factors are crucial in maintaining staff productivity and continuity, but many of the small things that tie the individual to the company are also important. Job satisfaction focused on challenges tends to be transient, since all projects end. Between challenging projects, there must be something else to motivate the employee to remain with the company.

For this reason, company benefits are very important. While these benefits vary from one company to another, they tend to be those elements which make life more secure and comfortable: insurance, pensions, and so on. However, while these offerings are certainly important, like salary they tend to represent background satisfiers. They are not very visible and are becoming increasingly standard among companies. This means that the manager must come up with new and imaginative ways to make the department an attractive place to work.

In many cases, the perks and benefits described in this chapter, from allowing work at home to supporting outside interests, require effective marketing to management. If management understands the true cost of turnover and the extremely competitive nature of the development job market, there should be little problem in convincing them of the benefit of these programs. However, if the marketing plan fails to succeed, or if it is obviously fruitless to try, the manager must find ways to market those perks that are provided in more attractive ways. If people can shift their working hours, they will not care whether the program is called flex time or taking advantage of open computer time. The advantages they gain will make it compelling to work for the department and the company.

None of the perks outlined in this chapter, taken one by one, are likely to reduce turnover substantially. However, a complete package of benefits that is unavailable elsewhere *can* make a difference. And when turnover is low, the manager has a greater opportunity to effect long-range strategies than when the department is constantly changing.

The benefits of implementing benefit programs include more than turnover, however. Such programs imply that the manager is willing to provide the best working conditions and opportunities to the staff. People respect that effort and tend to feel a part of the organization and its goals. The department and the company become part of their lives and make it possible to live flexibly. When that happens, the company's success is directly tied to the employee's success. That creates the most positive working situation possible.

Part III
Managing the Technology

11

END USER LANGUAGES

Conventional development—at least, what is commonly considered conventional—is based on procedures and methods designed to provide not only process efficiency but also product consistency and integrity. The mechanisms that accomplish this are the result of years of training and research. Additionally, and perhaps more importantly, the languages and skills necessary to develop systems have historically required highly specialized technical skills. These skills were limited to a select few.

That specialization caused the formation of systems development departments. Despite the stress and delays caused by this centralization of the role, it did guarantee the possibility of a common approach to product development. The gains go far beyond the simple use of efficient, rich languages and techniques. An environment is created whereby thorough analysis, prioritization and cost justification are ensured.

Had automation not accelerated so rapidly, the conventional approach to development would still be used. However, the gains achieved by centralized development implied a lengthy process for any system response. The need for more systems and shorter development cycles could only be satisfied by larger development staffs. The effective limits of staff size were quickly reached in an era where personnel costs outstripped capital expenses.

In order to compensate for the need for systems while keeping staff costs down, user-friendly languages began to appear. Initially, these languages were simply alternatives to procedurally oriented languages such as COBOL, Fortran, and assembler languages. Report program generators were certainly more friendly than the lower-level languages but still required fairly high technical expertise. The problem was that while process activities could be restated in terms more easily understood, the access to data still required significant knowledge of data processing concepts.

The development of database capabilities set the stage for the advent of end user languages. Databases provide a screen between the language and the data so that technical translation could be separated from process activities. These new languages, crude at first, became known as "fourth-generation languages (4GL)." These languages quickly proliferated and increased in sophistication with the advent of the PC. PCs were designed to be used by people who were not necessarily computer literate and therefore not development professionals.

There is no universal definition of a 4GL. In general, the definition consists of examples. The most obvious characteristic of 4GLs is that they allow end users without extensive data processing experience to utilize the product. This does not imply that every language is easily used by the general public. Some are specialized for use with a business or scientific discipline, and some experience in that discipline is necessary. Table 11-1 lists some of the more popular 4GL products. The list is not exhaustive, nor does it imply any ranking of quality. It simply serves as a definition/example of end user languages.

While the technical simplicity and nonprocedural nature of 4GLs were important, their availability allowed much of the development activity to be performed by the end user. This dramatically expanded the development pool to include all reasonably intelligent users. Unfortunately, this extended development group was neither trained nor necessarily willing to follow the designed rules to ensure integrity. The systems developed in this new style

Table 11-1. Examples of End User 4GLs

FOCUS—Information Builders, New York, New York
Database-oriented application generator and language

SAS®SYSTEM—SAS Institute Inc., Cary, North Carolina
Statistical analysis, spreadsheet, operations research, graphics, report writing, forecasting, data management

EXPRESS—Information Resources Inc., Waltham, Massachusetts
Modeling, financial analysis

ON-LINE QUERY/ENGLISH—Cullinet, Inc., Westwood, Massachusetts
Database-oriented ad hoc inquiry, language

INTELLECT—Artifical Intelligence, Waltham, Massachusetts
Natural language

SIMPLAN—SSI Inc., Chapel Hill, North Carolina
Financial analysis, modeling

P-STAT—P-Stat, Inc., Princeton, New Jersey
Statistical analysis

NATURAL*—Software AG of North America, Reston, Virginia
Database oriented application development language

*Natural is a trademark of Software AG of North America.

often lacked the integrity and consistency professional developers had been trained to provide.

However, despite their limitations and their sensitivity to problems, the 4GLs represent the wave of the future. Because of the acceleration of system needs and the rising costs of trained developers, the development and operation of application systems must be shared by developers and end users. Managers who wish to keep the development function as a central force in the corporation's future must include the use of 4GLs in their strategy.

When 4GLs are integral components of the strategy, their positive aspects can be used and their potential problems defused. Arbitrary refusal to support them or a severe limitation of their use will merely cause them to be hidden. They will continue to be used for increasingly critical business applications without the benefit of discipline. The development manager who hides behind the role of information custodian and takes no active part in 4GL use ignores a basic fact: data are useful only when presented as information. It is the 4GLs which, more and more, will be responsible for that presentation.

This chapter is concerned with 4GLs as an important technology that the development manager must deal with. It begins with a discussion of the benefits and problems of the conventional or self-contained development process. It is crucial to understand the advantages of this arrangement because it is precisely these characteristics which the development manager must attempt to replicate with end user development. Next, the advantages and disadvantages of end user development are discussed.

With end user developed systems, one of the primary problems is the certification of products. How can one tell if the displayed inquiry or report is correct when only final figures are acted upon? Conventional development provides this certification as a by-product of the process itself, with its gates and reviews. This is the subject of the next section—certification.

The chapter closes with a discussion of ideas for blending end user and conventional development to produce systems with the speed desired and the integrity required. It is unlikely that conventional development will disappear in the near future. It is likely, however, that the number of systems created within the development department will drop substantially. To ensure integrity while providing system solutions rapidly enough to keep pace with business dynamics, the development manager must effectively blend these two approaches.

SELF-CONTAINED, CONTROLLED DEVELOPMENT

In conventional development, most of the application system is constructed and supported by the development department itself. 4GLs may be utilized, but the actual construction is done by development professionals. End user inquiries may exist, but they generally involve single outputs, not the subsetting of data and manipulation for reports.

Regardless of the languages or methods employed, the key ingredient is that the process itself takes place within the development department. Procedures, standards and methodologies exist, extensive testing is performed and the people doing the work are skilled developers. The control this centralization implies, not the tools themselves, are the great strength of conventional developments.

When establishing a strategy which utilizes both end user and conventional development, it is important to understand the advantages and disadvantages of each. In that way, when that strategy is developed and implemented, the positive characteristics of each can be emphasized and the negatives avoided.

Advantages

The principal advantage of a controlled development approach is the ease with which procedures can be policed. Procedures provide a framework for developing systems which ensures not only that efficiency exists but also that all of the activities necessary to ensure product integrity take place. The easiest way to police procedural integrity is to complete each step before the next one begins. Failure to comply can be controlled either through forced revisions or, at the extreme, termination.

When development is not centrally controlled, procedural importance is downgraded. The manager of a non-MIS department will quickly compromise procedures to achieve the goal. User managers, though computer literate, are not professional developers and therefore find it difficult to appreciate the importance of procedures. The development manager who finds that a procedure was violated must defend that procedure against a working product, rather than internally before the product is visible. The former is a substantially more difficult position.

If procedures are easier to police in a centrally controlled environment, the same may be said of the implementation and evolution of methodologies. Methodologies provide consistency. Their adaptation and evolution imply that the lessons of one project are applied to subsequent projects. One can prevent the recurrence of problems while ensuring that the gains of good new techniques will be used in the future. When the development effort is dispersed throughout the user community, this process becomes much more difficult.

The use of methodologies requires some equalization of skill and understanding. Precise correspondence is not necessary, but the skills of those utilizing the methods must be somewhat consistent. In addition, the users of the methods must have some concern for the process itself, beyond the product being produced. With end users, the only concern is product. Since the user's career is totally dissociated from the methods employed, any gains to be carried over from one effort to another are difficult, at best, to achieve.

Much of the quality and integrity of the systems developed by a professional staff is due to the existence of quality gates. These gates force compliance with standards, review by peers and users, and formal control mechanisms. By discretely passing these gates, and thereby moving from one phase of the process to another, two things are accomplished. First, verification of the product takes place, so that small problems are not hidden in a wealth of output. When an entire system output exists, it is extraordinarily difficult to identify problems. Second, the developer cannot depart radically from the intent of the project due to misinterpretation or changing business conditions.

With end user development, these gates are far more difficult to use. The users are physically remote, are judged by different criteria and are less likely to document precisely what is required. Without gating, it is easier to experience the shift in commitment that one should try to avoid. The result may not be in line with the original intent, but so much effort has been expended that it is easier to change the scope of the project than redo the work. Eventually, the original intent will be satisfied, but generally in a far more convoluted fashion than is desirable.

With a centralized development approach, an adversary relationship exists between the user and the developer. Regardless of how cooperative the two groups are, the user is seeking errors in development's outputs and development is seeking inconsistencies in the user's requests and specifications. It is this constructive adversary relationship which ensures that all aspects of the problem solution are covered.

When the developer is part of the user's department, concessions are made because these individuals have a close working relationship. No one is as critical of friends as he is of strangers. When the relationship is close, testing becomes a matter of helping to prove that the results are correct rather than seeking errors. If one looks for errors, one is far more likely to find them.

Finally, with centralized, controlled development, the process of justification occurs with the proper level of review and the implied delay before proceeding further. Any project has a cost, regardless of how quickly the proposed system can be put on-line. The costs of justification include not only development but operational costs as well. When justification is bypassed so that the system can be developed quickly, users may end up with a system whose operational cost exceeds the anticipated benefit.

The cost justification process, when reviewed and analyzed between two competitive groups, tends to uncover hidden costs of a proposed system far more effectively than when the system is justified by the proposing group. Also, interdepartment justification includes a commitment to ensure that the proposed benefits really take place. This occurs because constant questioning takes place and because the future planning of two groups is based on those anticipated benefits and system scope.

Disadvantages

In centralized development, as in any service function, one significant disadvantage is the competition for scarce resources. If users have problems, they are forced to exert political pressure on development to gain control of those resources. As discussed in Chapter 9, development, by its nature, is extremely susceptible to political pressures.

Users quickly understand that in order to gain development priority, they must exert pressure either through benefit inflation or politics. The purpose of prioritization is to define projects based upon the relative advantage of each to the company. When the development staff is forced to respond instead to the relative strength of each user, prioritization is undermined.

A centralized development approach implies a bureaucracy. Since the department is judged on the quality and speed of product development, as well as on which projects gain attention, the department develops mechanisms to ensure success and the perception of success. These mechanisms, if they are to be effective, must be used for all projects, regardless of their scope and cost. In small projects some steps must be circumvented, but even a limited set of steps can create more overhead than actual work.

This bureaucracy not only frustrates users but, more importantly, can discourage them from making simple requests because the effort does not seem worthwhile. Significant advantages for a competitive corporation can be stillborn when imaginative ideas are frustrated by development's bureaucracy.

The remoteness of the developer from the requestor can become a significant problem with a centralized development staff. Regardless of how effective the specification method is, a gulf exists between the ideas of the requestor and the realities of the developer. This problem is not unique to systems development. Anyone who has played the parlor game where people, arranged in a circle, whisper a message to each other around the circle and compare the final message to the original can attest to the problem in communications.

With a large, specialized development staff, the original idea can be reinterpreted through several levels, including radically different approaches to business solutions. Programmers simply do not look at the business the same way as analysts or end users. Inevitably, they will interpret requests differently. No documentation review will totally overcome this problem. It is inherent in a multiple-stage communication process.

One of the more obvious disadvantages of a centralized development approach is the time required to fill a request. Often the user will conceive of a simple way to solve a significant problem, which may involve adding one item to an inquiry or revising a calculation on a report. The change is simple to describe, easy to make and nondamaging to the company. Yet in order to have the change made, requests must be filled out, justification provided, meetings held, priority established and resources freed. By the time all this is done, the change could be made and substantial benefit achieved.

The bureaucracy and communications problems described above account for much of this time delay. However, the net effect is that the user's waiting time is well out of proportion to the need. If the user could have made the change himself, the time lost would have been nebulous. It is true that bypassing the bureaucracy could do harm, especially if the change was not as simple as thought or in fact was damaging to the corporation. However, the user does not perceive that danger, only the time lost.

The advantages and disadvantages discussed here are summarized in Table 11-2, along with others. Obviously, they are somewhat situational.

Table 11-2. Conventional Development—Advantages and Disadvantages

ADVANTAGES

- EASE OF PROCEDURAL ENFORCEMENT
  All resources are under single control, so violations of procedural integrity can be dealt with directly.
- EASE OF METHODOLOGY IMPLEMENTATION
  With a common focus of technical expertise and commitment, methodologies can be implemented and changed with relative ease.
- QUALITY GATE ENFORCEMENT
  Enforcing quality gates involves prevention of next stage commencement. This enforcement is nearly impossible without total control.
- ADVERSARY RELATIONSHIP WITH USERS
  The fact that development and the user are in a competition ensures that extensive auditing and verification are performed.
- FORMALIZED COST JUSTIFICATION
  The formalization of cost justification ensures that, from an economic perspective, the proper projects are being worked on.

(cont.)

Table 11–2. (Continued)

- CONTROL OF NEW TECHNOLOGIES
  With a centralized approach, new technologies can be evaluated from a corporate perspective.
- CENTRALIZATION OF PLANNING
  All aspects of information technology can be integrated into a single plan with associated efficiencies.
- COMMON INTERNAL LANGUAGE
  All members of development use a common technical language.
- FOCUS ON CORPORATE INFORMATION GOALS
  The entire project can focus individual efforts on planned strategies at a corporate level. This ensures minimal redundancy in problem solutions both today and tomorrow.

DISADVANTAGES

- STRONG COMPETITION FOR RESOURCES
  With centralized development resources, all departments must compete for a limited resource pool.
- HIGH LEVEL OF OVERHEAD BEAUROCRACY
  Due to the checks and balances of the development process, many quality gates exist. The smaller the project, the higher the percentage of overall time this overhead represents.
- REMOTENESS OF THE DEVELOPER AND REQUESTOR
  Residence in separate departments and independent goals create a gulf between the person making the request and the person filling it.
- LENGTH OF TIME TO FILL REQUESTS
  Development is a time-consuming process. Often extensive benefits can be lost while that process takes place.
- HIGH INVESTMENT IN SOFTWARE
  The length of time and the cost of the effort automatically raises the cost of the system. This investment can delay replacement with newer, more advanced systems.
- SENSITIVITY TO PERSONNEL LEVELS
  Development is labor intensive. With the difficulty in justifying personnel increases, the number of requests that can be filled is limited by the number of programmers or analysts.
- FORMALITY OF THE PROCESS
  The formality of the process, with requisite justifications and reviews, can often discourage the user from requesting systems. It is simply not worth the effort.

For example, adding bureaucracy to a small project and, during one phase, finding that the results of the change would be catastrophic turns that disadvantage into a dramatic advantage. Thee are many reasons to do development in a centralized department, not the least of which is the limitation of risk.

END USER DEVELOPMENT

End user development means that the user analyzes and constructs a substantial portion of the operational system either personally or with the development department acting in a consulting role. Depending on the type of firm, this development may involve sophisticated code and data relationships, or it may consist simply of reporting or statistical subsystems independent of the operational data. This type of development has existed for years, but until end user, 4GLs became common, it was not widely used.

The development manager's primary concern is the fact that development is being performed by nonprofessionals, for whom the disciplines, procedural orientation and commitment to the process do not exist. Over the years, these aspects of the process have evolved to the point where they are nearly as important as the final product itself. When the end user performs the development, these by-products are either more difficult or impossible to affect.

Advantages

One of the advantages of 4GL, and therefore end user development, is that the gulf between the system need and the response is either eliminated or significantly reduced. Users can conceive the solution in their own terms and immediately begin testing it using the system. As problems arise, they can be highlighted and alternative paths chosen. Without end user tools, the process of testing and alternative selection must be done using pencil and paper, meetings or mental processes. This isolates the solution from the reality of implementation. Systems are different in a computer than in the mind.

During development, the people immediately available for help are also in the user department. The solution is interpreted by the users who understand the business environment. This approach generally results in a system which is more closely related to the user's perception of the solution. It exists in terms the user understands. It may not be the most technically sophisticated, efficient or consistent solution, but at least it is in accord with the thinking of the department. This is the principal factor of efficiency in the user's mind: how the system operates in his or her environment.

Regardless of the flexibility of the 4GL chosen, the real flexibility of end user development becomes apparent during the development cycle. Since 4GLs generally allow the preparation of sample outputs quickly, the user/developer can produce a sample of a system output and, with peer users, alter that output quickly. This allows the user group to alter a baseline system view rather than create that view with great care. Using conventional development mechanisms, that baseline must be painstakingly created, since it will be the basis of a substantial effort.

The initial version may or may not be easily altered in ways the users prefer. If that is the case, the user must make concessions in regard to output. In contrast, when the baseline is created by development, the user tends to force those modifications or start again. The net effect is that the system will match the user's desires more precisely, regardless of how critical those small components are. The closer the match, the more the user will be committed to the product.

This flexibility extends to the development schedules. There is no second party involved in discussions or reviews. Therefore, less preparation is required for meetings and they can occur on a more ad hoc basis. This process eliminates much of the time involved in getting two groups together.

When the user department is constructing part of the system, their contribution allows the professional development staff to concentrate on the more technically sophisticated aspects of the system. Much of the development staff's time is normally spent on the basic presentation aspects of a system. The format of reports, the physical attractiveness of screens and the usability of parameter strings are aspects of the system which require little technical expertise. They are often precisely those characteristics which inspire the rave reviews successful systems receive.

With the users involved, these cosmetic components of the system can be developed by the individuals who are most concerned with them. Naturally, they must coordinate their efforts with the professional staff to ensure that data are used effectively. However, having the users responsible for that development substantially reduces the burden on the programmers and analysts. In addition, the professional staff is able to dedicate more time to the challenging aspects of the development process. This division of labor increases the challenge of the job and heightens morale.

Disadvantages

The most striking problem associated with end user development is the multiplicity of problem solutions. Business problems can take on many guises. One of the functions of the professional analyst is to identify where commonality occurs so that one solution can solve many problems. With end user development, this professional analysis does not occur, and the multiplicity of solutions causes no particular concern. The only worry is whether the solution that does exist precisely fits the user's problem. If it does not, users will redevelop the system to solve the problem their own way. This is both expensive and dangerous.

This duplication of effort occurs for two main reasons—ignorance of another solution or departmental jealousy. Obviously, the existence of a knowledgeable development group provides safeguards against duplication caused by ignorance. This process is not automatic. It is necessary to maintain a portfolio of end user systems and conventional systems for referral before any development activity takes place. Departmental jealousy is avoided when a nonaligned force can intervene before construction of the new system begins. This is one of the benefits of centralized development.

Closely allied to the problem of multiple solutions is the issue of whether the product should be developed at all. As mentioned earlier, the development of software entails expense, regardless of who is in charge. In addition, a newly installed system may improperly disguise some of the benefit expected from a more strategically oriented product. How many times has a development manager faced the dilemma of the statement: "Yes we see the benefit of the new system but we have a PC solution which, although crude, does cover a decent portion of that need; therefore, that part of the benefit should not be quoted."

All systems should move in one strategic direction. Without this direction, opportunities are missed and comprehensive approaches are compromised. The process used to meld single projects into a comprehensive plan is the cost justification process. With end user development this process can be bypassed easily, since a large part of the system may be built before the development department is involved. By that time, a significant portion of the budget may already have been spent, skewing the cost/benefit analysis.

From the perspective of users, this particular disadvantage is often the primary advantage of doing their own development. It bypasses the bulk of the development department's bureaucracy and gives users a significant advantage when they finally go to the department for help. By that time, it is hard to fight the request. The problem is that the justification process is meant to serve a number of purposes, from bottom-line cost analysis to providing an alert point for strategy compromise. When the process is bypassed, all of its benefits are lost.

The greatest disadvantage of end user development, and the one typically used by its opponents, concerns data integrity. Although there are ways to avoid many of these problems (as will be discussed later in this chapter), there is no doubt that the risks of data misuse are substantially higher when development takes place outside the professional group. Data, even when extracted from a very secure database, can quickly become subverted through incorrect manipulation. By the time that information is finally presented it can look quite acceptable, and it is so remote from its original source that it is difficult to verify quickly.

While training and expertise can overcome part of this risk, even the most experienced data processing professionals make errors in data usage. The various gates and tests in the development function are designed to find these errors before they reach a business decision situation. When end users perform their own development, independent of these process gates and audits, the risk of misuse is substantially higher.

The advantages and disadvantages discussed here, as well as others, are outlined in Table 11-3. Due to the development department's historical control over the process, the disadvantages may seem to outweigh the advantages significantly. This is largely a matter of perspective. End user development tools are one of the challenging issues the professional development group faces for the future. They will be used—and extensively. The manager of systems development must come to grips with these issues and meld

Table 11-3. End User Development: Advantages and Disadvantages

ADVANTAGES

- ELIMINATION OF THE GAP BETWEEN NEED AND RESPONSE
  The development of the system is in the hands of those who need the solution, which allows adjustment of the response.
- FLEXIBILITY DURING DEVELOPMENT
  The type of tool and the intimacy of the developer and the requestor allow changes to be made more quickly and with less formal justification.
- CONCENTRATION OF PROFESSIONAL DEVELOPERS ON SOPHISTICATED ISSUES
  Development of the mundane aspects of the system allows professional developers more time to work on the technically complex issues.
- SEPARATION OF PRESENTATION AND MANIPULATION COMPONENTS
  With end users preparing the presentation components, changes in data arrangement have less effect on the overall system. This is due to the existence of a screening mechanism between the two.
- PROTOTYPE CAPABILITIES
  The simplicity of most 4GLs allows a version of the system to be brought into operation quickly. This allows effective and repetitive prototypes to be developed and tested in an operational environment.
- SHARING OF RESPONSIBILITY
  When end users produce a significant portion of the system they share in its success or failure. This dramatically increases their commitment to the project.
- EDUCATION INHERENT IN SYSTEM DEVELOPMENT
  Involvement in development creates a hands-on educational process.

DISADVANTAGES

- MULTIPLICITY OF PROBLEM SOLUTIONS
  Since user developers have only a limited (generally departmental) perspective on system availability, they will often develop overlapping systems.

Table 11-3. (Continued)

- ABILITY TO BYPASS THE JUSTIFICATION PROCESS
  Much of the validity of justification results from compulsion by an independent party. When that need does not exist, justification can become automatic and meaningless.
- RISK OF COMPROMISING DATA INTEGRITY
  Without professional expertise in dealing with data, and its accompanying care, there is a higher than normal potential for data to be compromised.
- WIDE RANGE OF DEVELOPMENT STYLES
  Much of the ease of maintaining and supporting developed software depends on the standardized approach to style. Without this training and discipline, the style varies widely, causing higher overhead in maintenance.
- NONCOMMITMENT TO DISCIPLINE
  There are always two commitments in a business discipline: to the company itself and to the profession. Users are committed to professions other than the one being used for development.
- DIFFICULTY IN ENFORCING STANDARDS
  Standards are enforced to ensure consistency in development and corporate business principles. Attempting to enforce standards without administrative control is difficult.
- EXPENSE OF SUPPORTING OBSOLETE PRODUCTS
  As products evolve, substitutes are implemented to replace less functional products. If substantial systems are in place using those obsolete products, those systems must be retained.

end user development and conventional development into an effective, comprehensive strategy.

CERTIFICATION OF SYSTEMS

Conventional development, a multiple-phase, audit-intensive process, provides a high degree of certification for its final product. By the time a system is installed, the user community can comfortably assume that it is correct. It will perform consistently and within the framework of correct business principles (at least in theory). While this result is due largely to the expertise of development professionals, it is also due to the checks and balances of the process itself.

With end user development, this situation may not exist. The opportunity for error is substantially higher because these multiple gates and reviews do not take place. For those systems which merely serve departmental functions, this risk is not overwhelming. The department's own knowledge of how things should appear will provide a safeguard. However when the information produced by these systems has corporate implications, errors introduced by faulty development can be catastrophic.

The Problem

The translation of data into information can be either direct or the result of manipulation and subsetting. When manipulation occurs, the relationship between the final figures and the original data can become extremely obscure.

As an example, in a system of order tracking, a key data item may be the order status, which can vary from entry in process to closed and cancelled. A closed order is one that has been shipped, billed and paid. Essentially, it appears to represent a sales figure. However, another system may track credits, which can represent a significant reduction in sales.

A cancelled order may also indicate that the customer has changed the order substantially, so that the original order was cancelled and a new one issued. The cancellation should represent a nonsale and should have no bearing on the total sales figures. While these factors may seem obvious to the application specialist, to a financial analyst new to the company they may appear relatively unimportant. If the analyst collects data on all orders "not open," both closed and cancelled orders will be retrieved, significantly distorting the sales picture.

On the surface, it may be obvious that these factors are wrong. However, if those dollar values are merely one component of a statistical comparison with industry standards and market penetration, they may be very difficult to see in a state which makes their errors obvious. When upper management views these figures in a marketing strategy meeting, they may make a decision which jeopardizes their market share. A bad decision of this type can easily affect the survival of a company in a competitive market.

Clearly, the more extensive the use of end user tools, the more susceptible the company becomes to this type of error. One alternative is to have the professional staff verify all output produced by end user systems. However, this approach greatly reduces the effectiveness of the end user tools themselves. It would be easier to have all development performed using conventional tools. Since that is not likely to occur, the development manager is left with the problem of somehow ensuring information integrity in systems over which he has little or no direct control. The manager may not even have staff expertise on the tools in use.

The Solution

Certification consists of the submittal of user-developed systems to systems development for review. When a system has been submitted, development reviews it and, if it finds the system to be correct, sets its stamp of approval on the output. The process does not stop there, however. Certified systems are moved from the end user's department to MIS for coverage. At that point, regardless of the language employed, the systems are supported by development and follow the normal change management process used with conventional systems.

Support is the mechanism utilized for control. It ensures that a system which was acceptable and within corporate guidelines remains so. Subsequent development and/or enhancements of the product may take place in the user community, but submittal of those changes follows the same route as original certification. Support of the system by a professional development staff generally provides adequate incentive for the user to submit to the certification process. Naturally, this entails conformation to standards and disciplines that the professional staff considers essential in providing adequate support.

This standardization increases the user/developer's work. This extra effort, as well as the visibility of the certification process, cause the number of submittals to remain limited. All systems need not be certified. Those of departmental scope tend to exist without support. In the user's mind there is no need for it, beyond development's normal consulting role.

It is when the scope of the system extends beyond a single department that certification becomes crucial, to the department and to the entire corporation. It is here that the development manager requires a commitment by upper management to make the program effective. Management must refuse to allow noncertified information to enter the decision-making process. When strategy meetings take place and presentations of key information are made, management must seek verification of the information's quality. This involves the professional group's certification that the raw data used, the way they were manipulated and the methods used to produce them are reasonably accurate. That is the purpose of certification.

In order to highlight properly the certification a system receives, screening mechanisms must be integrated into output production so that it is obvious that a certified product is being used. Ideally, this mechanism is a statement which appears on all terminal outputs and reports indicating that certification has occurred. It is analogous to the seal of approval seen on most consumer products today. That seal dos not guarantee that the product is perfect, but rather than the risk of failure is significantly lower than that of products without the seal.

The actual methods used to provide the certification stamp vary based on the product. Table 11–4 presents some rules to follow. Whatever method is chosen, whether active or passive, certification of end user developed applications is the key in melding these systems into an overall strategy for development. Since the use of end user tools will continue to grow, the ability of the development manager to balance their use with conventional development is essential.

Table 11–4. Rules for Implementing a Certification Stamping Process

- ENSURE THAT THE PROCESS IS AUTOMATIC
  The display of the certification stamp should occur as part of the inquiry or report, not through some external reference. The use of external review ensures that the stamp will be accessed very seldom.
- STAMP ONLY IN POSITIVE CASES
  A certification stamp should be applied only after a review and acceptance process takes place. This means that the stamp must not be displayed for any systems which are not certified.
- IDENTIFY THE DATE/TIME OR VERSION OF CERTIFICATION
  Since systems pass through multiple levels, the stamps should describe the level in question.
- OPTIMALLY, PROVIDE PASS-THROUGH STAMPS
  When systems feed others, they should pass on certification levels to subsetting systems. That way, valid data can be indicated for reporting products.
- NEVER CERTIFY UNPROTECTED SYSTEMS
  No system should be certified which development cannot control. Without control, continued validity cannot be guaranteed.
- CONDUCT PERIODIC AUDITS
  Review must be conducted, especially for PC-type applications. Without this audit process, security can be subverted.
- REMOVE CERTIFICATION FROM DUPLICATE OR OBSOLETE SYSTEMS
  When systems are replaced, the old systems should not be maintained in a certified state. This will create such a high maintenance burden that certification will be counterproductive.
- PUBLISH A CERTIFIED SYSTEM PORTFOLIO
  If certification is to be a positive process, all users should be given an opportunity to choose the use of certified systems over independent solutions.

BALANCING END USER AND CONVENTIONAL DEVELOPMENT

The manager's success in balancing end user tools and conventional development will be determined largely by the evolution of the technology itself. As tools continue to evolve and database technology begins to acquire some standardization, much of the difficulty in achieving balance will ease. However, these events will not occur in the near future, and if the development manager does not actively seek to establish a healthy balance now, a distorted environment will exist once product stabilization occurs.

The first step in creating a balanced environment is to recognize that simple, arbitrary rules and antagonism will not work. There is far too much demand for new systems in today's competitive marketplace to allow only a conventional approach in development. The reality of end user systems must be recognized and, in fact, fostered for development to meet the increasing demand.

Once recognition exists, a reasonable plan can be developed. This strategy must include several components, intelligently interwoven, to succeed. The first step is to choose a broad enough range of tools to make the development process productive and comprehensive. Categories should be established and one supported product chosen to cover each category. Categories consist of broad-range needs such as report writers, screen generators, database systems and other classes that support the specific industry. Only one product should be chosen for each category and support, at whatever level is deemed appropriate, provided for that product.

It may not be possible to prevent the use of nonsupported products, especially in a PC environment. However, the issue of support can be important enough to prevent extensive use of nonstandard products. When it is necessary to broaden the product coverage base, the manager can evaluate the options of continuing to support the old product or forcing its replacement with the new one. That decision will vary based on a number of factors, not the least of which is political necessity. Whatever the choice, the principal condition is one of support. If the manager is to support multiple tools, adequate staff must be provided. If it is not provided, multiple products are not a feasible option.

Selection of software products is not a simple process. Invariably conflict will occur when one user favors a particular product while another refuses to work with it. While the development manager cannot avoid this conflict, formal criteria can be established to be followed in making all selections. These criteria provide the rationale for choosing one product over another. The rules presented in Table 11-5 can serve as a baseline for establishing criteria for product selection.

Once the products are chosen, the second step is to establish guidelines on which parts of a system are to be handled conventionally and which ones by standard end user tools. The easiest way to do this is to determine which parts can be produced without conventional development. A guideline such as requiring the user to develop all reporting or inquiry subsystems is an example. With this type of guideline, justification must exist to force development to produce inquiries and reports. The professional developers are therefore allowed to concentrate on the technically sophisticated aspects of the system and to utilize the end user products to verify their work.

As each project request is passed through the initial investigation cycle, it is reviewed to determine the optimum approach: end user or conventional development. By doing this early, users can anticipate how much effort is

Table 11–5. Criteria for Selecting End User Software

- REQUIRE AN IDENTIFIABLE BENEFIT FOR THE PRODUCT
  A real justification should be required—not simply the quality of the vendor's sales effort or a competitor's choice, but fulfillment of a true need.
- ENSURE COMPATABILITY WITH FEEDER/RECIPIENT SYSTEMS
  Do not select systems which must stand alone when others exist which are compatible with installed products. This will result in multiple-step operations and higher risk.
- IDENTIFY SYSTEM EXTENSION CAPABILITY
  Products that allow for extended systems, such as databases with simulators as add-ons, are far better choices than single-thrust products. They allow simple, well-conceived interfaces.
- LIMIT DUPLICATE TOOLS FOR THE SAME CATEGORY
  The fewer tools used to support a class of need, the better. This not only lowers the maintenance cost but also avoids duplication of solutions for simple problems.
- SELECT ONLY PRODUCTS WITH A REASONABLE USER BASE
  It is best not to be the only user of new, unproven product. The end user system market is dynamic enough to avoid choosing a product with a limited expectation of market success.
- ENSURE AN ACCEPTANCE UPGRADING POLICY
  Since these products imply extensive evolution, upgrading will be necessary to maintain technical currency.
- ENSURE AVAILABILITY OF EDUCATION
  The more formal the educational process for end user products, the easier support will be, as the likelihood of user intelligence is higher.
- ENSURE ADEQUATE INTERNAL SUPPORT CAPABILITY
  It is essential that support personnel be available within development. If they are not, they must be trained before the product is installed.
- CHOOSE PRODUCTS WITH ACCEPTANCE SECURITY PROVISIONS
  Since the number of users will always be limited, there should be security in the product to ensure that limitation.
- CONTACT REFERENCES
  Verify the product's usefulness and viability in a real environment. Learn its limitations as well as the assets. Local contacts are best.
- IDENTIFY VIRTUAL FEATURES
  Judge a product only on the basis of its implemented features, not those planned or proposed.
- IDENTIFY CONFLICTING FEATURES
  Much of the marketing of a product can hinge on peripheral capabilities. If another product has been chosen to provide those features, they are of little value in the current product.

required of them for the project and how much professional expertise must be available. If the user lacks resources or experience, development can fill this need, but at a fairly high rate of charge-back. At any rate, resource needs are highlighted and the project is divided into responsibility areas.

The third step is to institute a certification process for end user systems. There is no doubt that, with the availability of end user tools, systems will be developed without development's knowledge or support. While this may be counterproductive at times, it is a situation that must be recognized. Certification will not prevent it; it will only control its impact.

The final step in balancing the development options is to utilize standard tracking mechanisms when end users and conventional developers work on the same project. This ensures that the principal parts of the system do, in fact, deliver simultaneously. It also helps prevent a shift in project scope as users change specifications in response to experience gained with the tools. A development staff can produce an elegant database and update system for which the user has changed all the ground rules during their portion of development. Regardless of who does the development, there must remain a single focal point of coordination. Otherwise, the system will not be comprehensive.

CONCLUSION

No invention has produced a greater impact on systems development than end user languages. This technology gives users the opportunity to perform most of their own development in response to needs. While there are many performance and integrity problems with end user products, these are not the principal issues facing the development manager today. Those problems will eventually disappear as the products evolve and hardware becomes less and less expensive.

The real issue facing the development manager, and the corporation, is that end user development via 4GLs allows the process control steps of development to be bypassed. These safeguards have been developed over a long period of time and are the result of both science and experience. In many cases, these gating mechanisms allow systems to be developed with a substantially reduced risk of failure. The gates were not devised for that reason, but rather to create predictability and maintainability.

Since industries are becoming more and more information sensitive, the development manager must successfully meld end user development with the more conventional process. This allows the benefits of end user tools, ranging from speed to their close relationship with the actual enterprise, to be achieved while still maintaining integrity and discipline. It is a complex issue and one that will not wait patiently for an optimum solution.

More than anything else, the manager's strategy for implementing and using end user tools must take into account their rapid evolution. Sensitivity and flexibility are bywords when developing a strategy. It is not certain how these tools will look in the future, but they will definitely form the foundation for continued system delivery.

12

PROCEDURES, METHODS AND STANDARDS

Procedures, methods and standards are three principal technologies of systems development. They are not normally considered part of technology simply because they are not oriented to hardware or software. However, they govern the way a development department operates, have a major impact on the department's success, and, more than the precise tools employed, determine its day-to-day operations.

Development and maintenance of these three items would represent a formal process. With their dedication to discrete activities and reviews, as well as the formality involved, they require considerable thought and effort. When viewed superficially, they can appear bureaucratic—and, in fact, they are. However, bureaucracy is not necessarily a negative factor. At the proper level, it provides the necessary checks and balances which ensure product quality, commonality and adequate review of plans.

However, over the years, bureaucracy has come to imply a commitment to the steps and not the product, the mechanics and not the goal, or the conservation and not the dynamic. For that reason, procedures, methods and standards have been relegated to a back-room role rather than providing the framework for the day-to-day operations of a department.

The purpose of these three elements is to provide consistency in development's activities. They do not represent inflexibility but rather a basis upon which to decide what constitutes exceptions and why those exceptions are justified. They provide the same form of stability that legal principles do in normal life. Without these rules, the result is chaos.

For that reason, the development manager must foster the development and evolution of procedures, methods and standards. In many ways, these are the elements which will define the department. Especially in large departments, the manager cannot hope to control the work of all members of the staff. Their performance will vary widely based on the personality, the pressure they experience and the specific situation. The quality and style of the systems they produce will vary widely as well. These variations can be positive and creative, or they can contribute to an atmosphere of inconsistency. It is through these three technological elements that the manager attempts to establish an environment which will foster creativity, when appropriate, and limit variations when they are either inefficient or counterproductive.

Development, as a dynamic discipline, requires procedures, methods and standards that can grow and match the technical environment. Therefore, they cannot be inflexible or arbitrary. Much of their maintenance and enhancement should be left to the staff itself and changed in response to both the discipline's growth and the staff's maturation. Basically, however, they must be administered by the development manager.

It is therefore extremely important that the manager understand the intent and the atmosphere that these three elements will foster. Procedures which allow for no exceptions take bureaucracy to its negative extreme, inevitably resulting in a nonresponsive department. Methods which are not adapted to the organization, the people and the industry they serve become so abstract that they cease to serve a useful purpose; their compromise by staff members becomes a form of aggressiveness in the user's eyes. Standards which are too rigid limit creativity and eventually drive imaginative professionals away.

Conversely, when procedures, methods and standards are too loose or poorly enforced, each new project becomes an exercise in the definition of how the department will operate. Each product is new, support becomes a major burden and quality is defined by the strongest rather than by the most knowledgeable.

Either extreme is a dangerous situation. The effective manager seeks a balance between them in which the department operates both efficiently and imaginatively. This balance must be fostered and protected or it will inevitably drift to one extreme or the other. Since the manager cannot realistically review every line of code or detail of analysis, he or she must define how that code or analysis will look globally. The important components must be identified and an atmosphere created in which their adherence is seen as productive for the department as a whole.

In this chapter, procedures, methods and standards are discussed as vehicles to provide direction to the department. Each is defined and discussed separately, and its intentions are analyzed. The discussions focus on the practical rather than the theoretical. The subject of creativity versus discipline is discussed. The two are far from mutually exclusive; in fact, constructive discipline breeds an atmosphere which promotes creativity rather than stifling it.

For most new managers, the administration of procedures, methods and standards represents a significant transition point in their careers. Administration is often viewed as a move away from the technical and, in many ways, the leadership aspects of the job. For this reason, new managers often choose to ignore it in order to avoid perceiving themselves as pure administrators. However, it is through procedures, methods and standards that the manager retains control over technical issues.

PROCEDURES

Formal procedures are developed to standardize and control the principal aspects of systems development. They provide the administrative consistency which would otherwise be missing in such a variable, dynamic process. Formalized procedures are extremely important for the manager. Without them, more decisions are left to project leaders and lower-level managers than is desirable. While it is important that project leaders be allowed some latitude, based on the situation, the development manager is responsible for applying measures which ensure product consistency across all systems. In order to achieve this consistency, sacrifices in individual projects may be necessary.

Managers of development tend to deemphasize procedure development and maintenance. As a background activity, this seems less important than highly visible technical issues. However, without adequate procedures, the manager must deal with these issues on every project that comes along because there is no basis upon which to operate. Therefore, the manager must ensure a proper level of discipline within the process so that all corporate requirements for all projects are met.

Once the commitment is made to develop or revise procedures, the manager must ensure that the level of formality and detail is in keeping with his or her desires and the corporate culture. When great attention must be paid to the precise equality of each project and product, the procedures should be more formal. This often happens when work is performed on a contract basis, with the contract defining how the work will be done and how precise the final product will be. The only reasonable way to ensure this is to define the steps in such detail that very little latitude exists. The process is time-consuming, but the final product will completely match the original specifications.

In other cases, especially when a small staff is involved, high precision is counterproductive. The product must be produced quickly and the users of the system are willing to accept some risk in order to ensure timeliness. When this occurs, procedures should be written which define primarily the external checkpoints that are needed. The manager must then perform a more detailed review before the product goes into production. The department must also have a clear concept of its priorities and responsibilities. When these issues are not formally defined, they must be implicitly understood. There are five principal elements the manager should be concerned with when dealing with procedures. These will now be discussed.

Gating Steps

Process gating means that discrete stages of the process must be completed before the next stage commences. These gates allow the manager to halt the process for any reason before any additional expense or commitment occurs. They are formal review points where goals are matched to performance by someone with a knowledge of the overall responsibilities and a perspective beyond the single project. It is at these points that project steps may be repeated or revised in the interest of standardized methods or good business practices.

The intent of procedures, methods and standards is to ensure that the gates are successfully passed. Regardless of how detailed the procedures are, they must define and direct the gating process. The gates should be defined explicitly, should delineate responsibilities and should require completion of the phase to which they apply.

The most critical component of the gates is their effective linkage to the methods and standards. The methods must support the gating steps and not dictate mechanisms which, by their nature, cause activities to take place around the gates. As an example, if the gates indicate that no system testing takes place before the coding is complete, the method cannot require testing to occur simultaneously with coding. Likewise, if standards are detailed, their review must be part of the gate at which they apply, not after the entire process is complete.

Periodic Review

Procedures must not be allowed to become stale. As changes are made in the development process, they should be incorporated as quickly as possible. Unless this occurs, there will be so many discrepancies between the development process components that the procedures will be ignored. Ignoring procedures is worse than not having them at all because the perception that they are being adhered to remains. When that perception does not match reality, system quality and problem response invariably suffer as plans and organizations are created with procedural continuity assumed.

Review and adjustment allow the procedures to remain up-to-date and procedural mechanics to reflect the reality of the workplace. The review should always occur in the same time frame so that users of the procedures understand when their methods must change. The frequency of review and alteration will vary depending on how detailed the procedures are. The more detailed they are, the less frequent the changes will be simply because they will cover more complex, broad situations. Review should take place at least annually, however, regardless of the level of detail.

Exceptions

When procedures are established, exceptions are necessary and inevitable. Regardless of how much time is spent in preparation, situations will arise which are not covered in the standard approach. Even if they can be foreseen, there will be times when situational decisions are more appropriate than compliance with written procedures. Too many forces are at play, from politics to technology, to attempt to spell out all decision factors in the development process.

Procedures should be developed which allow preapprovals for exceptions. This may involve stage combination, such as combining the specification and analysis gates for a project which has management approval regardless of the cost. It may also mean that programming standards will not be part of the code completion gate when a new language is first used. In any case, exceptions should be standardized so that the manager knows and approves them. In this way, they can be controlled and their implications evaluated. They should not be approved at the gate itself simply to cover noncompliance.

Scope

Procedures are the broadest in scope of the three elements discussed in this chapter. They govern the process of development from the receipt of a project request through its implementation and maintenance when in production. Methods and standards, in contrast, cover portions of this activity. Because of the broad scope of procedures, the manager must involve all persons and structures in the department when they are being developed.

Since personnel and organizational structures vary, procedures should be developed which avoid specifying individuals or organizational units as much as possible. Although this is not always possible, much of the relationship between procedure and organization can be defined by separately referenced current practices.

Current practices are variables in the procedure which are far more dynamic than the procedure itself and are intended to vary. As an example, the procedure may indicate that database design is to be reviewed at four different stages in accordance with current practices. The review is conducted by the manager of database administration. When that person's responsibility grows, the review may be conducted by specialists in different database languages. The current practices specify that the reviews will be done at different levels at each stage and which area will conduct them. In this way the details can change while the procedural intent remains consistent.

Style

The style with which procedures are developed has a major bearing on how easily they are interpreted, and thus on their effectiveness. Many corporations have elaborate rules governing their preparation. Often there are departments specifically set up to write procedures. If this is the case, managers should use these facilities or at least follow their guidelines. This not only simplifies the task but makes it more probable that development's procedures will be accepted.

When these facilities are not available, and generally they are not, the manager must develop the style of procedures as well as the content. No one procedural style is best. In general, the style depends on the degree of latitude desired and the way in which the procedures will be referenced. However, there are two factors of style which should be considered.

First, the "playscript" style should be avoided. It is too constraining and does not reflect the variability of the process. Second, a procedural manual is best developed as a reference guide, not as a start-to-finish description. The principal elements should be oriented around events that will prompt reference, such as walk-throughs, obvious stage boundaries and approval gates. With this style, they are much more likely to be referenced.

METHODS

Methods provide a standardized approach to systems development. The key word here is "approach." Methods should be chosen and implemented as an umbrella for major portions of the process, not as inflexible instructions about steps to be done. With this approach, they provide consistency for every product and, because they are proven in actual operation, quality assurance as well.

Without active, formal methods, each project may be developed with different priorities, different emphasis on specific aspects of the process and, consequently, different levels of success. Over time, project leaders tend to gravitate naturally to one method or another, self-developed or standard, which serves them well. Successful project managers choose successful methods so that consistency will be achieved—but that consistency will be by project manager, not across the entire staff. In addition, the consistency of the methods developed will be the result of the particular manager's experience rather than of research.

Methods are generally chosen from a standard marketed set. Some examples are YOURDON structured disciplines, JACKSON techniques and WARNIER-ORR. While these methods vary somewhat, they all share several characteristics which are far more important to the manager than the specific technique employed.

First, these methods are the result of considerable research and study. Therefore, they are applicable as a general development tool, rather than being tailored to one personality or industry. To be effective in specific circumstances they must be tailored, but not at the level of theory. Second, they are theoretical, with practical use resulting from adaptation and implementation. This theoretical basis provides consistency across the method rather than a cut-and-paste approach drawn from a body of experience. Third, the widespread acceptance of these methods provides a pool of semi-trained personnel in the job market. The manager can then include as a hiring criterion some experience with the method chosen and expect to find a qualified candidate. This lowers training costs and shortens the learning process.

Methods are part of the development process and therefore fit into a portion of the procedures. Depending upon how extensive their implementation is, they may cover a small fraction or nearly all of the project life cycle. Methods may also be mixed, such as using YOURDON techniques for analysis and specification preparation and WARNIER-ORR for code construction. Whatever method or mix is chosen, the manager should understand that methods do not supplant procedures. Rather, they enhance and enrich the project life cycle, providing consistency and safety throughout.

Methods differ from procedures and standards in that they generally involve little formal documentation. Instead, the principal components are integrated into the procedures and standards and documented in that fashion. Optimally, a document exists which describes the purpose, scope, and primary components of the method. It may be part of the department's policies or even a broad standard to govern the entire process. The primary mechanism, however, is the method's impact on the procedures and standards.

While some methods may prove more effective than others based on personnel preference, industry type, or philosophy, the overriding concern for the manager is that a method be followed; the particular method employed is of no concern. As with procedures, there are a number of issues to be considered in regard to implementation. There are many excellent textbooks dealing with the methods available today. From a functional point of view (that of managing a department where a method is or will be employed), there are three principal issues. These will now be discussed.

Implementation

True implementation of a new method should occur only after it has been tested in a pilot project. The results of the pilot are the basis of the implementation process. The primary reason for waiting for the completion of a pilot project is to determine how the method will be used. If proper analysis was done and a well-accepted product chosen, implementation will take place. The real questions are, which components will be implemented at what stage and which standards will be created to support the method?

These questions should be answered by the pilot project, but only if the results and experiences are thoroughly analyzed. Once that is accomplished and the decisions are made the manager must commit himself to the method. There is bound to be resistance in the initial stages, as well as a temptation to ignore the new product if a crucial project is to begin and the project team is unfamiliar with the method. However, if the manager fails to make the commitment to the product, it will probably never become the standard. So, managers must stand their ground and insist on compliance. The purpose is to ensure comprehensive project consistency, and this entails some short-term risk.

Adapting versus Adopting

One of the strengths of predefined development methods is their usefulness across a wide range of industries and applications. This characteristic increases the probability that it will be appropriate in any environment and ensures a qualified job pool. However, it also provides the greatest opportunity for problems in the specific environment.

Predefined development methods are not suitable in all situations. Components must be carefully reviewed and modified to suit the specific environment. Over time, aspects of the selected method will constantly change to match the experience of the developers, as well as technological evolution. It cannot remain static, any more than procedures can.

This adaptation process should be an explicit effort and should not be done by the manager. The manager should specify which aspects of the method are important and assign members of the staff to control and provide the final specifications. For example, the manager may state that analysis must proceed in a top-down fashion and in such a way that user review can take place at all critical stages. The actual adaptation should be done by the staff and reviewed by the manager.

Avoiding Long-Term Inbreeding

While adaptation of the standard method ensures applicability to the specific situation, it carries the risk that, as the product becomes more and more practical, it begins to lose its theoretical purity. As that takes place, the department slowly departs from the real intent of the method. A method operates best when the link between theory and practicality is evident. As it becomes more obscure, so the discipline weakens.

This inbreeding cannot be easily remedied by the influx of new staff. Their learning is focused mainly on their own adaptation to the department's method, and since they are (hopefully) hired at the junior levels, the emphasis is on learning the existing process, not suggesting alterations.

In order to maintain the theory–practice link, classes should be periodically conducted at the theoretical level. This can be done by stand-up instruction or videotape, but it should not be tailored to the specific implementation. Members of the staff who attend can then compare the internal implementation of the method with the theoretical baseline and recommend changes to bring the implementation back into line.

STANDARDS

Standards ensure either product quality or efficiency by adherence to proven mechanisms. These mechanisms can range from instructions on the preparation and content of analysis documents to the use of precatalogued program modules. The fewer options available for the component being standardized, the more effective those standards will be.

By establishing standards, the manager can limit the paths for the developer. The intent, of course, is to ensure that limitation is for productive purposes, not to hamper creativity. The paths that are eliminated are those that will make little difference in product quality. In other words, the alternative choices will be of no higher quality than the selected standard. In this way, the developer's ability to concentrate on the creative aspects of the system is enhanced rather than reduced.

Standards also aid in promoting consistency. On projects where standards have been strictly followed, any staff member can enter the project and, when gates are passed, move more easily from phase to phase. This consistency extends to operational characteristics as well. Reports and displays are identical, messages are produced in the same format and responses are consistent.

Detail versus Broad Standards

Standards, like procedures and methods, are instituted to produce results beyond the specific elements they address. They define a style and philosophy toward the development of systems, the latitude allowed the developers, and the level of discipline and consistency expected. When the manager institutes standards, these philosophical elements are being defined for the staff in ways that affect their everyday work.

Broad standards, such as defining the elements of a cost/benefit report, provide direction rather than specifics. The analyst is still allowed to determine how much detail is necessary for an appropriate analysis, but the manager is assured that all elements *will* be covered. During review, the interpretation of what should be in the report may vary and the report may have to be redrafted. This is the basic drawback of broad standards; they are open to interpretation and perspective.

However, for most analytically oriented activities, broad standards on direction are the only viable option. There is too much variability in the process to place tight limits on the content and level of the output. Broad standards also allow far more creativity to be displayed, and creativity is important for much of the process analysis in the development of systems. Control is best exerted at the inception of a phase by defining the level of detail expected for the standard gate to be passed. In this way, the developers know what the standard interpretation will be and can adapt their approach to that development stage.

Detail standards precisely define what is expected of an activity. Most commonly, this type of standard is applied to code construction or design aspects which derive a direct benefit from commonality. The developer is left with no choice but to follow an accepted path. When the manager institutes detail standards, that aspect of development is essentially removed from the thought process. Design and construction of nonstandardized portions of the system will be oriented toward those standardized elements, which become the cornerstone of the systems produced.

In this situation, the manager must be certain that the standards are best for the systems. If they are ill-defined, hard to interface with, or too numerous, the systems produced will be extremely convoluted in order to meet them—one of the situations standards were developed to avoid. On the other hand, too few standards result in systems with a high probability of variance in style, increasing support and maintenance costs. They should be carefully interpreted and evaluated in terms of what the manager is attempting to achieve overall.

Detail standards allow the implementation of efficiency programs with confidence in meeting expectations. When the manager determines that certain report formats or display designs will be allowed and supported, those components, and the code to produce them, can be catalogued in libraries. From that point on, this type of output is disallowed in any application program and the standard routines must be used. The effects are lowered support requirements for output preparation, reduced design time and less code production. Without detail standards, that type of program would be nearly impossible to police.

The principal technical benefit of detail standards, especially with precatalogued routines, is confidence that much of the system will work. During testing, this significantly reduces the number of logic paths that the developer must follow to debug a system. In terms of support, the knowledge that specific components of the system are bug free allows faster, more effective resolution of problems. These benefits inevitably result in a more rapid production of systems with a high probability of operational success.

Enforcement

For standards to work, they must be universally applied. At an appropriate gating point, whatever work is produced is verified for standard compliance. If a compromise with the standards is found, the work must be brought to an acceptable state before the gate is passed. Since standards are the responsibility of managers, who define departmental product consistency, managers must ensure their enforcement.

Enforcement is a passive process. Rather than presiding over reviews for compliance, the manager must justify any compromise with approved standards. In general, enforcement at this level will cause requests for concessions to be minimized. It will take less time to make systems comply than to achieve approval for variations. This is one case where bureaucracy has advantages.

If exceptions to standards are granted frequently, the standards are probably inappropriate. Standards are meant to be just what the name implies—standard. Any exception compromises the purpose of establishing the standard. When exceptions are frequent, either the standard is not really standard or the group requesting the exception is not committed to its use. In either case, the situation should be remedied.

Like procedures and methods, standards should be reviewed periodically. Technology, staff changes or philosophy will negate the effect of some standards while creating the need for new ones. The review ensures that the viability and applicability of standards remains high. It should be conducted by a committee of staff members, not by the manager alone.

CREATIVITY VERSUS DISCIPLINE: A HAPPY MEDIUM

It has been charged that strict standardization of the development process limits the creativity of developers. They do not have the freedom of thought and expression which promotes new and innovative approaches to the solution of corporate problems. Discipline, on the other hand, allows the orderly production of stable systems. Through this discipline, the company is given stable, accurate knowledge for making decisions and conducting business which allows management to be creative and innovative.

Both of these aspects of development, creativity and discipline, are necessary for an innovative, productive staff. The manager has two tasks when attempting to strike a happy medium between them. First, the purpose of the standard procedure or method, its benefits and its effects, must be effectively marketed to the staff. It is the staff that will make the process work regardless of the sense and utility of the procedures, methods and standards. Only in practice are they viable and organic. This marketing is necessary for many departments which already have some standards. Unless they were established with common sense and gained acceptance, they are not viable. The staff is probably ignoring all but the most visible elements and is following the letter of the law but not the spirit.

The second task involves establishing standards so they create the atmosphere desired and ensuring their continued evolution. The manager must understand what these standards should achieve. This knowledge will determine their level (detailed or broad) and their effect on the decision choices. The manager should present a written outline of their intent and allow a staff committee to define the standards, procedures and methods in detail. If such an outline already exists, it will form the basis of the review.

The staff committee must understand the need to build discipline into the process. The manager should discuss the elements of discipline necessary and the efficiencies they produce. It should not be an edict but rather a cooperative discussion which allows the committee to understand their purpose and intent. This will ensure control and consistency while protecting the staff's sense of craftmanship and self-expression in their work.

Avoiding Unnecessary Bureaucracy

One of the key questions the manager must answer when establishing standards, procedures and methods is how bureaucratic the process should be. The answer will determine the level of detail and the amount of latitude allowed the developers. The more detail present, the more bureaucratic the environment, since detail requires more verification than broad direction. Consequently, the process will be slowed as verification is performed.

Bureaucracy, although sometimes necessary, is relatively rare. To avoid too much of it, the manager should examine each formal step or aspect and make sure that the gain will justify the delay incurred by review. As an example, if the department operates on a charge-back basis and all projects must be scheduled prior to budget preparation, how necessary is it for development to apply stringent cost/benefit analysis to requested projects? The company's management mechanisms and budget process should do this very well. If the user can justify the development cost, that should be enough.

In this circumstance, it would be better to get an approved benefit statement from the user than to prepare it in the development department. In theory, the latter procedure is correct for allocation of resources, but the political reality is that the project has been justified. Professional analysis will not change that fact. Therefore, it will accomplish little and should be avoided.

Standards operate the same way. The manager must ask, "what is gained by doing this the same way every time?" If the answer does not justify the standard, it should not exist. When approaches to a problem are preferable but not mandatory, they should be presented in just that way, using the practices discussed earlier. The fewer standards that exist, the more likely they are to be followed. This does not imply some magical maximum number of standards. It does mean that whatever standards are applied should truly be required.

"Try It and See": The Dangers

The formality of creating procedures and standards often causes managers to take a "try it and see" approach to their implementation. A staff member suggests that it may be wise to standardize a process and the manager, unconvinced, does so temporarily, planning to review the results in a specific project. The hope, obviously, is to limit the risk of failure to one area. The concept is fine and conservative but seldom is effective.

The first problem is that standards, procedures and methods are designed for global goals. In an isolated situation, they may be more of a hindrance than a benefit. The results of the test will vary substantially based on the people involved in the project, the implementation, and the desire of the tester to see that the process works. The test will not prove the component's long-term applicability for the department as a whole, as intended, and its failure will jeopardize its future use.

The second problem is that implementation of the process focuses on a specific project. Enforcement is significantly different when implementation involves the entire department, and so are the priorities to be achieved.

The final problem is that when one tries an approach in a limited way, the basic theoretical evaluation is bypassed. One starts with the practical and therefore loses touch with the theoretical, cross-situational implications.

To deal properly with standards, procedures and methods, evaluation and analysis should be done. If a committee exists, allow it to do this work and prepare the targeted mechanism for implementation.

DISTRIBUTION

All procedures and standards should be on-line and available to the developers at their work stations. When development does not have interactive capabilities, printed distribution is necessary. However, without on-line availability, distribution will be a significant problem.

Standards are most effective if the issues involved can be verified as they occur. Otherwise, much effort can be spent on a nonstandard approach before the developer is even aware that a violation has occurred. When that happens, one of the prime goals of standardization—efficiency—is compromised.

If the standards are implemented in a database, additional long-term benefits can be achieved. Systems can be passed through the standards database to verify compliance. This capability provides automated verification and greater assurance of gate passing when those stages occur. The developers themselves can pass system components through the database after major portions of the system are constructed. This way, corrections can be made long before schedules reach the crisis point.

CONCLUSION

The development manager is constantly seeking ways to bring adequate discipline to systems development. When this is done, schedules can be prepared with reasonable certainty, plans can proceed on schedule and the expectation/result ratio so critical to management can be satisfied. Software development requires as much stabilization as possible without infringing on the creativity and innovativeness of the developers.

Discipline can be achieved with the appropriate implementation of procedures, methods and standards. These elements of process control ensure that, regardless of the complexity of any particular project, consistency and reasonable efficiency will occur. These elements have a pervasive influence on both the work and the effectiveness of the products.

Involving the staff is the primary objective in the creation and enforcement of procedures, methods and standards. It ensures that the procedures are not bureaucratic, that the standards are relevant and productive, and that the methods facilitate the development process. However, the manager must lead the way, understanding the goal to be achieved and the atmosphere to be created. The manager must also make sure that the procedures, methods and standards are enforced. Exceptions cannot be granted cavalierly. The purpose of these elements is comprehensive and long-term. Short-term sacrifices must be made to ensure their effectiveness.

13

MANAGING IN THE DATABASE ENVIRONMENT

In the early 1970s, database technology provided the best opportunity, data processing professionals believed, to control and stabilize systems development. The ability to isolate data and data structures from application code allowed the application to change without risk to data security and integrity. Although the database was originally marketed as a method to reduce or eliminate excess storage for redundant data, the primary gain is the isolation of data.

Few data processing departments today lack database management systems. Their products are numerous, ranging from simple file structure systems to sophisticated management systems providing automatic recovery and supportive 4GLs. The technology has created the role of database managers, analysts and planners to protect and enhance the use and distribution of data assets. It has made the use of 4GLs viable for development, since the management system provides protection and security, allowing the manipulation of data by nonprofessional users.

With all of its benefits, database technology has yet to achieve its main goal. Much corporate data are still unprotected, either because including predatabase systems in an integrated environment is considered too expensive or because the data analysis and generation involved are seen as too time-consuming to justify. As a result, some parts of system referenced data are contained in a database and others are independent.

The development manager must also deal with a wide range of organizational structures to support that database. In some cases, the database function is provided by a separate group, while in others it is part of development. In still other cases, there is no independent function. Each of these arrangements creates both benefits and problems for the development manager.

Database technology will probably achieve its original goal at some point. Until then, however, the development manager must operate in an environment of rapid transition, changing organization structures and diverse approaches to data management. Many of the problems facing the manager will be solved outside the development function. Development will be expected to make concessions and foster the transition to an independently managed database. Regardless of the difficulties of supporting this transition, the development manager should be actively involved in making it work.

In this chapter, several issues are discussed in order to clarify the database concept. The idea of a fully integrated database is reviewed, concentrating on the benefits for development. The modern database environment is then discussed to highlight the difficulties of this transitional stage for the manager. The difference between the data and database administrators is then examined, emphasizing how the development manager deals with each.

The next three sections discuss technical and organizational problems that occur in the transition from conventional mechanisms to the database environment. Probably no subject has spawned more professional literature than the database concept. It is imperative that the development manager understand both the theory and practice of database management. This is basic to the continued effectiveness of systems development.

This chapter does not provide an exhaustive treatment of database technology. Instead, it highlights the principal issues facing the development manager in the database environment. Throughout the chapter, the terms "comprehensive database" or "fully integrated database" are used. They imply that all data are under disciplined control, *not that they reside in a single, monstrous, all-encompassing database*. Integration can be achieved using bridges across multiple databases, active dictionary/directory mechanisms or various other means. The main advantage of integration is that data can be identified and controlled.

The advance of fiberoptic technology, allowing for high-speed, long-distance data transfer, implies that in the future data can be integrated despite a remote hardware location. This capability will force a redefinition of the term "integrated." That technology, as applied to databases, is in its infancy but will certainly evolve rapidly as it fills a dramatic need.

The probability of achieving a fully integrated database in the conventional sense is highly unlikely, for reasons to be discussed later in this chapter. However, it is important for the manager to understand the benefits this goal implies. The attempts to achieve integration will yield enough benefits to justify the effort even if the final goal is never achieved.

THE FULLY INTEGRATED DATABASE

With a fully integrated database, the principal gain is the opportunity to eliminate variables in the construction and support of systems. Developers are allowed to concentrate on the manipulation and presentation of information, knowing that a stable base exists. Since a key ingredient in project success is the elimination of variables, this is a major goal for the manager in establishing a comprehensive database environment.

In a support environment, the existence of stable data allows workers to search for problems in the component of the system which displays the problem. There is no need to spend valuable time searching feeder systems and update/edit programs to find out where bad data were introduced. That is generally where most support time is spent: not searching for the problem itself but for its origin. With the knowledge that the data are valid, the problem is dramatically reduced and resolution is speeded.

The advantage of application independence allows development to proceed, in many cases, without worrying about introducing new data elements into the system. This permits the continued use of end user inquiries and reports even if a new system is created. When new data elements must be created, significant time and expense, not to mention risk, are avoided by the ability to concatenate the new data with established data structures.

Application independence also allows developers to concentrate on the new system rather than trying to modify older ones to support the new data arrangements. This problem is quite serious in terms of the overall project. When a wide-ranging new system is being developed, many operational systems may be affected. The new data or their interpretation are necessary in the existing systems.

While the new system is under development, the affected systems and programs must be frozen. During that time, and generally for a period following implementation, the affected program is unavailable for enhancement and susceptible to support problems. The existing program is certainly stable, but any changes introduced independent of the project must be retrofitted into it. These changes may negate significant portions of the design. In any case, freezing components of the system introduces more variables into the project.

Most modern, sophisticated database management systems permit the editing of data before they are recorded. When preestablished data conditions and ranges are not valid, the update is rejected. Obviously, there are limitations to this editing capability, especially in relating data from one database to another. However, the fact that data fields pass edits independently of the more error-prone application code provides great integrity for data.

The broader the integration across systems, the greater the assurance of integrity. As the automation of a company grows, data elements become more closely related. For example, the validity of a customer's financial status, both as a true customer and as a vendor, may be closely related to the customer's open order volume. If this value is not a determinant in the editing of the financial status code, this relationship is lost. When the data are contained in a tightly integrated database, the relationship is possible. If the data are independently maintained, this tie is difficult, if not impossible.

A comprehensive, integrated database also provides for greater data availability than exists in a nondatabase environment. When a system is being developed or enhancements are being made, data can be easily transferred to the new system from external ones. There is no need to develop the convoluted, complex interfaces necessary to match companion systems' cycles and run characteristics. The new system can be designed and constructed from scratch, without extensive dependencies.

This situation has many benefits. First, project life cycles can be compressed because one of the main complexities, cross-system interfaces, is reduced or eliminated. Second, with data elements immediately available and defined, developers in one application area need not become experts in another area (the one controlling the issue data). This substantially lowers the risk of misuse or misinterpretation. Third, data redundancy can be avoided.

The problem with data redundancy is not excessive storage requirements. The ready availability of low-cost mass storage has essentially eliminated the problem (except in the most gross cases) in making development plans. The real problem occurs when redundant data are actually not redundant. For instance, finding an order status code in two places is a problem only when the values disagree. When that happens, theoretically equal systems yield unequal results and decisions are based on invalid information. With database management systems, this problem can still exist, but the tools are present to reduce the risk.

The totally integrated, comprehensive database has enormous benefits for users and for corporate information control. These gains deserve major consideration. From the development manager's viewpoint, this is a given but, with or without this database, the manager is responsible for providing these benefits to the company. What is important to the manager, and what this book emphasizes, is the benefit to be achieved in developing and managing systems.

A comprehensive, integrated database makes it much easier to develop systems. Given the long-term, stragegic nature of development's service role, the difficulties in changing to this environment are easily justified. However, few managers today find themselves in a situation where they are dealing with a comprehensive, integrated database.

TODAY'S DATABASE ENVIRONMENT: THE REALITY

Very few data processing departments today have a comprehensive, integrated database. At best, a large portion of the data exist in several loosely related databases. The remainder is housed in files developed years earlier which have never been transferred to the database. These relatively uncontrolled files can have either a slight impact on the process of development, by requiring extra interfaces, or a major impact by placing the data' validity in question.

This arrangement creates significant problems for the development manager. The abstract need for a comprehensive database is generally recognized by all concerned; otherwise, no database system would exist. However, the tendency often develops to protect the integrity of the few existing bases to the point where little or no change is justifiable for that base's expansion or integration. At the same time, new projects, when examined in their own narrow terms, do not justify the expense and cost of subdatabase generation or upper-level integration.

In such an environment, standard files, independent of the integrated database, are developed simply to keep project requests moving. Once those systems exist, the eventual problem of integration becomes even more serious. Strategically, it is difficult to justify such an approach, but tactically, the manager is committed to project success. This can quickly become a no-win situation.

The separation of the database and applications further increases the problem. Database specialists concentrate on data integrity alone. Application systems are often viewed as a threat to that integrity. Development managers then find themselves at odds with data administrators; the developer needs to produce systems quickly, while the data analyst seeks to study new data implications at length. The result of this conflict is generally the creation of two database functions, one within development and one outside.

Given the recognized benefits of an integrated, comprehensive database, it is difficult to understand why this situation exists. The long-term benefits are well accepted by data processing workers and generally accepted (to varying degrees) by corporate management. Yet, despite this recognition, separate database functions still exist and continue to plague the development manager.

The principal reason for this situation is cost. Developing an integrated database costs a lot of money. To truly integrate the data, several steps are necessary which cannot be tied to any short-term economic gain. The entire company must be studied to establish information relationships and needs. Ownership of information must be determined and responsibility for integrity identified. Current data structures must be mapped to corporate structures in order to identify gaps and inconsistencies. All this takes resource dedication and time, both for MIS and for users and management.

There is no inherent or recognizable benefit from this exercise. It sets the stage and prepares the company for future development projects. In a competitive environment, management generally has little patience with such an effort. They prefer to spend money on tangible programs with quantifiable benefits. Therefore, the framework is never developed, and implementation of database programs tends to be haphazard at worst and fragmented at best.

Changes within the company also make it difficult to implement a database program. Since such a program takes several years (in general, the payback period is 3 to 5 years), a long-term commitment by management is required. During that time, there are likely to be many changes in management. New priorities and personalities will emerge, and the likelihood of a continuing commitment for an integrated database is low. These organizational changes may also necessitate changes in the database, leading to new maintenance costs.

Finally, regardless of management's commitment to data integration, inconsistencies in database technology remain. The principal database vendors define the technology, despite the forward-looking research of database theorists. There is little or no consistency or real interface capabilities between the popular database management systems today. This means that, for the foreseeable future, the problems of data integration will remain.

These and other issues define the reality of database management today. In order to achieve the long-range benefits of an integrated database, the development manager must either overcome the problems or live with them. Much of the development of the database will be beyond the manager's control. It will be governed by the skill and perseverance of the MIS director and the data/database administrator. This process cannot succeed without the development manager's active support and sacrifices. The benefits for the manager are real and will be appreciated for years. Without a database management system, many of the technologies of the future, such as end user languages and the information center, will never achieve their true potential.

THE DATA ADMINISTRATOR VERSUS THE DATABASE ADMINISTRATOR

In a database environment, not only are data separated from applications, but data structures are separated from the developers as well. In general, a database function of some sort exists and is responsible for the integrity and stability of the databases. Typically, this function is equal in importance to development. However, because of its immaturity, it exists in a variety of reporting structures.

Whether the database function is external or internal to development, data separation is typically coupled with responsibility separation. This separation implies another level of bureaucracy in the project life cycle and therefore must be of concern to the manager. That separation, and how well it complements the process of developing systems, will have a major impact on the manager's success.

Today there are two independent database functions: data administration and database administration. Often they are combined into one person, department or group but, for the development manager, functional separation still exists. Therefore, whether dealing with one area or two, the manager must understand the different priorities and directions of each.

Data Administration

Data administration is concerned with strategic issues. It is responsible for identifying the information requirements of business areas and for ensuring that the information is available and properly used. It is also concerned with coordinating long-term projects to ensure that the implementation of databases supporting applications is consistent with company strategies.

Data administration deals with information and business models and subject databases. It plots the relationships between various databases and datasets so that management can understand database needs for the future. Thus, the data administrator is responsible for convincing management of the need for an integrated, comprehensive database.

The development manager deals with data administration primarily during initial project planning and scope definition. At that time, the project is mapped to strategic plans and additional criteria are added to the project based on that strategy. Enhancement of a financial system, for instance, may cause the data administrator to lobby for the elimination of a subsystem with conventional files in favor of enhancing database files. Such an extension of project scope would provide no short-term benefit for the users but may pave the way for future systems and enhance data integrity.

Database Administration

Whereas data administration is strategically oriented, database administration fills short-term tactical needs. When development determines specific data requirements and their relationships, database administration organizes the data efficiently to fulfill those needs. Typically, these administrators are experts in the specific database management systems in operation.

They form a bridge between the logical view of data and the physical arrangements utilized to provide it.

Database administration is by far the more common arrangement. Given the complexities of database technology, this expertise is essential to the use of a database management system and therefore has a more perceptible benefit for the company. Therefore, this is nearly always the first requirement covered when a database program is initiated. The most common next step, after the scope of the database broadens, is for the strategic database needs to be met by extending the responsibility of this group.

Development managers work most often with database administration. The data requirements are given to this group, either as formal documents or by active participation in analysis, and test bases are provided for the project. Throughout the project, the database group monitors performance and adjusts the structures, distribution or relationships of the data. It is crucial for the development manager to remain actively involved with the database group throughout the project. Only in this way can an adequate system be developed.

The role of support shifts constantly between data/database administration and systems development, since the data have little value except in presentation. Databases and strategies will change based on application needs, and applications will change based on the need for integrity, security and end user access. To ensure that progress is made, this relationship must be cooperative and effective. Since data responsibilities usually fall within development, it is this group which must make most of the sacrifices in terms of reduction of scope and retraining.

The development manager must understand that, regardless of the structure of the database area, two functions always exist: the day-to-day database function and the long-term data administration function. Each has its place, and each involves different perspectives and priorities. For the strategic goals of the database concept to be realized, both must be active in systems decisions and supported fully by the development manager.

CHANGING TO A DATABASE ENVIRONMENT

Given the many advantages of a database environment, and understanding that it will probably not be established following a dedicated project effort, the development manager must take steps to spearhead its development. If a database function already exists, the initial steps will consist of formulating a plan.

That plan should first identify the company's data needs and the shortcomings of the current data arrangements. Without a specific data modeling effort, need identification will be somewhat superficial, but it is better than nothing. With a plan in hand, projects that have already been justified can be adjusted and adapted in order to shift to the database environment. After a certain period, enough of the data will be under database control so that final integration will require far less effort and cost. In most companies, in order to be effective, the corporate data model and plan must be fairly flexible in order to change in step with the company's organization and product changes.

There are several ways in which the development manager can facilitate this slow, unobtrusive shift to the database. These activities will provide intrinsic gains and can be by-products of normal projects. All that is required is the commitment of the manager and the staff.

Subject Databases

Subject databases are information models of business data needs. Data are related by business function, consolidated by the most common relationships and identified in terms of ownership and responsibility. To be effective, the information model must support a business model that describes in detail how the business operates and interrelates common business functions. The information model, and therefore the subject database, support this business model. Since the flow of information in a company is itself a description of the business, the two models are inseparable.

Subject databases become the basis of all future project efforts. When project requests are made and the initial analysis takes place, the subject database is reviewed and the project woven into its framework. For database purists, subject databases essentially define future projects. The purpose of the database is to provide information needs, and all requirements will be met as a by-product of that information availability. Once end user languages are fully effective this situation may exist, but today the reality is that a database supports an application as much as the reverse.

Subject databases do provide a valid, consistent framework for the future development of application databases. They are necessary strategic tools for the development manager who wants the systems produced to work together rationally, rather than needing constant retrofitting to support future projects. In most cases, management will be loath to underwrite an extensive effort to produce an enterprise/information model.

The development manager can gather most of the information necessary to create the information model through the day-to-day analysis of most projects. The analysts would be required to fill in gaps in the model on a constant, scheduled basis. Regular meetings would be held to continue development of the model, and the program committee would direct the effort. If application groups are separated, this program would operate independently, and the manager of each group would be required to dedicate a preset amount of resources to it.

This puts responsibility for the development of the subject databases squarely on systems development. Since a subject database is not necessarily an implemented product, but rather a description of relationships, it can easily be part of a concept-oriented program. This approach, however, is not optimal. A separate project, involving dedicated management for a specific period of time, is far more successful. However, if this is not feasible, developing the subject databases within a program structure is far better than doing nothing at all. It can also provide a stable starting point once that involvement is achieved.

Control Databases

To begin to benefit from the local use of a database managment system, the manager can create a control database to ease maintenance burdens and set the stage for a comprehensive approach. This is done by consolidating variable control data, which, without this approach, generally requires considerable resources for table maintenance and program changes. Once the database is established and some simple rules for variable control have been defined, the physical maintenance of this database can be turned over to the end user.

Creation of a control database generally begins with a specific project or a regularly scheduled maintenance cycle. During that effort, the variables for the program or system are removed and isolated in a database. Then standard code is developed to present the variable data to the programs that use them. Once that method is established and the security/control mechanisms for data control are put in place, the need to maintain that code is eliminated. Future maintenance or development efforts then build upon this database in order to eliminate all internally controlled variables.

As an example, consider a company manufacturing and marketing consumer products throughout the country. Most of the sales and distribution reports are based upon sales territories and the regions in which they occur. Originally, these territories were codified in order to relate them directly to the regions but, as the company grew, that codification included as many variations as consistency. In addition, some products are sold only in special territories, such as "government sales," and must be separated. As new products are introduced, many programs must be changed accordingly. Many do not change, however, since they simply list or cross-reference sales and orders for auditing and control.

To simplify the maintenance effort and move to a control database, a structure is developed to house all territory codes, their description, and three or four codes to identify them further. One code may be sales type to subset government sales, or several mutually exclusive codes may exist for separate departments to provide their own hierarchy. In a separate structure of the database, all regions are defined; they also carry several subsetting codes under the control of the separate departments. Proper audits and controls are established so that changes made in one relationship structure do not compromise others.

Next, code is developed to retrieve this database structure, under variable identification, and produce reports, screens or systems based on the newly housed data. Programs which simply report and identify territories or regions are unaffected or require only simple changes to retrieve descriptive titles. Once these routines are employed in the programs, the user is given control of the database to change codes and relationships at will. As each program that uses territories or regions comes up for maintenance, this new structure is embedded. Eventually, few enough programs remain under the old method to justify their change for consistency's sake.

Over time, any new table or control type data which can vary is entered into this centralized database. In this process, the gains are usually minimal. However, the stage is being set to relate cross-application data at an integrated level. As this occurs, the amount of data outside of these related structures is slowly reduced until total integration of all data reduces the overhead for a dedicated effort. The benefits are also being slowly displayed.

Building Upon What Has Been Done

When the objective is to achieve a strategic goal, no project can be viewed in isolation, especially when that goal is a comprehensive, integrated database. It is necessary to build constantly upon what has been done in the past, utilize existing database structures and make concessions for data usage.

In the example just described, new reporting or analysis programs may be quickly developed without the benefit of the control database for territories and regions. All that may be required is a simple listing or display, and the user sees no need for pulling in the control database. The manager must force projects to utilize that base, both to ensure its complete use and to avoid fragmentation in the future. It is nearly impossible to predict how enhancements will change the flavor of any single application. Bringing everything under the database umbrella uses resources today to avoid potential compromise tomorrow.

Each project must also be viewed in terms of its contribution to the future database environment. During project review, the question should be asked

"Can any aspect of this project enhance the integration of data across the applications?" These opportunities should be taken any time the cost of the extra effort is not overwhelming. Over time, these efforts will create the basis for the integrated environment.

When the manager decides that an integrated database is desirable, fostering this environment requires constant, long-term management. These efforts will remain largely unseen until final integration occurs. At that point, the spotlight will be on that specific integration, and much of the manager's efforts will fade into the background. The effort involves stage setting, not the high-visibility, high-recognition situation it truly deserves. However, if the manager's goal is to provide a better environment for developing high-service applications, the reward will be in the improved development capability.

ORGANIZATIONAL PLACEMENT OF THE DATABASE FUNCTION

The database purist believes that data and/or database administration departments must report to the highest possible level of management. Optimally, this would be outside MIS entirely, or at least outside of systems development. However, while there may be some sense in going outside of MIS, in most cases it is placed somewhere within data processing itself.

For the development manager, the importance of the reporting relationship is whether it occurs inside or outside development. There can be subtle implication in regard to external reporting, but the principal difference is the need for a peer relationship in developing major components of a project.

Database Within Development

Database reporting within development is the most common initial organizational step. This arrangement is useful because the tie between data and application is extremely strong unless independence was a design objective. The general trend is to separate the functions after a while and move the database outside development.

It is not unusual, however, for the database to remain within development. This arrangement facilitates communication, simplifies the project life cycle, and for users seems less like a technical specialization. For the development manager to make this arrangement work, the database and application functions must remain separate even though the reporting structures dovetail.

Without this functional separation, the two components of development, application and data, will be compromised at equal levels. Managers tend to ensure an equalized compromise between competitive groups under their control. However, database rules and regulations cannot be as easily compromised as the application aspects of a project. If the two are equalized, both will be equally unstable and changeable. The long-term desire is to stabilize the data portions of systems to allow more flexibility for applications. Therefore, managers must favor data over application when issues of data integrity and stability occur.

This perceived favoritism is difficult to manage unless the staff clearly understands what is being accomplished. The strategies and purpose of integrating all data management should be fully communicated to staff members in order to achieve the desired results without creating ill will and dissent. A major component of development is taken away with the insulation of the database function. That will not be agreeable to either staff or managers unless they fully understand the benefits and are committed to making the strategy work.

Database External to Development

Obviously, the favoritism discussed above is not a factor when the database is independent of systems development. When separate managements are involved, each is allowed to operate with his or her own priorities. For the development manager this has two positive effects. First, there is no need to worry about the development and acquisition of strong technical expertise. Second, the development manager can concentrate on application development with the assumption that someone is stabilizing and controlling the database environment.

There are certain problems, however. First, an independent database creates another level of bureaucracy on all projects and strategies. When the database function is aggressive and supportive, this produces little difficulty. Attention remains high and the existence of an independent group tends to speed the projects rather than slow them down. However, the likelihood of all priorities being addressed at equal levels diminishes over time. When the database group begins to operate more independently, it has its own priority lists and strategies to consider. The development group must then depend upon procedures to ensure that its schedules are maintained when it depends on the database group.

The second problem occurs when issues of power and control arise. This situation occurs continually with peer management and must be handled with sensitivity and political adeptness. However, it can be particularly acute between the database and development managers because it is difficult to draw the line between the responsibilities for data and information created via applications. It is generally applications which place the data in the database and massage them into presentable form. Therefore, despite the isolation of data and applications, the two managers may conflict fairly regularly.

Regardless of the advantages or disadvantages of an independent database group, it remains the most logical choice for a final organizational arrangement. It separates the responsibility to match the intended separation of the components serviced and better allocates work in developing new systems. The development manager who is responsible for the database activity should understand that it will eventually be managed by an independent peer. With this in mind, the manager can establish the procedures governing future relationships before a competitive environment exists. This will go a long way to ensure a positive, cooperative relationship later on.

DATA DICTIONARIES AND DATA DIRECTORIES

Much of the strength of a database environment lies in the fact of identification and definition. The fact that a database creates a stable data environment implies that the definition of the data is stable as well. The potential values, ownership, cross-data relationships and scope have been thoroughly investigated before the element was placed in the database. If this is not the case, the data are no more stable than the applications, since they will inevitably change as new information about that element surfaces.

If nothing else, a database justifies the effort to create it by this definition and identification. In today's competitive world, understanding the information relative to the company's operation can be as important in maintaining or achieving a market share as the operation itself. Therefore, reporting that information in a timely, consistent manner is critical to success. That cannot happen without clear identification and definition of the data which make up that information.

Data Dictionary

A data dictionary is a compendium of definitions for the data in a database. It generally defines the element in English business terms, as well as its ownership, where it appears, and its characteristics and valid edit ranges. In most cases, the data dictionary is part of a database management system. Therefore, many of its components relate directly to the technical and administrative characteristics of that system. Optimally, the dictionary is active in the day-to-day operation of the database.

For the dictionary to be active, many of its components must directly define the data in the base. Data elements are added to structures only through the dictionary. That is, the dictionary contains the mechanics to make database changes so that data cannot be entered without being defined. In addition, the edit criteria defined in the dictionary are used by the management system to add or modify data. If these criteria are not met, the addition or modification fails.

When the data dictionary is passive, its validity is totally dependent upon the discipline of the managers. If discipline is high, one can assume that the definitions are present, but there is no way to ensure that the edits between the dictionary and the programs performing the updates agree. Therefore, validity is always in question. Passive dictionaries are better than none at all, but they certainly never approach the utility and control value of active dictionaries.

Data Directories

Directories describe where data can be found. They may be held in controlled databases, conventional file structures or manual filing systems. The purpose of directories is to simplify the analysis needed to find the proper data sources for systems, as well as to prevent unnecessary duplication of information. As described earlier, duplication is considered a problem, causing incorrect control and requiring extra storage.

Directories, like dictionaries, can also be active or passive, but most of the information in the base is passively controlled because most sources of data are outside database systems. Therefore, some reliance must be placed on the managers of all data sources to maintain data currency. Since few database management systems today provide comprehensive directories, the road maps described by the directories must be generated within development.

A directory's principal strength is the richness of its indexing mechanism(s). The developer, whether a user or a professional, can access a directory that provides keywords or known definition points and be guided through the storehouse of data. He or she may know only that the needed element has something to do with customer credit codes and, by entering keywords such as "CUST-CRED," will eventually be directed to a data element called "PURCHASE-LIMIT-CUST." Since data element names are based on uniformity and specific constructions, whereas the English language is notoriously vague, the directory and dictionary combined should provide the needed translation.

Optimally, dictionaries and directories are machine based and integral to the database management system. However, the manager of development does not always have a formal dictionary. If one does not exist, the creation of a manual dictionary is highly advantageous, if for no other reason than to prepare for a future mechanized dictionary.

CONCLUSION

Few data processing professionals are unaware of the benefits to be achieved by a comprehensive, integrated database. While databases have never lived up to their expectations, there can be little doubt that, in time, they will be accepted and expected by all companies. Creating the integrated database will be an arduous, difficult process whose burden will be borne mainly by the development staff.

Development is a business function, like all others. It dedicates resources to efforts when there are perceivable benefits to be gained. This goes beyond project servicing, which is the principal purpose of development. A long-term movement to a database requires efforts which, at least initially, provide little visibility for the manager. In many cases, the concentration on database migration will add risk to project cycles by adding another variable. Before attempting this effort, the manager should be confident that a database will help fulfill development's responsibilities.

An integrated database can make life much simpler for the manager in developing systems. It creates an independent, stable core for all systems. This stability allows problems to be isolated more rapidly, focuses attention on data manipulation and presentation, and significantly reduces the analysis phase of projects. It also provides an additional layer of sophistication for projects, that of the database analyst.

A database function does somewhat restrict the scope of the development manager. Data management is no longer the manager's responsibility, and that can be somewhat intimidating. The manager must develop a new interface mechanism, accept additional project dependencies, and compete with another peer manager. Since the database function typically begins within development, these issues can be worked out under controlled conditions. If the manager addresses the subject of database development intelligently and pragmatically, a cooperative relationship with the new manager can be developed.

The benefits of a database management system far outweigh the problems of maintaining it. It should be fostered and embraced by the development manager. Any opportunity to enhance that development should be actively pursued.

The future of MIS will undoubtedly change dramatically in the next several years. One of these changes will undoubtedly be the separation of data from applications, both in design and in organization. The development manager can either be a part of that future or fruitlessly fight it.

14

THE INFORMATION CENTER

The information center is a concept which has developed in the last several years. Its creation is due primarily to the advent and increased sophistication of end user languages and the PC. These two factors have transferred a great deal of computing power directly to the nonprofessional developer. As discussed in Chapter 10, this movement has not only increased the potential universe of development resources but has also separated the capability to develop from the discipline of development. Basically, the information center was developed to extend the potential of end user computing while providing discipline based on practical experience.

Since the information center as a concept is still in its infancy, definition of its function depends on the company. In one organization it is little more than a walk-in center where PCs are placed at the user's disposal. In another, it represents a full transition to another style of systems development. Over time a median between these two extremes will occur and a balance between information center responsibilities and conventional development will be found. In the meantime, the definition will depend largely on the ability of the development manager and the staff to take on a new role in the production of application systems.

The organizational placement of the information center varies nearly as widely as the definition. Conceptually, its relationship with development is tenuous. In theory, they represent alternative solutions to business problems. However, in practical terms, it is difficult to separate them. The systems developed by users, whether on PCs or using mainframe languages, inevitably tie into conventional systems. The tie can be through parallel database use, feeder systems, or the need to apply development discipline to extensive end user projects. Therefore, for efficiency's sake and until computer literacy begins to approach computer expertise, systems development remains the best location for the information center.

The information center has a pervasive influence on systems development. It provides a new role for the developer: that of consultant to the user. It also has the potential to act in a transitional role, allowing professional developers to act as certifiers of system solutions and custodians of corporate information.

It is certainly no accident that the information center developed when it did. Since the end user could now produce systems without extensive professional involvement, a stabilizing factor was needed between the new technology and the discipline to control it. Thus, the development manager must recognize the realities of nonprofessional development and provide the transition of the staff and strategies to an information center orientation. The center is a stepping stone, not a finished product.

In this chapter, three aspects of the information center are discussed. First, seven broad functions which touch upon the development manager's role are reviewed. These functions transcend organizational placement and will be issues for the manager whether the center is under direct control or external. The next topic considered is project distribution—the stage where projects are initially targeted for either end user or professional development. Finally, the primary issues involved in the transition from conventional development to information center support are reviewed.

PRINCIPAL INFORMATION CENTER FUNCTIONS

While an information center can have a wide range of functional responsibilities and report in a number of structures, not all of these responsibilities concern the development manager. There are, however, a number which directly affect how the manager performs the job and deals with the user community.

The issues are not always obvious. For instance, if the end user develops PC applications without consulting the development department, the obvious problem is that the resultant application will misrepresent some critical corporate information. However, even if that application has complete integrity, the manager faces a more subtle problem. The resulting system may conflict with justifiable portions of a planned, internally developed application of the future. The manager then has the thankless job of justifying the removal of a working end user system in order to match the scope of the internal system.

The only simple way to avoid this situation is to become involved, at least peripherally, in all end user projects. This ensures that all aspects of the system portfolio are understood. The end user will call on systems development only if that involvement is to the department's advantage. If development places obstacles in the user's path, the user will simply avoid the issue. The development manager must therefore place the department in the position of actively seeking to help the user and to maintain positive visibility throughout projects.

The seven information center functions discussed in this section, like the information center concept itself, represent a different role for the professional developer. The manager must recognize this and allow many of the procedural and administrative aspects of that role to develop through practical application rather than through edicts resulting from a conventional process perspective.

The Consulting Role

In providing direction for end user developed systems, the development department cannot ask the user to follow its mechanisms and procedures and to inform development of his progress and the scope of his systems. This simply adds steps to the process and, though it may work on the first few projects, will quickly fall by the wayside. As a result, many systems will be developed and produced of which the systems development staff knows nothing.

Providing consulting support can greatly reduce this problem because users gain some advantage from their extra efforts. They will tend to request help on a continuing basis if they feel it is to their benefit. This active involvement allows development to track, understand and direct much of the information center's development. For development, the gain consists of having an input to all developed systems, regardless of who does the developing. For the users, there is no need for the in-depth expertise needed for independent development.

This consulting support is provided at three separate levels. The lowest level consists of responding to simple questions, generally of a technical nature. Typically, these concern which software is most applicable, how data are best organized, where stable input data can be found or who has already addressed a similar problem. This type of consulting should be provided as needed, avoiding long queues so that users are not forced by delays to find their own solutions. Such questions can often be answered in a few minutes and require little extensive justification or planning.

The second level of consultation requires more time and dedication. It involves review and involvement throughout the user project as problems arise. Typically, time can be broadly planned for the process, but the actual amount of consultation will vary based on the complexity of the problem and the personnel required to answer the questions. As with any other project, development's involvement must be project oriented so that time can be allocated and resources apportioned.

The third level of consultation varies from conventional development only in terms of who is responsible for the project. In these cases, development personnel are assigned to user projects, either full time or part time, at project inception. Typically, they are given highly technical or project control problems. The situation is directly analogous to the user representative role in a conventional development project. In that case, the user brings business expertise to the development-controlled effort. With information center consulting, development brings technical expertise to the user-controlled project.

Certification

Certification, which was discussed in Chapter 10, consists of the review of a product developed without the disciplined, self-auditing process used by a professional staff. It recognizes that the resultant product may well be as effective and controlled as that of a professional developer, but applies a set of criteria to the product which allow its integrity to be verified. Once verified, the product is protected from damage, by MIS and development, in a controlled production environment.

In an information center, nonprofessional development is fostered. Training and consulting are provided, quality products are selected and a stabilized database is accessed. Much of this effort is designed to ensure a quality product. Users are given an opportunity to achieve much of the discipline that professional developers have spent years acquiring. Of course, this does not guarantee that the product will be any more valid than it would be without it.

End user projects generally have a life cycle similar to that of professional projects. The main difference is that they are typically much less controlled and disciplined. They still go through a construction phase, and until there is a need to approval-test the product, the decision as to whether it meets quality specifications rests with the developer; there is little direct external control. With these projects, the approval-test is the submittal of the product for certification.

Certification is therefore the normal final gate of any development project, but in reverse; the user is submitting to development rather than the other way around. For a certification process to work, several elements must exist; some can be controlled by development, but not all. Most of these elements were discussed in Chapter 10 under the heading of end user development. From the perspective of the information center, the salient aspect of end user computing and certification is the final gate.

If certification provided no particular benefit, few systems would be submitted, and those few would be from users who desired technical recognition of their product. Management's refusal to consider noncertified system results for corporate decisions is one of the two principal benefits of certification. The other benefit is support of the operational product. Support is the next topic of discussion. From a certification perspective, support means that end users can now use the product as they would any professionally developed system. If a system breaks or questions arise, the user simply calls development for help or an explanation. The user should expect a response equal to that received for conventionally developed systems.

Certification must be a formal process. It should have all the characteristics of a normal testing phase for any development effort. Change management, procedural review, standard assurance and sign-offs should be as much a part of certification as they are of any project turnover.

Support

Is is fine to defend the procedural integrity of a justification/certification process but, in the final analysis, one of development's responsibilities is to support corporate data usage. Cavalierly telling users that, since proper procedures were not followed, they will receive no system support exposes the corporation to the risk of improper data interpretation. Regardless of how justified development is in refusing support requests after the user was warned, it is still necessary to respond in some fashion when the risks of ignoring standard mechanisms are realized.

Obviously, when conventional development methods are used or when consulting support is provided during project cycles, most of this risk is automatically avoided. However, products developed completely by end users are ripe for high-risk problems. It is to these products that information center support is directed.

There is little difference between question-and-answer consultation support and the support described here. The principal differences lie in how the user is charged for those services, as well as the predictability and scheduling of responses. Beyond that, the servicing of support requests is identical. It probably will be handled by the same individuals.

Users must be charged directly for service received against noncertified systems. Certification was probably avoided because it is known that certification submittal would fail. This could occur because proper procedures were not followed or because strategic plans were ignored. The most common strategic conflict occurs when systems are produced in place of approved corporate systems. For some reason, the user chooses to develop a new system despite the existence of another product. Since this would automatically involve refusal at certification time, the system is never submitted.

Charges should be at a premium rate, for two reasons: (1) the user is technically in violation of an established system intent, if not a policy; (2)

it is necessary to take into account the second element described above: unpredictability of service requests. This unpredictability does not vary substantially from that of normal systems. The only rational way to staff for this type of failure is historical precedent. However, seldom will development or the information center be allowed to staff for the support of uncertified systems. This is against stated procedures. Those procedures will be violated if need arises, but it is extraordinarily difficult to convince management of that need at budget time. Therefore, the charges received for uncertified systems support will generally be needed to hire outside workers to round out the support staff in the form of co-ops, part-time workers or contract staff.

Support and how it is allocated to systems is a key issue to be determined when establishing an information center. It is difficult to justify because it involves a picture of highly paid specialists sitting around waiting for something to break. Support is critical, however, and should be a prime issue defined in the information center's charter.

Portfolio Management

The fourth function associated with the information center is portfolio management. This function, discussed in earlier chapters, is extremely important in an information center. For users, an information center is a place to glean information about systems and computing tools. In order to direct users to proper business solutions at the lowest possible cost, it is essential to understand what tools are currently available and how each of them can fill a system need. Then and only then can the user be properly directed to existing solutions and shown how to use the data.

As systems are produced or certified, they are entered into the portfolio. This process requires analysis by both information center personnel and professional analysts. Noncertified systems are entered as well, though they cannot be identified as specifically as certified ones—they can never actually be said to be operational. Reaching an operational state implies a level of stability that uncertified systems do not have.

With the portfolio in hand, information center specialists can direct users to solutions which either match their need or provide input for their systems. This limits the number of parallel systems and provides some consistency across corporate information systems. Most users do not seek special solutions when existing ones are available; they follow accepted paths. The portfolio allows them to find those paths.

A systems portfolio should exist whether an information center has been formed or not. It is simply good administrative practice. The information center allows the portfolio to become more comprehensive, since knowledge of end user systems tends to focus here. Therefore, once an information center is formed, the portfolio maintenance should be moved there. Conventional developers will provide information for portfolio maintenance just as end users do.

Information Custodians

As systems move into the user community, the integrity of information becomes more important for the development staff. The proper updating of databases, sophisticated data manipulation and consulting become the primary roles of the development staff. The information center is responsible for presenting information about the data to users for their development and use. It is analogous to the marketing arm of an organization.

Having data efficiently housed in a database and well defined does not imply that they will be properly referenced or used. Theoretically, nothing can ensure proper use. However, directing potential developers to the appropriate data at least eliminates the primary cause of data misuse: ignorance. A user attempting to evaluate a customer's financial position, for example, does not want to pick up invalid data. Nor does that user generally look for shortcuts at the risk of making an error. However, in a veritable sea of data, he or she may simply find it difficult to determine precisely which data are most appropriate and where they are located.

Nor is a user willing to wait a long time to be directed to the correct data. He or she may have a question or need, of which the data, though important, are only a minor part. For example, a customer may be in the office trying to negotiate a major contract. The answers to questions must be found immediately and, quite often, without the customer's knowledge that the questions are even being asked. This need for immediate help generally eliminates the possibility of contacting the development group. That group's schedules are set and structured, and it takes hours or days to get results. In many cases the information may cross several disciplines, requiring the analysts to seek help elsewhere, further slowing the process.

As an information custodian, the information center provides access to information about data on a responsive, end-user oriented basis. The user calls the information center and specifies the data need. The specialist can then review data dictionaries and directories to determine what data are needed and how they can most easily be accessed. If necessary, additional personnel can be called in to help, but this action must be based on the department's knowledge and, to the user, the focus remains the same: a single person in the information center. If the specialist determines that the question merits a data dictionary entry, this can be done to simplify further responses. If the issue requires more in-depth analysis, this can also be done.

It can be seen that, as end user products mature, the role of information custodian becomes the primary role of the development department, rather than conventional systems construction. Eventually, this role will strain the resources and expertise of the information center. As a starting point, and as a means of transition, the role of information custodian is extremely valuable. It transfers information interpretation and protection further to the user community and thereby makes interpretation more responsive and less bureaucratic.

Education

The plethora of end user tools available today greatly increases the opportunity for poor systems solutions and difficult support situations. Regardless of how effective any one tool may be, most computer professionals understand that the fewer options available in a process, the fewer chances there are of failure. This knowledge causes most managers to limit the number of languages or database management systems available in any department.

However, while the number of languages and tools can be limited for mainframe products, the PC environment is very different. Support guidelines will provide some limits but not a total ban. If the user has a strong enough justification, additional languages will be chosen. The information center can at least reduce the risk of this broadening of language choices by educating users.

Education can be an important weapon. Without it, whatever tool is chosen by the user is naturally limited in its use. Little exposure is possible in a cross-department environment, and few users will choose a package if their ability to use it fully is limited.

The information center can coordinate, contract and schedule classes for all approved products, as well as for general-use products not on its supported list. It can therefore control the curriculum and attendance, and direct the postclass extension of capabilities. Few users want to get directly involved in this process. Most of them would rather be given a schedule and register for a class than seek out qualified instructors, schedule meeting rooms and ensure adequate hardware and software availability. They will quickly accept education from a separate group.

Since education is necessary to use a product adequately, the information center, by default, has some control over which products will be used. If nothing else, their use can be delayed (while educational schedules are being established) until classes are conducted. In that way, knowledge of the product exists before the product is used.

Product Selection and Installation

The final function of the information center is product selection and installation. While many products must be selected by the development department due to their close ties to the database and existing applications, PC software and hardware fall in the realm of the information center. When the two groups have the same manager, there is no conflict. Otherwise, the responsibilities of each group should be well defined in order to avoid overlap.

Given this mix of PC and mainframe software, duplication of software tools can and should exist. Tools such as spreadsheets are available on mainframe systems and convert the terminal to a PC. Spreadsheet analysis is also the mainstay of PCs. When this type of duplication exists, the only important factor is the ability to transfer data between the two without complex interface requirements. If intelligently chosen, the parallel software on both types of computers will allow considerable networking ability utilizing both technologies.

The subject of selection and installation was addressed in Chapter 10. It is very important in extending and directing the end user environment and in effecting an appropriate mix of software and conventional systems. When choosing software, the information center should not be limited to supported products. There may be products to be installed on systems which will not be supported by development or the information center. If users want or need those products badly enough, they will get them. PC software is inexpensive enough to be purchased, in most companies, as an expense item and may easily show up on a weekly expense report. In this situation, the products will be installed. With the information center performing the installation, at least the product will be environmentally sound.

PROJECT DISTRIBUTION

When a great deal of end user development occurs, projects tend to follow multiple paths. Conventional projects are evaluated, initiated and constructed within a standard development life cycle. Each component of these projects, and the resultant product, are well understood by the department and controlled by established procedures. End user projects with substantial involvement of the development department are less controlled but can at least be directed effectively through accepted procedural practices. Their scope and limitations are well understood. Total end user efforts can be identified at initiation time but seldom appear until implementation time—and often not even then.

It may not be known which path a project will follow until the request or intent is evaluated and established. Once that occurs, the project can be distributed along the appropriate path and steps taken within development to monitor and direct it. Even when the project is external to development, its progress and problems can at least be known. Without effective distribution, important projects can disappear until they have a substantial impact on the strategies and growth of the company. In order to distribute these efforts properly, with a full understanding of the implications of that distribution, the information center must analyze requests and apply the appropriate disciplines to select paths for projects.

This process, of course, implies that projects of all types are centrally directed for distribution. To ensure that such activities occur, the process of receipt and distribution must be efficient and responsive. Optimally, a project is terminal logged and routed to a central database for information center evaluation. After evaluation, the project is described, logged and identified, with appropriate notification to the affected parties. These parties are identified by management. Upward or cross-department notification may be required when data or information will move across departments. This allows the impacts to be understood by the entire company and proper steps to be taken when responsibility lines are crossed. It has the added benefit of removing development from the political problem of trying to stop one department's efforts to protect another.

The information center, or its functional equivalent, is chosen as the focal point because it has the opportunity to view all projects—those involving systems development and those oriented to the user. It has no axes to grind and no business allegiances. It merely acts as an expediter.

The mechanisms used in the receipt and distribution of projects vary substantially based on the physical structure of the company and the formality of project requests. They also vary based on the technological sophistication and capability of users and systems development. Despite these variables, there are three important issues to consider when distributing projects: mechanisms used to classify projects, the implications of supported versus nonsupported efforts and the monitoring of projects.

Classification of Projects

Project requests must be classified quickly and the user notified about the result as soon as possible. Classifications are established at this initial level for two reasons: (1) to separate requests that will follow obvious broad paths and (2) to notify the user of the implications of the path chosen.

Broad paths can be established fairly simply. Projects requiring conventional development or substantial professional involvement are immediately routed to the appropriate project queues, as outlined in Chapter 2. These efforts are understood to require significant analysis in order to produce definitive estimates. They should also be entered against the requesting department's budget and resource allotment. The important point here is that notification is provided, control numbers established and an agreement on project scope is reached. It is possible that the user did not understand that such a request required development help. With this new knowledge, the requestor may wish to alter the request in order to move it to a less costly classification.

When the request implies or explicitly indicates end user development, the second reason for classification comes into play. The information center specialist evaluates the request and defines its implications for the requestor. These generally include the availability of alternative solutions that will have significant impacts on the user's resultant support, compliance with standards and potential for certification. The results may also be communicated to other parties, especially when procedural integrity is threatened. Often this communication is enough to alter the request.

The results of this classification may cause the request to be altered or cancelled, or other normal actions in the project cycle may be initiated. In any case, the information center specialist is seldom involved in the next steps unless they require justification of the classification.

Supported versus Nonsupported Projects

Probably the most important reason for classification is to identify the kind of support the requestor can expect. This information is based largely on initial product selection and identification. If software product A is evaluated and found to be either redundant or unacceptable, and the user intends to use it, notification of nonsupport will be a major determinant of its use.

Systems development is not in a position to prevent a product's use directly. Its only practical weapon is the refusal of support unless premium costs are paid. Only management can prevent the product's use, based on its commitment to operate only with supported products. Management may state, for example, that certain classes of systems must follow approved lines. Only purely internal or personal use of unapproved products may be allowed. Alternatively, management may decide that the perceived benefit of the project is more important than the support implications. In either case, it is a decision of management, not of development.

In terms of project distribution, the support implications must be communicated to the user explicitly and strongly. These decisions must then be adhered to by all members of the department. An analyst who helps the user with an unsupported product for any reason weakens development's only weapon in dealing with an ever-growing variety of system solutions. Once support decisions are violated, development can no longer control or direct the company's information processing systems.

Project Monitoring

Project monitoring with nonconventional development is difficult at best. There is practically no way to do strict monitoring on a formal basis. The information center, and therefore development, must maintain an active stance, querying the status of the project and then reporting it for their own internal purposes. External reporting must be done carefully, avoiding any implication of failure or delay. Reporting negative results will only eliminate communication and will not change management's view of the effort. Management's attitude will be determined by the success or failure reported by the user management. Development should not interfere with that structure even when they know that the stated progress is questionable.

The real purpose of monitoring end user projects is to try to judge their impact on future projects and to gain some knowledge of product use for future classification. If it is found that every time product B is used many problems or delays result, that product may be removed from the approved list or stronger warnings provided when a request is made. As monitoring becomes less threatening and users come to perceive its benefits, it may become a formal part of all projects. Like other aspects of end user development, monitoring is best developed slowly and without edict. When users perceive its benefit, cooperative monitoring of projects will take place, not before.

MAKING THE TRANSITION TO THE INFORMATION CENTER

The information center represents two different things for the development manager. First, it is an element, either organizational or functional, positioned between the user and development communities. This location provides a balance between the nontechnical user and the technically oriented development staff. It was spawned by the extension of professional tools to users, making a buffer more important than ever.

Second, it represents a picture of the future, characterized by the use of friendly, directly accessed development tools that allow end users to meet their own information needs. The development person becomes a consultant and information specialist who directs and proposes paths for the nonprofessional developer. End user products and the current expertise level of users indicate that this situation is a long way off (in terms of technology, this can range anywhere from 6 months to 10 years). However, an effective transition to the future must be evolutionary and not revolutionary. The development manager who wishes to direct information usage and systems development must begin taking steps to foster that future environment to-day.

These steps are small. They do not involve hiring hundreds of people to establish and staff a comprehensive information center. Rather, they involve emphasizing characteristics which may have been ignored or altering the philosophical approach to user/professional involvement.

Altering Skill Sets

Professional developers, through years of training, display specific personality traits and skill sets. These typically evolve from the environment in which they operate. A conventional development staff is characterized by painstaking attention to detail, wide-ranging considerations of impact and strategic implications and project orientation. These characteristics work well in an environment where most of the work is procedurally defined and effectively controlled.

To function well in an operational, end user environment, developers must be prepared to move to a mode of constant minor adjustments in existing operations. The predominant emphasis is on specific business tasks, and automation is used to solve narrowly focused problems of limited scope. The craft of development is seen only as a mechanism for solving specific problems, not as an end in itself.

In order to effect this transition, developers must move into the user's environment and become immersed in the activities of that department. They can then solve problems from the user's perspective and become far less technically specialized. Since it is the environment that hones skills, immersion in the user's day-to-day world is the only rational way to develop those skills.

Because the information center environment will take years to develop, it is neither feasible nor practical to simply shift developers to users' departments. Nor is it efficient so long as conventional development processes still provide most corporation's information solutions. The most effective method for developing these skills is to rotate staffing of the information center instead of creating a permanent group of specialists.

This rotation accomplishes a number of other things as well. It introduces the tools to all members of the staff and avoids progressively greater specialization. It also ensures broader corporate exposure, since information center personnel deal with various disciplines rather than concentrating on a single area. The exposure of conventional staff to end user environments allows the information center to realize its primary benefit—a practical transition of the definition of development. As end user development becomes the primary force for new systems, the staff is already trained and has already made the mental transition.

The Key: The Database

Making database knowledge a primary determinant of success aids in the transition to a new method of development. However end user tools evolve, the centralized characteristics of stable data will remain the key to effective corporate usage of those tools, as discussed in Chapter 13. This means that the development manager must seek to move database expertise into the group in all phases of the process and at all levels of understanding. Segregating that knowledge and experience within a separate group will only make the future transition more difficult.

With the current approach to database technology, this is a complex problem. The sophistication of most database products requires a high degree of specialization, and the development manager will be forced to accommodate some separation between the development staff and database management. That does not mean, however, that developers should simply shift all database issues to a separate group. The developers should be active participants in defining data needs and determining how they can best be achieved with current technologies. They cannot be passive.

Moving database contact into the information center helps effect this transition. Maintenance and communication of capabilities and the use of dictionaries are effective first steps in educating all development personnel. During the staff's periods of coverage in the information center, the dictionaries can be enriched and extended to include as much corporate data as possible.

Providing Project Management

As much as developers must adapt to a new method of developing systems, users must adapt to more stringent project control. Managing end user projects will be a cooperative effort, including project specialists from development and project managers from the user community. This consultation and coordination role for developers can be honed while serving in the information center.

The mechanisms used to accommodate consultive-type project management are based on an active knowledge of project control. Procedures must be created that accept this style of control and direction. The situation is different from conventional project management and must be adapted over time and through exposure. When large end user projects are begun, the development manager should seize every opportunity to provide help in controlling projects using accepted methods. This will not always be satisfying for the developers, since much of the actual control and decision making will be the result of political pressure and not technical considerations. However, the exposure will be invaluable and pave the way for future undefined roles.

CONCLUSION

The concept of the information center has received much publicity in the last few years. Like any concept, it has emerged in reaction to perceived problems and opportunities. The principal motivation is the advent of end user tools, either mainframe or PC-oriented products. In many cases, the information center is an independent unit, while in others it simply involves increased responsibilities for systems development.

More than anything else, however, the information center indicates how systems development is evolving. As such, it is important for the development manager to gain a clear understanding of the functions involved and how those functions alter the way the department operates. By understanding the implications of the information center and its functions, the manager can use the center as an effective transitional vehicle for the staff.

15
PLANNING FOR TRANSITION

Managing systems development requires that the processes used, the people managed and the technologies employed be melded into a comprehensive approach. Understanding all components and ensuring that they operate well together allow the responsibilities of the department to be met and the company's information needs to be serviced.

However, development is an extremely dynamic discipline. The approaches used today will not adequately service the needs of tomorrow. To manage a development department successfully for the long term, the manager must adapt to ever-changing opportunities and challenges. Obviously, this entails planning and evolving to match that plan.

Typically, one thinks of planning in terms that relate to the business. Whether short-term or long-term, project plans are matched to the business plans of serviced departments and of the company as a whole to ensure that adequate systems will exist to support those plans. The success of this type of planning depends on a number of variables, not the least of which are the feasibility and consistency of the corporate plan itself.

This level of planning is best termed "application planning" and is one of the development manager's principal tasks. Unless this is done, each new project will represent a new and isolated thrust for the corporation. Application planning, however, is generally determined by the business. As the business evolves and technological opportunities are perceived; development must be ready to respond to these opportunities.

As experts in technology, developers are also expected to spearhead a portion of application planning. This means analyzing those technologies which are seeking problems to solve. By evaluating new products and understanding their applicability to the industry, opportunities to use these technologies can be incorporated into management's strategic plans.

However, as has been emphasized throughout this book, the manager does not simply manage the development of systems or the use of technology, but also a business function. The management of that function requires planning as well. The impacts on planning for development come from a variety of sources: the business plans of the company, emerging technologies, new or enhanced methodologies, the advance of computer literacy and availability of trained personnel. Because so many forces influence development, and because it is a relatively young discipline, planning for the department itself is even more difficult than planning for most business functions.

The development manager must recognize that the future means dramatic changes for the department. Those changes may not be obvious, but they can often be predicted by historical precedence and the logical evolution of technology. The manager must therefore plan a constant transition for the department based upon future roles and potential opportunities. This is what is meant by "transitional planning."

This chapter begins with a discussion of applications planning in general. The three principal levels of this type of planning—strategic, tactical and transitional planning—are reviewed as they directly involve the development manager. These are the planning components most often implied when planning is discussed, and all three focus on future plans for applications. Planning occurs on a number of fronts, from hardware to communications, but, in general, the development manager's participation is as a reviewer. For applications planning, the development manager spearheads the effort. That is his or her particular expertise and responsibility.

The levels of application planning are not reviewed in depth; many fine books are available on this subject. This discussion puts those levels into perspective in relation to planning for a transition. The balance of the chapter deals with transitional planning—both in definition and in terms of examples of innovative directions the manager may follow.

APPLICATION PLANNING

For development, planning always has two sources. First, the user has a problem which can be solved by a new technology; second, a technology exists which shows promise in solving problems. The manager must understand the needs of the business well enough to identify new technological opportunities and their applicability in both of these areas. For example, if the company is widely dispersed and communications are difficult and slow, the availability of electronic mail promises a rapid solution to these problems. The technology is mature and is directed to a specific problem.

Conversely, technologies exist for which there may be no application. However, as a technologist, the manager can predict a global application and a benefit to the company because that technology is the harbinger of a wave of solutions. As an example, "expert systems," a branch of artificial intelligence, allow the introduction of business expertise into computer systems. The technology is in its infancy but nevertheless implies the ability to automate enough of the decision-making process to allow executives to concentrate on longer-range issues. The manager must seek opportunities to apply this technology to isolated functions in order to test its applicability and be ready for future enhancements.

Strategic Planning

Strategic planning deals in long-term time frames, typically 2 to 5 years. It has two purposes: ensuring that system plans support and enhance the company's strategies, and melding short-term plans into those strategies. To some extent, the effectiveness of development's strategic planning is governed by the formality and effectiveness of the business plans.

If corporate planning is merely an exercise, the development manager's main concern is to provide flexibility in his strategy. Drafting and marketing specific, time-scaled plans will result in very little gain for either the manager or the corporation. Plans must exist for development because too many independent activities are occurring to allow a helter-skelter implementation of systems. The approach must be disciplined and strategic planning is the only way of providing that discipline.

However, if corporate planning is informal, the manager's application of his strategy must remain in the background. It will generally take the form of intradepartment meetings to ensure that the direction is followed. Very little information will be provided to upper management to indicate this strategic thrust. The best indication that a plan is being followed is that when reactive changes in direction are specified by management, development will be able to respond. This is the key to successful strategic planning in a corporation with no strong overall plan. In a reactive environment, one must plan to allow reaction without creating confusion.

When formal corporate strategies exist, the manager's job is considerably easier. The first task is to apply technological solutions which will support those plans. Concrete time frames can be used and measurable goals established. The manager must remember the second aspect of strategy described earlier and seek opportunities to apply new technologies to the business even though their specific application is not obvious.

Tactical Planning

Tactical planning includes the period from the present to the beginning of the strategic period. Its main purpose is to ensure that short-term efforts meld well with the long-range strategy. In most cases, tactical planning is seen in the prioritization of selective aspects of projects.

An example of tactical planning involves the database. If an integrated database is considered strategically desirable, each project will include the transfer of data references to a slowly evolving database. In many cases, this reference will add time and effort to the project. However, the goal is long-term and comprehensive, with benefits achieved only over time and only if all projects include this thrust. Therefore, the price is paid and the projects all contribute (often as a by-product and in very small ways) to the overall strategy.

It is the tactical level that is most often ignored in the planning efforts of development. It is at this level that compromise becomes an important issue. Users want projects completed as quickly as possible, so any extraneous efforts are considered counterproductive. In project planning, it is somewhat difficult to consider strategies because all user needs are immediate. Therefore, the integration of these tactics as part of an overall strategy is often subverted to get the job done as quickly as possible.

However, without a strong tactical plan, prepared before project pressures are exerted, there can be no effective strategic plan. It may exist and be entwined with the corporate strategy, but it cannot succeed. It is this fact that has placed strategic plans on the shelves in development managers' offices, never to be referenced. Without effective short-term direction, long-term goals will remain goals—not become realities.

Project Planning

Project planning is relatively simple and straightforward, and has been discussed throughout this book. Its goals are specific and its success is easily measured. The entire process of project planning focuses on the procedures and methods employed to develop systems. If these components are effective, project planning will work. If they are vague and ill-defined, project planning will be sporadically successful at best.

To meld project plans into tactics and strategies, the effort must be made in the early phases, before commitments are made and schedules produced. Each project must be interpreted in terms of its opportunities to contribute to the overall plan. The contribution is, of course, limited by the size of the project itself. Trying to fit a project into an overall plan may make it so costly that it will never be done. Therefore, some reason must be used.

TRANSITIONAL PLANNING

With the emphasis on technology and servicing end user needs, it is easy to lose sight of the fact that the development manager is also planning for a department. This type of planning is governed, to a large extent, by the application plans. Large projects planned for the year require additional staff to service them. Additional functions being serviced may involve reorganization.

However, systems development, and all aspects of MIS, are in a somewhat different position from that of most departments of a company. They deal not in products but in information. Since information distribution is becoming nearly as important as the product itself, having a single department control that distribution actually slows the process. Much of development's work is designed to speed that process. Since the only logical way to realize that goal is to eliminate all barriers to information distribution, development is faced with the unenviable task of ensuring its own elimination—at least the way it is defined today.

Since there are many complex issues surrounding information distribution, there will always be a need for specialists in information technology. This need is not likely to be satisfied by the way in which development operates today. There must be an entirely different definition of what systems development is, how it services the company today and how it will operate tomorrow. The explosion of technology and the opportunity to apply it not only to specific systems but the development process itself ensure that fact. It is difficult to predict how these changes will happen and what the future functional requirements of development will be, but one thing is certain—they will be radically different from those existing today.

This is where transitional planning comes in. It assumes that systems development is currently in transition and is likely to remain so for years—if not indefinitely. This premise must dramatically alter the way the development manager plans from the way other managers plan. Whatever the manager does to improve the department's operation will not have extremely long-term impacts. A new methodology will invariably be replaced long before it can reach fruition. Organizational arrangements will invariably become obsolete and unmanageable before they can stabilize. Specific skills, which may take years to develop, will be obsolete before they can be disseminated throughout the department.

Planning for transition requires one paramount skill—imagination. The manager must understand the implications of emerging technologies and the changing business environment. The attempt must be made to predict how those changes will affect the company and to take steps to position the department accordingly. This involves doing little things now which will allow alternative paths to be followed in the future.

Transitional planning implies taking risks as well, since much of what the manager will infer about the future will be wrong. There is a need to proceed carefully and evaluate the results of each step taken toward the future. Radical changes breed radical failures, and few managers survive many such failures. The key is to be in step with the future and be prepared to take advantage of opportunities as they occur.

The balance of this chapter deals with a number of issues and solutions based on possible definitions of development in the future. Each is based on a specific premise, but generally on the fact that the definition of future development will be substantially different from what it is today. These solutions are only a few of many, and are presented as much as examples of transitional planning as of probable future conditions.

In attempting to define the future, much of what a development manager must take into account is peculiar to each situation. If a company is planning to allow customers to access their databases, the manager must determine what impact that will have on his department's skills and on the approach to the process. Once this step is taken, the manager will be in the same business as software companies. That step represents a radical departure from purely internal systems construction. The manager must be certain that the appropriate changes in skills and procedures take place.

Despite the difficulties in predicting the future of MIS, and therefore of the development department, certain reasonable conclusions can be drawn. First, given the overriding need to gather, protect and present information about the business and its process, a strong orientation to comprehensive database technology will prevail. As noted in Chapter 13, this environment implies different talents and strategies than those seen today.

Second, as discussed in Chapter 11, most systems development (the analysis and construction of system solutions) will be done by the end user. The technology of 4GLs and the database must evolve for this to occur, but the probability is strong. This implies a smaller development staff and considerably different skills.

Third, the skills and direction that database technology and end user languages will require from development are most closely aligned with the information center concept discussed in Chapter 14. The roles of consultant, tool set developer and certifier of systems may be the only functions of development in the future, although wider responsibilities are more likely.

All three of these scenarios imply a need to prepare for the day when development will meet its responsibilities with a much smaller staff. However, to reach that point, a greater number of special resources will be required. Much of the development manager's challenge is to fill short-term (which may mean 5 years) needs while avoiding long-term resource commitments.

In any case, the key to these and other issues is to understand that development is changing and will continue to do so. In order to be prepared, the manager must take steps today to meet the challenges of the future.

PROVIDING DEVELOPMENT RESOURCES

One of the chronic problems facing the development manager is the recruiting and training of competent professionals. There are more jobs than applicants. Finding anyone at all is difficult, much less finding competent people.

This problem will continue in the foreseeable future. Not only will trained personnel become increasingly scarce, but the manager is faced with an additional complication. This problem springs from the fact that the need for conventional programmers, who code or develop from specifications, should decrease. This reduction should be due to the anticipated increase in the use of 4GLs coupled with the increasing computer literacy of the average employee. Thus, it will be necessary for analysts and consultants to help the user develop solutions and a core of senior developers to build and manage tool sets.

However, the timing of these changes is very difficult to predict. Today most development departments still require additional personnel to do conventional development. In fact, the lack of workers often determines whether systems are built at all. Most companies wish to keep permanent staff to a minimum. The development manager also prefers to minimize the number of conventional developers on staff given the steady movement away from internal development.

The problem becomes one of filling this short-term need for trained workers while limiting the number of full-time programmers and internal designers. Much of the manager's success depends on how well these seemingly conflicting needs can be satisfied without excessive expense. One obvious solution is to use outside contractors and consultants, but while this practice does reduce the full-time staff, outside workers are expensive. The manager is left with finding imaginative ways to solve the problem.

Two potential sources of personnel are discussed here. Certainly, there are many others—in many cases, purely regional sources. The development manager knows that trained workers are hard to find. It is necessary to explore every possible solution and to evaluate its feasibility.

Cottage Industry

One of the most dramatic developments of recent years is the two-income family. When both spouses work, many problems occur because of the general desire to have one of them remain home, caring for the children or doing domestic chores. In many cases, couples are willing to sacrifice a great deal of money to accomplish this. Benefits seldom become an issue because one of them can provide adequate benefits for both.

In many cases, one spouse has put a career on hold to raise a family. In most cases this is the wife, but a growing trend is to have the husband take this responsibility. In either situation, a skilled individual exists who would like to work but cannot because of the need to be at home.

In both of these situations (the individual who must work but wants to remain at home and the individual who is at home but wishes to work), a resource exists (sometimes within the manager's own department) which may solve the manager's problems. There are many cases where an employee leaves for maternity reasons and never returns but would like to remain active in the business. Often there are married employees who wish to return to school full-time but cannot give up the second income. In Chapter 10, the subject of home terminals was discussed as a potential benefit. The concept of a cottage industry simply takes that idea one step further.

Terminal capabilities can be provided in the individual's home for programming purposes. These workers are given assignments in any appropriate fashion and do most of their work at home. Periodically and on a scheduled basis, they come into the office for review, further instruction or whatever personal involvement is required. Assignments are given on a piecework basis, and rates are established for each job. The individual agrees to produce a unit of work (program, system, documentation or enhancement) in a given time. When that work is satisfactorily completed, the worker is paid.

The rates of these workers can be expected to be reasonably low. The primary objective of these individuals is to work out of their home while maintaining some technical expertise. Therefore, their rate tends to be a secondary consideration—within reason. Their ability to retain their contract depends on their performance, and the manager can cancel the contract if the work is not satisfactory. No benefits are provided, no space is occupied, and there is little concern for providing career paths and opportunities, as with permanent employees.

For a department in transition, this is an excellent arrangement. As the shift occurs from conventional to end user development, fewer and fewer outside people are retained. The manager need not worry about retraining, but can concentrate on the continued development of internal employees. This significantly lowers the dependence on transitional skills.

There are many issues to be considered in such a program, not the least of which are security and the corporate culture. However, using the cottage industry to fill transient resource needs can solve a major problem for the manager who needs conventional resources but either cannot or will not hire permanent staff.

Correctional Institutions

In many situations, workers are needed but little or no money is available to hire them. Analysts are usually permanent employees, with easy access to users. However, if procedures are well established, programmers can be nearly independent of close user contact. That is one of the principles of the cottage industry approach. It is still necessary to pay people who are working at home, although at a reduced rate, and the location of terminal devices may prohibit this arrangement. One option for the development manager is to seek a source of personnel in a controlled environment where the benefit for the developer is independent of salary.

Such an environment is the correctional institutions. In minimum security prisons across the country, a primary goal is to provide training for a career after the sentence is served. In most cases, career training is geared to trades, but there is no reason to believe that it could not be directed to professions—such as program development.

The company would need to provide terminal capabilities in the same configuration as that at the central site. Someone would also need to guide the remote facility's efforts. This guidance would be substantial at first, until experience is developed, and would gradually decrease as the remote unit became self-sufficient. Some training would be necessary, but probably no more than that required for any inexperienced development candidate.

These issues are identical to those which must be addressed in any development situation. While the cost of training is not low, much of it is a one-time cost and payback is tremendous. Such a program has the added benefit of reducing the company's long-term commitment to a development approach which is dying—that of the large conventional programming staff.

If nothing else, such a program is an excellent public relations effort. The company is seen as being committed to social improvement. At the same time, it gains needed workers at a very low cost. Everyone benefits. Certainly this approach must be pursued delicately. It will be perceived as unconventional, and that in itself will trouble upper management. However, it does solve a significant problem in the rapid deployment of applications systems. The bottom-line improvement will overcome a great deal of trepidation.

Development Centers

While the development manager faces the problem of providing conventional development personnel while planning for their elimination, the corporation often faces analogous problems of finding and/or housing those people even if they are available. In many cases, for a variety of reasons, the corporate location does not attract many people. Small towns, cities with a blue collar environment, environmentally unattractive areas or crowded cities often have difficulty drawing computer professionals. In addition, the cost of space in large cities often makes the maintenance of a large development staff prohibitive.

The sophistication and dependability of long-distance communications eliminates much of the need to have development personnel (those who do not require close contact with users) located close to users. It allows program development staffs to move to where the people are rather than moving the people to the corporate headquarters. Establishing development centers in remote locations is a good transitional strategy and lowers the manager's dependence on the local job market.

These development centers are small—five to ten persons. They are managed by a full-time development professional but can be staffed by either part-time or full-time employees depending upon the number of employees projected for the future department. Facilities can be kept relatively spartan in comparison to those of the headquarters. Hardware and communications capabilities need not be as sophisticated as those at the central site. When the development department must be reduced, the company need only relocate full-time employees, reducing the cost of the transition to the future end-user development environment.

The location of development centers can vary in response to local situations. They can be placed in suburban areas to eliminate the need to travel to the central city. If a certain part of the country has a large talent pool, a center could be located there. It can even be established to handle temporary needs.

Examples of such a transient condition can be seen in the quality-of-living indexes for metropolitan areas across the country. Asheville, North Carolina, was recently rated as the top small city to live in out of 277 rated. Yet that city, due to its size and somewhat remote location, has a very limited market for computer professionals. Natives of the city or people who wish to move there are often unable to do so because there are more candidates than jobs. Locating a development center with part-time personnel in such an area would provide a substantial job pool because at this time there are few other opportunities. If this situation changes and it becomes too difficult or costly to staff the center, it can be closed.

Each of the three scenarios described here assumes a set of procedures and standards which allow the isolation of system development phases from users. But for a future which emphasizes end user development, these are precisely the phases which should be isolated. That separation allows the manager to concentrate long-term programs on the elements that will exist in the future while the conventional processes still continue. As the conventional process is phased out, the procedures will also disappear, with no impact on future-oriented ones. As those elements decline, the people performing conventional work will be phased out as well, with no effect on the department.

The manager will not find it easy to market programs which deviate from standard personnel policies. Unionization issues, personnel implications, conservative personnel attitudes and legal questions all encourage management to move slowly in personnel matters. However, these and other imaginative programs can provide the resources necessary to compete in a technology-based market place. They merit considerable attention.

DISPERSED DEVELOPMENT

In future end user development environments, one possible arrangement involves having specialists act as members of the department they service. This means that there is a development specialist in human resources, finance, manufacturing and any other department which has a reasonably high level of system need. These specialists act not as the sole source of development but rather as consultants and for the construction of the more sophisticated components of systems.

The user/developer would be placed on the user's budget and managed by the user. In most cases the responsibilities of this individual would be somewhat spread so that normal departmental duties would be within the scope of the job. A functional reporting relationship would remain between the individual and the development manager. This ensures some consistency of approach and direction.

Such an arrangement provides significant benefits. The developer located in the user department is able to concentrate on the most important tools and issues in the functional area. Engineering functions specialized in computer-assisted design/computer-assisted manufacturing (CAD/CAM) applications, financial areas requiring heavy modeling exposure, and marketing concentrating on statistical inquiry capabilities all require specific technical talents which do not logically occur across the company. The background, skills and career goals of individuals interested in these functions vary widely, and these persons tend to be associated more with user disciplines than with MIS anyway. Common cross-discipline applications would continue to be supported within the development department, as would database availability and its associated maintenance and development.

There are obviously some major issues which must be addressed before dispersed development becomes a reality. A standardized approach to database technology must be developed. Standardized interfaces must exist between software products so that communications and data transfer are simple and straightforward. A relatively disciplined approach to education about technology must occur so that all users and developers use the same process in developing systems. The probability of all of these issues being addressed in the near future is minimal, but it is not difficult to foresee an eventual solution.

The dispersed development department is dramatically different from what one generally sees today. Its matrix characteristics can make direct management and control difficult. However, part of that environment does, in fact, exist—although not formally. Each time a user develops a system and uses it to operate part of the company, the effects of dispersal are felt. The development manager who does not take steps to bring the department's organization in line with this operational environment is at considerable risk.

In order to anticipate this eventual dispersion, the manager can select a few appropriate departments and begin its implementation. Candidate departments are those that already perform much of their own development or rely heavily on information center consultation. An individual could be transferred to such a department, reporting directly to the user but reporting functionally to systems development. This would allow strategic control while preparing for the eventual transition to principal resource residence within the user departments. As the products in use evolve, that form of organization, and its supportive procedures, would evolve in step.

TOOL SET DEVELOPMENT

The picture of a future where the majority of the development takes place in user departments does not imply that no professional development exists at all. Even if 4GLs evolve to the point where they completely supplant conventional languages, the need for professional, independent developers will remain. The product those developers produce may be different, but there will remain a demand for common, single-approach routines to be utilized by anyone developing a systems solution. These centrally developed routines will become the tool set for all systems, regardless of who develops them.

The concept of tool sets is not new. It has been used by programmers and analysts for years. Date conversion routines, standard heading routines, service charge algorithms and table searches are all well-known examples of cataloged tools for standardizing and simplifying programming.

The programmer or analyst calls the preestablished routine, passes specific parameters and receives the results for further action. The routines always perform as intended, maximize efficiencies and produce results in accordance with standards and policies.

The only difference between this arrangement and a future development function is that the tool sets would represent a primary role for development. The development manager would be responsible for evaluating corporate policy and creating approved routines, accessed by all developers, to enforce those information-oriented policies. The manager would also respond to requests from users who need a common approach to a task. Much of the tool set would also be dedicated to the proper presentation of data for user applications. In any case, the development of tool sets as a primary role implies discipline in maintenance and portfolio management, an issue the manager can begin to address today. There are several elements which must be considered in beginning such a program.

First, the tool sets will be interpreted by nonprofessional developers who are not controlled by the manager. For this reason, ease of use and understanding is equal in importance to functionality. This is analogous to the difference between internal software and marketed software. Tool sets developed for use throughout the company require far more stringent quality control than those used by professional developers. When placed in the portfolio, they must be well documented, easy to use, easy to access, addressable to all situations and, most importantly, fail-safe. When the user accesses the routine, the response must always be consistent and always right.

Second, a tool constructed for a specific situation must support that situation regardless of which 4GL is used. If the company supports five separate languages or products, the function addressed by the tool set must be accessible by each of the products. In some cases, this may require the development and support of five independent tools, while in others it may simply require interpretation within a single module. In either case, when the maintenance of a tool set portfolio is the product of development, the function must be served, regardless of the complexities and difficulties.

Third, tool set construction relies on skills which have recently been discounted by most development staffs. It requires a reemphasis on the technical aspects of programming and analysis rather than on business knowledge. Developers of tool set portfolios work in the background, following particular specifications for their products. They are concerned with efficiencies, commonality and technical sophistication. In many cases, this need re-creates the gulf between these developers and the analyst/consultant who deals with the user. It requires some division of the staff, and the organization of the development department must support this arrangement.

DEVELOPERS AS AUDITORS

In Chapter 11, the implications of end user languages were discussed. One of the principal problems was seen to be not the languages themselves but rather the bypassing of the checks and balances found in the conventional development cycle. Improvements in fourth-generation products are not likely to change this situation substantially.

Chapter 12 dealt with the importance of procedures and standards. They are the prime mechanisms to overcome the difficulties of end user development. By establishing appropriate procedures, ensuring that they are both easy to use and productive, and keeping them sensitive to the tools in use allows the development manager to bring some discipline to the process.

Simply publishing procedures does not ensure that they will be followed. Their adherence is dependent not only on their simplicity but also on how well they are enforced. To a large extent, certification means enforcement. However, certification applies only to software that the user wishes certified. It also occurs at a final gate, at which point so much money has been spent that development may be forced to accept the product due to a management edict.

As more and more development is done by the end user, the development department begins to fill the role of auditor of the process and the resultant products. In this role, the department assumes the responsibilities generally taken by the MIS auditor. Procedural steps are verified for compliance with standards, audit reports produced and implications of noncompliance communicated to management.

This role is somewhat unfamiliar to development people. Typically, they see a problem, propose a solution and act upon the acceptance of the proposal. They are judged on the success of the installed system and are ultimately responsible for making it work. As auditors, however, they merely state the condition of systems and the implications. Whether their audits are acted upon is incidental to their primary task. This change in approach requires some retrenchment of personnel.

The development manager must allow the analysts to perform audits on end user development. The evaluations would take place and be presented within development itself. They would not be published to the outside world. The implications could then be evaluated over time until a case history is built and the skills necessary to conduct audits properly are honed. When end user development becomes great enough so that systems development assumes the auditing role, the results of these audits can become the basis for proposals to upper management. At that point, the proper organizational and procedural moves can be made so that the transition is smooth and productive.

CONCLUSION

A development manager must manage the department as if it will be his or her domain for the long term. It cannot simply be a short-term career step—even if that is what it turns out to be. Moving the department into the future requires understanding and imagination, not only in applying technology to the user community but in applying it to the department itself. Unless this is done, the company's information needs cannot be properly met.

While this chapter deals with planning, it is not an isolated subject. Planning must be the theme that runs through all aspects of department management. It is especially important in a dynamic discipline such as systems development, since an effective plan can often represent the only stability the department possesses. When the staff and users see only reaction, they will quickly lose faith in the department's ability to provide long-term service.

It is the manager who is ultimately responsible for planning. Aspects of planning can be delegated to lower-level personnel, but it is the manager who sets the tone for the entire process. This requires commitment and active participation.

EPILOGUE

In 1970, Alvin Toffler's book *Future Shock* described an environment in which one of the most pressing psychological problems was not only change but the staggering speed with which that change was occurring. The business environment experiences these changes most obviously in the rapid evolution of its use of technology. Because of pressures created by the ever-diminishing differences between competing products and services, the importance of information about the business and its market has risen dramatically. In some cases, the importance of that information rivals that of the product or service itself.

While the ability to apply technology to the information need has evolved rapidly, it is not keeping pace. It is probably unreasonable to expect this. The appearance of a new technological solution immediately opens the door for further advances simply because more opportunities are perceived as the judgment baseline moves forward. This characteristic of technological evolution, coupled with the need for and awareness of the importance of information, indicates that the pace of change will accelerate in the foreseeable future.

The systems development manager is a key individual in this advancement and evolution. Much of the pressure to retain or create a leading-edge posture for the corporation in information usage falls on systems development. This pressure will continue regardless of the advances in database technology, information centers, and end user languages. Despite the picture of development as a technocracy, its major contribution to the corporation has been and will continue to be the fact that development is a professional group, knowledgeable and skilled in the development of systems. The fact that end users as well as developers can now create computer solutions does not lessen the importance of this professional expertise. In fact, its importance is amplified.

The most pervasive trend today is the evolution of development into a major business function. It no longer represents the disjointed and reactionary management of projects and implementation of products. It is a centralized (regardless of its organization) source of systems expertise for the company, as well as a guide and protector of corporate information assets. As such, its management requires a cohesive, well-conceived approach—just as any business function does. The department's responsibilities to the company must be understood, and the process used to meet these responsibilities must be both clear and flexible enough to react to the changing business environment. Its workers must be skilled in the mechanisms needed to fulfill these responsibilities. In the development department, with its rapidly changing use of technology, people must be intelligently managed and its staff retained for the long term. Finally, the technologies used to perform development, and their implementation, must be thoroughly understood and applied to achieve maximum advantages for the company.

It is safe to assume that the reader who has reached this point understands the sometimes subtle differences between managing a business function and managing a group of programmers and analysts. For the manager (or future manager), the task of melding these professionals into a proactive, cohesive group is not easy. It requires skills and determination that many managers may not yet have achieved. The successful development manager is not a superior project leader or analyst, but a manager—a role that requires the learning and development of new skills and talents. Due to the dynamics of systems development and its importance to the company, these skills must be developed rapidly.

Despite the difficulties and pressures involved, systems development will remain an exciting and satisfying discipline. Development's success, and the skill with which it is managed, will determine the competitive success of most businesses. For those who choose a career path which seeks a major contribution to the corporate future as a goal, development is one of the best places to be.

It is difficult to predict precisely how the evolution of technology will change development's role in the corporation of tomorrow. What can be stated with certainty is that development itself will be a major force in shaping that future. Few business functions can claim to have that impact. For the systems development manager today, the major challenge is to contribute effectively and imaginatively to the shaping of that future.

The key to this effort is a thorough understanding of what it means to manage development as a dynamic business function. The purpose of this book, as mentioned in the preface, is to bring some of the factors in managing this function into perspective. If readers have gained an insight into these factors and, more importantly, how they affect the situation in which they operate, the effort of preparing this book has been worthwhile.

APPENDIX: DEFINITION OF SYSTEMS DEVELOPMENT

Systems development is the functional unit responsible for the delivery, support, ongoing maintenance and auditing of certified computer systems.

Although this definition may seem somewhat simplistic, it covers a substantial amount of ground and deserves analysis. Some of the elements are qualified purposely and others are stated in generic terms. This is the definition which will be used throughout this book and is the basis for the charter discussed in Chapter 1.

It is of paramount importance for any organization to clearly understand this definition. Otherwise, direction and focus invariably wander to the point where every member of the company defines responsibilities and scope in whatever manner is most convenient or profitable. Unlike the older, more time-proven functions of finance, personnel, staff and others, MIS, and therefore development, do not have a historical definition. Everyone knows what the accounting department does, where its boundaries lie, and how to deal with it. MIS and systems development are less clearly understood.

Let us begin by breaking down the components of the definition. Each component has significant weight and should be thoroughly understood.

Functional Unit

The development function may occur in a separately managed department or may be dispersed across a number of departments. The reasons for dispersal are varied, ranging from divisional alignment to political necessity. However, whether it is dispersed or not, there should be a common definition of responsibilities and of the methods used to perform development activities.

Delivery

Delivery is the analysis and construction of the system through the implementation of the product. The product may be a new system, enhancements to an old system or replacement with a technically superior product. Generally, the conceptualization of a system occurs outside of the development group—either in user departments or with the announcement of an emerging technology.

Involvement of the user in delivery is one of the keys to success. Over the years, we have seen attempts to either highlight user sign-off of products or to move the responsibility for implementation to user departments. These attempts have generally been unsuccessful, since MIS is, in fact, the corporation's systems resource and is the most competent group to determine the validity of system solutions. In addition, many systems have multidepartment impact, and this trend is accelerating. In this situation, a central group must validate implementation. Users may exercise veto power, but they seldom actually implement a product.

Support

Support includes the investigation and correction of errors in systems, consultation in user analyses or development, evaluations of technological opportunities, and general aid and assistance to the company. Placing the support responsibility in the development department takes advantage of two key attributes of systems people: an intimate knowledge of the application systems and inherent analytical qualities.

Maintenance

Maintenance includes the changes made in systems to keep up with the business environment. It is typically determined by outside forces such as regulatory changes, business expansion/contraction or the need to ensure application currency (new releases of packages, etc.). It can range from an hour's worth of effort to a year-long conversion.

Auditing

Auditing means periodic review of the health of software systems. Are committed performance levels being maintained? Is the documentation still relevant? Is user-developed software being properly used? Are system outputs still relevant? Software, like hardware, has a limited life span. However, it seldom breaks as cleanly. It must be periodically evaluated to ascertain that it still serves its intended purpose.

Certified

Certification is more pervasive today than ever before. With the advent of user-friendly languages and the emergence of information systems as a key element in business strategy, important aspects of data/information usage have left the relatively disciplined realm of MIS. Users can now develop and use software systems without the knowledge of MIS and without the protection of rigid testing/validation procedures.

This presents a significant problem for the company in general and systems development in particular. Any software used in company decision making should be audited and controlled by MIS. In this fashion, it can reasonably be supported and, more importantly, certified as to correctness. Any software without this certification is outside the scope of the development group and should be viewed by management as carrying a higher level of risk.

Certification is dealt with in more detail in Chapters 11 and 14.

INDEX